Days Gone By

AIKEN, TEXAS AND THE OUTSKIRTS

PAMILA HOOPER ADKISON
AND
BARBARA WILLIAMS SCATES

AIKEN
PUBLISHING
COMPANY

Days Gone By
Aiken, Texas and the Outskirts
All Rights Reserved.
Copyright © 2024 Pamila Hooper Adkison and Barbara Williams Scates
v6.0

The opinions expressed in this manuscript are solely the opinions of the author and do not represent the opinions or thoughts of the publisher. The author has represented and warranted full ownership and/or legal right to publish all the materials in this book.

This book may not be reproduced, transmitted, or stored in whole or in part by any means, including graphic, electronic, or mechanical without the express written consent of the publisher except in the case of brief quotations embodied in critical articles and reviews.

ISBN: 978-0-578-27658-8

Cover and interior images © 2024 Pamela Hooper Adkison. All rights reserved - used with permission.

Aiken Publishing Company

PRINTED IN THE UNITED STATES OF AMERICA

On the cover: On February 3 of 2020 a truck turned the corner off of Hwy 7 West onto CR 1210, and his trailer went through the old store in Aiken. Emma Wilburn wanted to do something special for her grandmother, Delma Fountain Wilburn. Emma painted a canvas of the original way the store looked with its original sign…..Sonya War Wilburn

*In loving memory of
Jan Adams Akridge, Kelly Chandler Hancock, Henry
Faye Hooper, Jerry Holt, & Gene Akridge*

To my husband, Howell Maurice Adkison for his patience, encouragement, and kindness.

Table of Contents

1 - Aiken 1
- The Danley Store in Aiken, Texas 2
- Aiken, Texas 5
- Digging 'Taters 10
- My Childhood Memories of Aiken 12
- Growing up in Aiken, Shelby County 14
- James Danley and his Pets 17
- J.R. Gray's Store 18
- Where Did Aiken Get Its Name 23

2 - Our Neighbors 25
- Jewell Chandler Brown 26
- Cletus Sharpton 27
- Clarence Fountain 28
- Troy Chandler 33
- Marceline Crenshaw 34
- The Good Old Days 35
- Cotton Picking Trips 50
- Delano Warr 51
- Wrinkled Memories 52
- A Tribute to My Hero 58
- Grit in Your Spit 61
- Where Do I Start 62

    Annie-Go-Go 69
    Ura Lovell 75
    Earl Campbell 76
    The Akridge Boys 78
    Jess Warren 79
    Ms. Eller 83
    Carter Hooper 84
    Leta Lucas 85
    Barbara Scates 86
    Wayne Powdrill 89
    The George Adams Family 92
    Idell, Johnnie, and Yvonne Fults 102
    Fannie Mae Adkison 103
    Mattie Warr, Ruby Warr and Mary Warr Scates 109
    Mae Lee Vandygriff Goodman Taylor 112
    Sisters Lily Fountain Kitchen and Mattie Fountain Warr ... 127
    Jack & Rachel Fountain 128
    The Fenleys 130
    The Four Mints 131
    That Kid That Got Lost That Time 132
    Buster and Era Fountain 140
    Gathering Eggs 140

3 - Excelsior School 143
    The Old White Building at Excelsior School 149
    Excelsior/World History Since 1895 153
    Excelsior Common School No. 47 161

4 - Entertainment 163
    Golden Spur Rodeo Arena 164
    Respect & Rodeo Days 166
    Tree Carvings 167
    Gone Fishing 168

Jess Warren's and the Old Outdoor Theater 169
Louis and Ruby Fountain 171
The Fire Tower 171
Friday Night Volleyball 173
Powdrill's Saturday Night Dances 175
Deer Season 177
Pig Latin 179
No Swimming 180
The Pine Tree Challenge 182
Where There is a Will, There is a Way 182

5 - Lillie Mae Williamson 189
By Joyce Wilson Bright 190

6 - Mt. Herman 197
Jess Warren Memories 202
Pear Pie? 204
Living off the Grid 209
Mt. Herman School 212
Mt Herman School 1949 213
Mt. Herman Tragedy 218
Mt. Herman Community 220

7 - Employment 227
Farming 228
The Ride 231
The Three Mile Bridge 233
Watermelons, Grit Newspaper, and Snake Root 235
J.T. and Eldora Koonce Holt 238
Cooking on a Wood Burning Heater 243
Hay Bailing 245
Army Years (1966-1968) 246
Sand Hill Plant Farm 247

    The Sawmill 250
    West Shelby County Fire Department 254

8 - Jericho, Camp Worth, and Mt Pleasant School 257
    Jarry Co, Jerico, Jericho 270
    Mt Pleasant School 272
    1930-1945 Mt Pleasant School 275
    Jerico-Mt Pleasant History 278
    Dr. Bailey 282
    Dr. Sidney Lafayette (Fate) Bailey 283
    A Younger Generation's Perspective 284

9 - Jericho and World War II 287
    World War II Louisiana and East Texas Maneuvers – 1941 288
    World War II Louisiana and East Texas Maneuvers –1943 289

10 - W.R. Rudd Grocery Store 293
    W. R. Rudd Grocery Store and Service Station – Jericho, Texas 295
    The Jericho Community – A Vital Contributor
    to Shelby County's Economy 302

11 - Tabernacle School 307
    Tabernacle I 309
    Tabernacle II 313
    Tabernacle III 316
    Lena Anthony 317
    History of Tabernacle School 317

12 - Old Salem School 319
    Cemetery 323
    Funeral Wakes and 24-Hour Vigils 324
    Lost Near Ole Salem 330

13 - Grigsby and Martinsville 333
    At the Foot of Grigsby Hill 334
    Memories of Grigsby 337

14 - Waterman 341
    The Waterman Train Wreck... 342

15 - Other Topics 349
    Road Runners in Southwest Shelby County 350
    Little 'Gator 352
    Who's Been Eating My Fish 353
    Elections 355
    John Woods Park 357
    McSwain Hill 358
    Nicknames.. 362
    Three Counties Junction at Attoyac River................................ 363
    Early Trails and Roads Across Shelby County Texas 365
    Thanksgiving... 371
    Christmas 372

16 - Church 375
    Providence Church 376
    Aiken Pentecostal Church.. 377
    Summer Revival.. 382

Bibliography.. 389
Acknowledgments... 391
The Ones Behind Our Book 393

The call to remember was sounded by Barbara Scates after the Danley's store in Aiken, Texas, was damaged. A one-ton pickup had smashed into the building as the driver lost control.

Our friends and neighbors wrote stories and commented on each other's post via social media. Can you imagine having over 100 people in one room working on such a story? There seemed to be an urgency to record our oral history, though humble, before it became lost. A comment by one would jog the memories of others. Then they in turn added to the narrative.

Shelby County, once known as "No Man's Land", is a small area of the United States of America. Through our family stories you will understand how our lives are intertwined into the historical fabric of the USA. We have versions of small businesses, farmers, itinerate laborers following the cotton or the oil fields, the timber industry, teachers, large-scale farming, trains, and interstate commerce

As you read, you will come to know the people of Aiken and feel like you are amongst friends.

You will see that the work was hard, that neighbors helped neighbors, and that families were strong. We have had our tragedies and differences, but Aiken is a good place to live.

Enjoy the trip back to a slower time, through the eyes of the Shelby County residents.

*I may not have gotten to grow up in Aiken, but
I got there as fast as I could.*

Mila Justice Smith

1
Aiken

Days Gone By

The Danley Store in Aiken, Texas

By Barbara J. Scates

The skyline in Aiken, Texas, will be forever changed in 2020. In case you haven't been through Aiken in a while, the old Danley Store was recently damaged when a truck overturned, and pretty much, wiped out the front half of the store. There is so much structural damage that the demise of the store is inevitable.

The Danley Store was an icon in the community. Many memories were made at that store.

Since this historic store was such a big part of our Excelsior School Community, we would like for you to share your memories in honor of the Aiken Store.

Delores Harris Brown: So sad to see it destroyed. I went there many times in the '60s & '70s.

Kimberly H R: We would stop there before starting the hayride we had every year.

Lonnie W: I remember walking with my grandmother to buy a grape soda when I was small, and then later in life, starting my family with Christina, and bringing home my first child, Allen, to the home in the rear of the store.

Joy Tarver: Everyone should get 4 planks and build picture frames and put its picture in it.

Kelley Hancock: I remember going to the store to get gum, candy, and trading in Coke bottles for 10 cents. I loved going to the store.

Elaine Belanger: Ron and I enjoyed running the B&B as a small part of its history. That was back when renting VCR tapes was popular. The twin sisters and their families were very easy to rent from.

As East Texans would say, "Good people."

Lonnie W: Elaine, Delma and Thelma are still good people.

Jennifer M: I played Pac-Man.

Carolyn E S: My sister & I would sometimes walk to that store to get a Coke & candy bar, back in the '50s. We lived down the dirt road across the highway from Danley's.

Cindy Scates Eubank: Randy and I would stop there every morning before we went to Excelsior. I remember Mrs. Danley, and then, her daughter and granddaughters owning it. I love the twins as they were my mother's best friends growing up. I love this entire family. So many memories.

Joy Tarver: Would somebody save me 4 small boards please.

Barbara J. Scates: Joy, maybe someone will save you some boards...I think it is too dangerous at this time for anyone to approach.

Kevin Hughes: Joy, contact my mother or Aunt Delma and Tappy Wilburn.

Jean R A: I was there from a young age. The twins used to beg my mother to let me stay with them. Later years I would go buy Coke and peanuts and visit.

Barbara J. Scates: Wasn't it always amazing how Mrs. Danley could add up all your items in her head? And then make change from her apron pocket? She had quite a skill with numbers!!!

Days Gone By

Shannon A C: I don't remember Mrs. Danley there, but I do remember Mrs. Delma's and Aunt Thelma's mom there.

Shellie Burns: Ma Danley always let us kids have 1 thing every day for a snack. Good memories.

Kelley Hancock: I remember Mr. and Mrs. Danley. They were so sweet.

Joy Tarver: I bet nobody remembers Mr. Danley's name, all of it.

Joy Tarver: Barbara, Oad was what he went by, but he and his brother had about 6 or 7 names each. My mom knew, but I could never remember.

Barbara J. Scates: Joy, or was it Ora? Mrs. Danley's given name was Allie...

Joy Tarver: Barbara, they called him Oad, and she was Allie. I bet the twins would know his full name.

Barbara J. Scates: Joy, the Danley's were good, hard-working people!!!

Joy Tarver: Barbara, they probably saved our lives a few times. She gave me eggs and bologna, when we didn't have food.

Delores Harris Brown: Barbara, that's the name I remember being on the store, Ora Danley's Store. He was kin to my best friend's dad.

Shellie Burns: Yes, his name was Ora Danley.

Nina Jo Hudspeth Walker: Everyone called him Oad...he & Mr. Arce (Janet's, Leroy's & Cathy's dad) were brothers ... they were distant kin of mine, & yes, they were sweet folks for sure!

Linda P D: I too remember this store when going to see Grandma & Grandpa Hooper in Aiken.

Aiken, Texas

By Pamila Hooper Adkison

Aiken, Texas, with no zip code is a community west of Center, Texas, zip code, 75935. It developed on the crossroads of Highway 7 and the Arcadia Road. At one time there were three grocery stores and a switchboard for the telephone company that occupied each corner of the junction. The switchboard had closed before I moved to Aiken. The stores closed over time.

The small, country, grocery store was essential to the surrounding community. These general stores became the heartbeat of the area. One could drop by for a pack of gum and find out about weddings, births, and deaths before the news came out in the local newspaper. I am speaking of a slower time. A time when one might go into town once a week for supplies, but may go to the store every day. In the rural areas the stores were around five or six mile apart, which was within walking distance of many homes. These stores did not have an imposing presence like Walmart, Kroger, and Piggly Wiggly do. They were about the size of the neighboring houses. In many cases the families owning the stores designated the front of the building for the store and sectioned off the back for the living quarters. Everyone referred to a store by the name of the woman who run it, i.e.; Mrs. Danley's, Ura's, Vivian's or Lillie Mae's. These were the stores along Highway 7 from Center to Martinsville. These women would welcome you into their store every time you came by, but would not tolerate horse play nor disrespect.

We lived two houses down from Mrs. Danley's at Aiken. We lived there from the time I was in the second grade until I became a sophomore in high school. When Mother (Ann Hooper) needed milk and bread, she sent me to the store. At first I walked. Later Jimmy, my brother, and I saved and pooled our money together to buy a bicycle. After that I biked to the store.

My good friend, Joy Chandler Tarver lived on the Center side of Mrs. Danley's. I lived on the Nacogdoches side. Mrs. Danley's store was about the half way mark between our houses. We would call one another, and make plans to meet there. We bought candy, but sometimes we would get a package of peanuts to add to our Coke. As the peanuts plopped into the clear, green bottle, we watched the Coke fizz up and foam over the top. Straddling our bikes, we hung out under the portico until we had finished the drink. Then we took the glass bottle back in for the two cent return deposit.

We weren't the only ones who met at Mrs. Danley's. Kids were always around the store. During the school year, the Excelsior bus and the Center bus exchanged students there to carry them on to their respective campuses. Mr. Leman Chandler drove the Excelsior bus. He picked up the students from the Attoyac River to the store. Mr. Author D. Youngblood in the Center bus picked up those down the Arcadia Road to the store. The high school students continued on to Center with Mr. Youngblood. The younger ones went with Mr. Chandler.

During the summer the farmers brought kids by Mrs. Danley's. Teenagers from the rural communities could earn extra money working for the nearby farmers. Mr. Cletus Sharpston hired many of us to harvest his crop. Purple hull peas was his specialty. Like the school buses, he had his route that he followed. Then he'd carry us to his fields. He started out early. He came by my house about 6 am. That was an hour and a half before the school bus schedule.

"Hop in the back," he said through the window, barely coming to a stop.

He made his rounds until he had his pickup bed full of pickers. It was best to start picking early while it was still cool. Those fields got hot. If one doesn't keep hydrated, working outdoors in the sun in the south can be dangerous. Around noon we finished the field. Mr. Cletus settled up with us before we left. As he tallied each of our earnings, we stood around under a tree or sat on the tailgate of the pickup. At 1 ½ cents per pound, we had to pick 66.66 pounds to get a whole dollar. Then we loaded up to head home. Mr. Cletus stopped at Mrs. Danley's for us to spend the money we had earned that morning. A dollar would get a Coke and a honey bun.

When my kids were school age, I stopped at Muggin's after taking them to school. Muggin was the daughter of Mr. and Mrs. Danley. Mr. Danley nicknamed her that when she was born, because she was no bigger than his coffee mug. Her given name was Laverne, but no one in Aiken would know who you were talking about, if you had asked for Laverne. She opened the store after they had retired. Every morning I visited with her until customers started coming in. We had many discussions about the status of the world and about how we would solve its problems.

Daddy (Billy Wayne Hooper) was a truck driver as I was growing up. Mostly he was an over-the-road driver. He would be gone two or three weeks at a time. Mrs. Danley let Daddy keep a running account at the store. (Try to get the Dollar Store to do that). Mother never sent any money with me for the milk and bread. Mrs. Danley put it on the bill. One day I remember watching her as she added the ticket. With a short stub of a No2 pencil dancing above the receipt book, she added ten to twelve items in her head in seconds and handed the copy to me. With my fourth grade experience of the multiplication tables and long division, I questioned her accuracy. When I got home, I added up the ticket to prove her totals. She was much faster than I was, but I am proud to say that my numbers matched her's exactly.

When Daddy returned home from one of his trips, he would send me to the store for cigarettes. (The law against anyone under eighteen purchasing cigarettes did not pass until later. At that time a two-year-old could buy them). Mother doesn't smoke, so Mrs. Danley knew he was home.

Mrs. Danley would ask about Daddy, then say, "I haven't seen Billy Wayne in a while, tell him to stop by."

Was this a secret communication between them? As a kid I thought it was Mrs. Danley being nice. It was more than that. She was one of the underpinnings of Aiken. Many of the families in the community were part of the foundation of Aiken, but my guess is that the families leaned upon her more than any other person in the area. That's the thing though. She was always willing to help.

After the one-ton pickup rolled over into the old store, I was shocked when I saw the damaged store.

My first question was, "What happened?"

After looking around, I thought, "What has happened to my community?"

The Aiken that I knew as a child is not here anymore. With the improvements in the gas mileage of the automobiles, we don't have to fuel the cars as often. Plus, the State of Texas raised the speed limits on the highways. Travelers zipped pass the stores on to the next town, without stopping for gas and snacks. The advances in the automobile have limited the extra trade to the area and have led to the closing of the stores. Aiken, like any other rural community, is slowly changing.

That is not to say the changes are bad. I don't think the community is declining. It is merely different. The Excelsior School draws us together with extra activities and events that it sponsors. The local churches are filled with thoughtful and caring people. They volunteer for the school events. They volunteer for the fire department and help to raise money for it. When a tornado blew through last year, neighbors helped clean up around each other's homes. In the spirit of Mrs. Danley, Aiken is still strong and thriving.

Ora Danley Store in Aiken, Drawing by Pamila Hooper Adkison

Days Gone By

Digging 'Taters

By Pamila Hooper Adkison

One morning after I had taken the boys to school, I stopped by Muggin's. It was spring and our conversation turned toward gardens. She had one, but I didn't. Hers was west along the highway past Pa Danley's house. She had kept it watered and weeded, making the plants lush and the area between the rows clean.

"My potatoes are ready to dig," she said. "Go and dig you a mess."

As she handed me a small paper bag and her digging stick, she added, "Dig where the ground is cracking and disturbed. The ones there will be big enough to eat."

I made my way down the row, pushing the vines back to reveal the signs on the ground that she had mentioned. I rolled the top of the bag down a couple times to keep it open as I dug. Not every vine was ready, but by the end of the row there was enough in my sack for supper that night.

At church the next Sunday, Tappy Wilburn, Delma's husband, began telling me how someone had gotten into his potato patch, and he could see where that someone had helped himself to his potatoes.

Astounded, I replied, "Who would do that? There was no sign of anyone being there when I dug mine."

Tresa Danley Konderla: These are such wonderful memories. We would stop and visit with Uncle Ode and Aunt Allie, regularly, and I loved to wander around the store and outside. The grownups would sit outside and catch up with whatever the news was at the time as we ran around being kids. I thought Muggin was just the coolest name ever and, I must admit, I had totally forgotten she had a 'legal' name. She and Daddy were big buddies and I think they were pretty close in age. Thank you for writing this and sharing it.

Grace R: I was born and raised in Aiken, Texas, with my brothers and sisters. There are 8 of us in all. Dad was a Baptist preacher. He preached at White Rock Baptist Church. We went to church on Sundays back then, unless we were on our death bed or having another baby. I remember going to the Danley's Store. My brothers usually got to go to the store. We lived only a mile from the store, but it seemed like 20 miles back then. Really, this brought back so many good memories. Thanks. I still have a brother in Center.

Terry R W: Yes, I grew up in Aiken, picked purple hull peas for Uncle Lowell and my Pawpaw Clayton Russell, but got six cents a lb. I would pick a hundred pounds before I went to my job. When we were putting up for the family, all we ate morning, noon, and night was purple hull peas. They would let us kids sell a bushel, so we could get a Coke and candy bar, or my favorite orange pineapple ice cream. Lots of good memories.

Tresa Danley Konderla: I am so glad you mentioned orange pineapple ice cream!!! Not many people know this. I remember stopping in Martinsville and Mrs. Henry Faye would give me a huge scoop. This crossed my mind last week. Now, I am hooked on mixing pineapple juice with orange juice.

Kimberly S P: Her two scoops were more like three. My mom, Lillie Smith, loved orange pineapple ice cream.

Rhonda Chandler: We lived on Highway 7 most our life. The Aiken sign was across the highway from my daddy's and mama's (Charles & Joyce Chandler) place. My daddy would set a trailer of watermelons at the end of the driveway and people would stop and get them a melon and put the money in a coffee can that was attached to the trailer. Those were definitely the better days.

Joyce Bright: I use to catch the school bus at the Danley store, when I was going to school in Center. When the large stores came into the towns, it killed all of the Country Store business.

My Childhood Memories of Aiken

By Jimmie Nell Adkison Lee

Thank You, Pam, for taking me back to my childhood memories of Aiken, our friends, our bus drivers, and Excelsior School. I remember we could leave school and walk to Rachel Fountain's or Mrs. Danley's store, if we had a note from home. Walking down Hwy 7 wasn't anything to worry about then. I started to school in one of the old white buildings, and it seemed huge then. Here were Mrs. Eddings, Mrs. Lawson, Mrs. Holt, Mrs. Hughes (music), Mrs. Wheeler and our beloved, Mr. Billie Bo Barbe. All of these wonderful teachers helped shape my life. Many of the students were family, and the rest were like family. Not many schools were built in a cow pasture, and you had to go over the old cattle guard to get to the school. The cows were moved to the pasture behind the school. We could go barefooted and did. I remember the outdoor toilets too.

I started my very first day of school alone. My mother (Marie Adkison) was very sick. The school bus then was a pickup truck with a little house built on the pickup bed driven by Mrs. Rachel Fountain. I climb in, not knowing anyone, and registered myself for 1st grade. Later in the morning Mrs. Lawson caught me trying to cross the cattle guard to go home. I told her my mama was sick, and I needed to get home. She led me back in and had me stay with her until the bus came. She was afraid I'd get away again. LOL.

So many good memories, from the old white school house to the new school with indoor bathrooms. No air conditioning but windows always open. The red oiled sawdust was strewn on the floor at the end of each day to keep down the dust, while sweeping the concrete floors. That is a good smell I still remember. When the trail riders came through on their way to the Houston Rodeo, we were let out of class to run to the fence and watch the riders come through.

Another wonderful memory is the respect we had for our teachers and each other. I never remember one episode of bullying and there were 8 grades. The "big kids," we called them, helped to look after us younger ones. If you were stupid enough to be disrespectful to a teacher, you got a paddling. The worst was you knew what was waiting at home, and that paddling at school was nothing compared to the a$$ whooping waiting at home.

I'm 73 now with 15 grandchildren, and I so wish they could experience all that we experienced of the simple good life; even picking peas, loading watermelons, cantaloupes, the outhouse in the middle of the night, no phones, no TV, sometimes no vehicle nor electricity.

Those of us that came from that day and time are survivors…today's generation would greatly benefit if they could totally live in our time for a while.

Thanks again for all the memories. I had let the cobwebs grow on. We didn't know it then, but we grew up in a wonderful, safe and caring place. Our families had some very hard times, but everyone pulled together to help each other get through them. We're in a different time today, and I do long for the simple life I grew up in.

[LOL is shorthand for "laugh out loud". It is used on Facebook and in text messages on cellular phones].

Growing up in Aiken, Shelby County

By Mildred Hooper McSwain

I have many memories of growing up in Aiken, Shelby County.

We always looked forward to the county fair in October. They would turn out all the schools at lunch on the first day to go to the parade. I enjoyed watching all the marching bands. Then it was off to the fair grounds. There were people everywhere. The rides were going, kids squealing, people trying to win a prize, and cotton candy. It was an exciting time even though I didn't ride any rides. My sisters, Marie and Georgie, would ride a kiddie ride sometimes.

My daddy, George Hooper, was a farmer. I had to go to the field to help with planting and gathering. Marie and Georgie did too when they were older.

"I will never marry a farmer," I said.

In 1953 we got our little Pentecostal Church at Aiken. Brother M. D. Lamon of Lufkin was the pastor. There were several pastors over the years. During revival in 1955, we had a big baptizing when Marie and

I were baptized in Jesus name. Georgie was baptized the next year. Our Aunt Jewel and Uncle Ivy Chandler lived above the church. They had a pond and this is where the baptizing was held. There were also baptizings in Bridge Creek which was below the church. Later there was a baptizing in Lowell Russell's pond where my oldest sister, Joyce, was baptized. The camp meeting was held at the Aiken church for a few years. Later, Brother and Sister Lamon moved to Center out on Fulsom Chapel Road and established a church there. The camp meeting was then held there for several more years during July. In the '80s, our little white church by the side of the road at Aiken closed its doors for the last time.

At one time, there were three stores in Aiken. One had been vacant for a while. In 1953 or '54, Joyce and her husband, Velt Warr, opened the old store. That is where I met James Lee McSwain. We were later married in 1956. I didn't know this would mean rising at 4:00 am to cook breakfast and make a lunch.

There was a Pentecostal Camp Meeting going on in Center at the fair ground in the exhibit building. One evening my cousin, Essie, and I were at the store when James Lee and his friend came by. They asked if we would like to go to town. We thought that if I told my mama we were going to church, she would let me go. We were right. We went to church and this was our first date.

Again, since the fair always came to town in October we decided to go. We met James' friend, Ray Adkison, and he went with us. I think we rode every ride there.

The Texas Prison Rodeo in Huntsville was held each Sunday in October. One Sunday we decided to go to the rodeo. Ray didn't have a girlfriend at the time, so I asked my cousin, Dessie, if she would like to go, and she went with us.

James Lee was a logger and hauled logs before I met him. They skidded logs with mules and loaded logs with mules and skid poles. Auvie Adkison worked for him at this time. Mr. Minyard of Jasper built James' first loader. Then they came out with big tractors (Log Hog), the chain saw, and skidders, making the work easier on loggers. He used log wagons to haul logs out of wet bottom land and onto better ground to be loaded.

Marlie McSwain, Courtesy of Mildred McSwain

Michael, Stevie, and Kevin McSwain, Courtesy of Mildred McSwain

James Danley and his Pets

[James and Ester Mae Danley owned the store across the highway from Oad and Allie Danley. In Aiken most families had a couple of dogs and a few cats for pets. James' pets were different. Over the years he had an orangutan, a chimpanzee, a spider monkey, and a big talking parrot…..PHA]

Bruce Britt: One of them was mean. It would take your candy away and eat it.

Ben Burns: The wife just walked in and said that it was James Danley's monkey, and she grew up next door to him. She said that he had a spider monkey which ran free, and a chimpanzee that wore diapers. The chimpanzee had to stay inside because in her words, "he was mean as the old devil".

Tresa Danley Konderla: The monkey had a pet cat and it "picked fleas" off the cat until there was a bald strip down its back.

Lea Osborne: The monkey dressed as a cowboy and rode a dog at Halloween.

Debbie S A: James Danley had the monkey. He also drove the bus. He was my best friend growing up. LOL. He let me sit by him on the bus every day. We were the last ones to get off. He would tell us stories all the time, even about the monkey.

Nadine Windham: Rhonda, I remember throwing pears at the orangutan.

Janette, It looked hungry. Most of the time it would throw them back at us. It could aim!

Rhonda Chandler: We were really trying to feed the poor thing.

J.R. Gray's Store

Jan Akridge: This might be on another post, you can let me know. There was a J.R. Gray's store in Aiken in the '40s and '50s. Regular gas was 16 cents and Ethel was 18 cents in 1944. It was said at one time it belonged to Charlie Hooper. In 1946 Mr. Gray traded his house and store in Aiken to Bob Warr and wife, Mattie, for their farm in South Jericho Community.

Elaine Belanger: Was the J.R. Gray store the dilapidated building just across dirt road from the building that was hit by the truck just recently there in Aiken? Nina Jo, didn't they have red-headed children? I was always told that my grandmother married a Gray after her husband was killed, the daughter's name is Dovie?

Nina Jo Hudspeth Walker: Elaine, my memory isn't so good any more, but I do remember Dovie. She was my neighbor for a while, when I lived in Center. If memory serves, she had red hair. I think, Lillian Bittick is her sister. She worked for Dr. Oats for a long time. Both were sweet ladies.

Rodger McLane: Does anyone have a picture of the store? Mr. Warr and Mattie were my great-great grandparents.

April S: Rodger, have you checked with Betty? I know Mary has some taken on the side of the building that said "Coca Cola".

Rodger McLane: April, Yes! I've seen that one somewhere of, maybe, Betty and Jimmy? I would love to have a big picture of the front of the store for my office.

Helen Windham Rodger, I have one of my mother that shows the round-topped gas pump, but I am not sure where it is. I have never see a good picture of the store, but I would love to see one!

Rodger McLane: Helen, that's cool! I think someone told me the house is still standing, but a new house has been built around it?

Days Gone By

Rodger McLane: Royce Lynn, they must have been good people!

Royce Lynn Johnson: Rodger, They were…I remember both of them…. the store also.

Helen Windham: Roger, I think the porch has been enclosed, and maybe they have built additions.

Rodger McLane: Royce Lynn, I actually have her obituary framed. My dad remembers her at Aunt Essie's toward the end of her life.

Karen Bittick: Rodger, I last saw Grandma Warr at Aunt Essie's not long before she passed. She was very tiny and frail. This was in 1965.

Jana Ivy: Rodger, I am praying for the Warr gene of health and longevity! Hooker Warr was my grandfather and Mattie my great grandmother!

Rodger McLane: Jana, me too! My line is Robert and Mattie, Ernest, Ruby, my dad Rodger, then me.

Becky B: Across the dirt road?

Elaine Belanger: Becky, the building/shack that is on the same side of Hwy 7 as the Danley store- next to Danley store, but the other corner- not going toward Pinkston!

Eldora Gilchrist: Didn't Mr. Gray have a redheaded daughter, seems like I remember her.

Delores Harris Brown: Eldora, a lot of the Grays were redheaded. One of my grandpa's sisters had red hair. Their mother was a Gray.

Rodger McLane: Delores, my oldest sister and I are red headed.

Delores Harris Brown: Definitely in the family genes.

Gwen Taylor Stewart: Eldora, her name was Dellie. There was also a red-headed Gray girl named Agatha.

Joy Tarver: Our little community was very colorful. We had the Gray, Brown, White, Black, and Green families. That's all I can remember right now. Charlie Hooper was my granddad. When he had the store, Bonnie and Clyde came there several times for gas. They were always very respectful and caused no trouble.

Rodger McLane: Helen, I didn't know Great Grandpa Warr owned a store. I never heard that before. Dad has told me he remembered Grandma Warr when she was dying.

Helen Windham: This is Patty McClain and Jimmy Warr standing beside the Warr Grocery Store in Aiken. Rodger, our great grandfather owned it, and he sold it to my dad.

Patty McClain & Jimmy Warr, Courtesy Of Helen Warr Windham.

Where Did Aiken Get Its Name

Jan Akridge: "Aiken was founded in about 1895 and was named for Herman Aiken. He was a Captain in the Mexican War. Note of interest; a Venorah A. Williams was appointed postmaster on June 5, 1902. Grigsby was established about 1905, named after an employee of the Waterman Mill. Waterman was founded in 1905 named after the owner of Waterman Lumber Company".

Makes you wonder if Mt. Herman was named after Herman Aiken! (*Shelby County History Book II*)

Venorah, is this who you are named after?

Venorah McSwain: Yes, Venorah Williams was my grandmother and after she became ill, my Aunt Vida Williams Wakefield resumed postmaster duties.

Jimmie Nell Adkison Lee: Love learning the history of where we were born and raised.

Royce Lynn Johnson: You ever heard Aiken called "Hurtin"?

Mark A: Royce Lynn, yes sir. That's all Daddy ever called it, but he had an alternative word for almost everyone and everything.

William Rudd: Royce Lynn, J.B. Taylor often called it "Hurtin" ... (with a grin) ... when he was my teacher in the 7th grade.

Royce Lynn Johnson: William, J.B. Taylor..... Taught my mom at Salem and me at Center.

Delores Harris Brown: Royce Lynn, I always heard, "Once you get past Aiken you go to Hurtin. "

2

Our Neighbors

Days Gone By

Jewell Chandler Brown

<u>Nadine Windham:</u> My Mawmaw, Jewell Chandler Brown, lived in the white house where the Aiken sign is. I spent all my childhood playing the backroads in and all around that area.

I remember going with her, Charles Devlon Tarver, Rhonda Chandler, Kelley Hancock, and Relissa B when the farmers would pull the plants up at the end of harvest and picking the beans off the vines and getting paid. I got into a bull nettle once. Mawmaw told us how to ease the stinging pain, and she made me turn my head. I was crying more because I didn't want Dev to do that! Also, we used to always go to the dumps and bring back more stuff to build and play with than what we hauled off.

I remember spending the nights. ALWAYS, before you got into her bed, you better have your face, neck, hands, behind, and feet clean. Just saying.

The well at Aunt Francis' place, where Kelley Hancock lives now, has the best well water I've ever tasted. Also, Mawmaw had a huge pomegranate tree next to her house. We had all we wanted, until the well caved in. Uncle James wouldn't let us get near it after that.

I broke my tailbone, when I was little, jumping off a hay bale onto bed springs in the big barn behind Mawmaw's house. When I was five, Aunt Joy, Dev, and I got chased by yellow jackets and got stung bad. I swam a million times in the pond with the cows and snakes.

<u>Joy Tarver:</u> I bet I drank a 100 gallons of that mud. We all had such a good time. Mother [Jewell Chandler] made some of the younger ones

bring a note from their parents saying it was ok for them to swim. How did we survive that and many other things that would get our parents locked up now days? Playing volleyball was another big pastime. Going to the school and getting a ball out of the office, we were trusted to put it back and lock the door. Wouldn't that be nice now? Everyone watched out for the smaller kiddos. And they were all safe as could be. I even walked at night from my house to the school to play. Sometimes, Tommy Chandler, my brother, would get permission to drive the truck to the games. That was a treat. I can't begin to name everyone that played. Most of that same group swam in Pearl Lake too. We liked it better, not so muddy and away from the house. Someone built a float out of old barrels and plywood that was so much fun to jump off of and try not to drown. LOL. I couldn't swim, but that didn't stop me. I knew someone would save me.

Rhonda Chandler: I wouldn't swim in that pond now for nothing!

Cletus Sharpton

Adam J: I appreciate you sharing this information. You mentioned Cletus Sharpton. He was my great uncle. He also hauled pulpwood, when farming was over. He never hauled more than 2 loads a day. Sometimes he'd only haul 1. I'd ride to the wood yard with him. Also, my wife and I live in Uncle Cletus' old house.

Nina Jo Hudspeth Walker: Adam, I used to pick peas for your Uncle Cletus, when I was a just a kid. He would pick up all of us kids early morning. We rode on back of his old flatbed truck. LOL. I thought the world of him & his wife. Although I hated picking peas, but that's how we earned money to get school supplies & shoes. Back then, I would only wear shoes to church and school, and most times only in winter. A lot of kids didn't wear shoes in the summer back then, though.

Adam J: Nina Jo, Uncle Cletus' old truck is in the woods behind my house. His first wife was named Juanita. She passed away in '79.

Tammy Fenley: After Cletus' wife & my grandfather died, he married my grandmother, Effie Mae Fenley. I'm not sure how long it was, but they were married until he died. It seems like it was a good long while. He was a good and very kind man. He was just what my grandmother needed, after my grandfather died. I have a lot of good memories of the house.

Adam J: Tammy, they got married in 1981. He passed away in 1993. Your grandmother was a good woman. She was a good cook. She took good care of Uncle Cletus when he got down.

Tammy Fenley: Yes sir, she did. She had taken good care of my grandfather too. She was a good nurturer.

Nina Jo Hudspeth Walker: Tammy, I thought the world of your grandmother. She and I used to kid each other about being the shortest ladies in the community...sweetest lady ever! Mrs. Effie May was a little shorter than me. LOL.

Clarence Fountain

[Even though he lived most of his life deep in the piney woods of East Texas, Clarence Fountain lived life large. He farmed and worked in the log woods. He was an expert at all of the survival skills: fishing, hunting, and trapping. Oh yes, he made whiskey! Many of the locals have a story to tell about Clarence. Visitors express disbelief when they hear one. After two or three others reassure them that they witnessed the event too, the newcomers want to hear more.

Sheriff Nathan Tindall paid tribute to Clarence in 1996 in the *San Augustine Tribune*.

Here are a few true accounts of Clarence that Sheriff Tindall wrote: He wrestled bears at a carnival at Camp Worth. After someone shot him in the jaw, he just spewed the bullet out. While trapping during the winter, he would get his clothes wet to allow them to freeze. He said that after frozen, the clothes kept him warm. Clarence was bitten by snakes multiple times. When another moccasin bit him, he caught it and spit snuff into its mouth. Clarence went on his way. I don't know that the snake made it...PHA] (Tindall, 1996)

Clarence Fountain (in chair), his brother, James Alsie, and an unidentified female, Courtesy of Matt Sim

Days Gone By

[These are our stories about the legendary Clarence Fountain. .....PHA]

Royce Lynn Johnson: It was John Hoyt who caught Clarence. John hid in a stump hole all night. The next morning here comes Clarence with an old hound dog. The old dog treed John in the hole. Clarence thought he was barking at an armadillo and went on to his still. I heard this story from both of them when they met 20 years later.

Clarence said, "If I had just listened to that old dog!"

Rodger McLane: Perhaps one of the most colorful characters in that bunch. We've always heard stories about Clarence Fountain.

Linda Winder: At the Johnson Squirrel Camp in the 1970s. Royce Johnson and Irron Jimmerson encouraged Clarence Fountain to dance.

Royce Lynn Johnson: I never saw Clarence with shoes on. I was trapping on Tupelo Gum Slough years ago. It had frozen the night before and ice was around the edges. Here comes Clarence wading around running his traps...barefooted!

Fred Borders: I met Clarence a few times. I had a first cousin about 20 years older than me named Crook Parker. He worked for my dad and me throughout the years. He would work for a few weeks and would disappear. We could always find him down at Clarence's house.

Hoyt Hooper: I went to school with his son, Lubbert Earl, and his daughter Maurene, and heard his brother preach a lot of times.

Matt Sims: Hoyt, Maurene was my grandmother. All I remember about Uncle Lubbert is he would give me a $10 bill every time he saw me.

Howell Adkison: Lubbert Earl flatheaded for me at one time.

Our Neighbors

<u>Royce Lynn Johnson</u>: Howell, lots of people today don't know what "flatheaded" means. Spell check doesn't either....

<u>Russell Andrews</u>: Howell, Lots of [people] probably don't know what a flatheader is, but I do.

<u>Howell Adkison</u>: Run a chainsaw, sawing timber.

<u>Rhonda Chandler</u>: Clarence Fountain was one of a kind. My most favorite stories are about this man right here.

<u>Sharon Fenley Prince</u>: Rhonda, my biggest memory of Clarence Fountain is that he was always barefoot.

<u>Nina Jo Hudspeth Walker</u>: Sharon, yep, barefoot even in winter. He wore overalls, most times no shirt, & with one strap undone. At least, that's how I remember Clarence. When he would come to our house, he was always clowning with us kids. A very funny guy!

<u>Joy Tarver</u>: Nina Jo, did y'all know he was in the history books? He got bitten so many times by so many snakes they would use his blood as anti-venom serum.

<u>Rhonda Chandler</u>: Joy, the Center library has a book with him in it... very interesting book.

<u>Mitchell Anthony</u>: I remember going with my dad to Clarence's. Goats, chickens, and pigs were just roaming through the house. Everyone there was drinking, playing cards and dominoes. The cigarette roller had just come out. You put the paper down in a holder, then sprinkled the tobacco in, then pulled a handle and it rolled the cigarette to form! I think it was his wife that smoked the most, but I never rolled so many cigarettes in my life. That day everyone wanted a cigarette. Maybe that's why I never smoked. Except for the time Daddy caught me and

my brothers acting all grown up smoking alfalfa hay. He made each one smoke a King Edward cigar! None of us ever smoked again.

Jan Akridge: This is my tale about Clarence. I went with my 2 best friends down to his house one night. We went for our husbands! I was a town-country girl when I married Billy. Clarence's house was wayyyyy down in the woods. My friend had a little red and white car that high-centered every sand hill between his house and Mt. Herman. I was scared to death. Do you know how scary looking he was? I just knew we were going to high-center and have to walk home.

Jimmie Nell Adkison Lee: I went to Clarence's a few times with my Papa Taylor, and Mama and Daddy. All of us kids would load up. Clarence would walk out behind his house and come back with the goods. I clearly remember how he was dressed and animals running everywhere. God broke the mold when he made Clarence.

Sharon Fenley Prince: My grandfather, Big Bud Fenley, was good friends with Clarence back in the day. Don't remember any stories about the 2, just that they were friends. My grandmother, Effie Mae Fenley Sharpston, is a Fountain descendent. Her grandmother was a Fountain who married a Battles. Joe Fountain told me one time he got a lot of old Fountain photos from my grandmother when he was doing his Fountain family research.

Linda Winder: There is a page on Clarence Fountain in the book on the history of the Fountain family that was done by Christine McSwain Mahan. The book has several hundred pages of information and photos on William Fountain and his descendants. A copy is available to see at the Shelby County Historical Museum. The book is very well researched and has hundreds of people in it. I prepared the photo pages for the book.

Russell Andrews: Linda, my brother, Pete Andrews, used to spend the night with Clarence and Miss Jewel. He woke up one morning, and a big hog was staring him right in his face. I asked how it got in the house.

He said, "It [the house] doesn't have any doors on it."

For some reason, he wrecked his car down there in the woods. I wonder why.

<u>Russell Andrews</u>: My cousin, Steve Tomlin, named Joseph, his son, after Clarence, CJ Tomlin. Mr. Clarence was buried in brand new overalls.

<u>Howell Adkison</u>: I learned to drive by going to Mr. Clarence's and to a couple of other bootleggers for my dad.

Troy Chandler

By Pamila Hooper Adkison

Troy was blessed with many talents. He was a barber, a truck driver and he owned a trailer dealership in Nacogdoches. His special talent was the gift of persuasion.

He persuaded Daddy (Billy Wayne Hooper) to go into the rabbit business with him. They bought one rabbit and built the first cage themselves. They then bought the whole business from a willing, dare I say, relieved grower. It took a few days to move the rabbits and cages. An old chicken house had been razed behind our house in Aiken. They put the cages there tucked under the trees near the back of the property. Some of the cages were about 8' high with "apartments" on four levels.

They both had jobs, so they recruited me to take care of the rabbits. The rabbits had to be watered twice a day and fed in the evening. They paid me 50 cents an hour.

When the cages started filling up with baby rabbits, they built a holding pen about 20' long to keep the fryers. Time came to take them to market. Neither Daddy nor Troy had a pick-up nor coops to deliver them anywhere. What now? I mentioned Troy's gift of persuasion. He convinced a retiring Army Sargent to buy the whole enterprise and move it.

Marceline Crenshaw

By Tammy Fenley

Let me tell y'all something.... I was just on the phone for an hour & half with a lady from my church who is 92½ years old. Now let that sink in a minute... 92½ yrs. Old!!! & at 8 o'clock at night! If you ever saw this lady, you would not even come close to guessing her real age if you didn't know it. She still plays the piano at our church every Sunday morning, Sunday night, & Wednesday night too. And I just learned in our conversation that she has been losing the feeling in her hands for 25 yrs. Now, now, did you get that... a 92 yrs. old that can still read & play music on a piano with limited feelings in her hands & fingers? I also learned that she learned to play the piano from a school music teacher when she was going to school at Excelsior who taught piano lessons (apparently not as an extra job outside of school hrs.) during lunch & break time hrs. She had that & only 5 other lessons outside of school, in which she learned to play the piano. Just her playing the piano is amazing to me, but she also is still the secretary for the White

Rock Cemetery & her chapter of the Eastern Stars, which is an organization that is very near & dear to her heart, & she has been a part of for years. Those are only a few of the things that she still does. Truthfully speaking, her memory is even better than mine! I have often thought & said that no telling what all someone could learn from her life, vast knowledge, & experiences. I told her that she needed to start making recordings of the things she knows & remembers. That they would be priceless to her kids, grandkids, & many others, including me. Anyway, I just had the urge to share a few of my feelings about this remarkable woman with y'all. If you know her, then you are blessed indeed, & I'm sure that you share my feelings concerning what an amazing woman Marceline Crenshaw is?!

The Good Old Days

By Paul D. Hooper

As told to Pamila Hooper Adkison

Jessie Adkison, your husband's uncle, and I were friends. We worked together. Of course, he was older than I was. At one time he and Jewell, his wife, lived the other side of Pinkston off the Arcadia Crossing about 300 or 400 yards next to where Author D Youngblood and his family lived. They lived on some property with a pretty good sized open field, which he planted in cotton. He hired me to help him to chop his cotton...he and Jewel. He was going to pay me 50 cents a day and feed me dinner, pick me up each morning below Ma Parrish's, where I was living at the time, and carry me home in the evening. Which I don't have any idea how many days I worked. I was about 12 or 13 years old. It was about 1947 or '48. That was my first paying job.

Days Gone By

Now, I picked peas for Cletus [Sharpston], Ed Johnson, Owen Bradshaw and Elton McSwain... Me and your daddy, Billy, brother Don, all of us worked, usually, for the same man, at the same field and every day for the grand total of 1 cent a pound for the peas we picked.

Watermelons, we worked for the same people, you know, watermelons and cantaloupes. I don't even remember what we got paid for that, probably so much an hour. We worked from can 'til can't. Whatever we made we spent it on ourselves; for blue jeans, for our shirts, shoes, socks, shorts, and etc. to carry us through the school year, until next season it started all over again.

I guess you could say, Jessie and I were good friends. At one time he and Jewell lived up there on the hill above Ma Parrish's [Willie Mae Choate Parrish], somewhere along about where The Lillie Farm is now. Of course, I lived more with my grandma, than I did with Mama and Daddy [Pearline and Willie Hooper], after I got on up in school. Jessie and Jewell and their son [J.W. Adkison] would walk down to Ma Parrish's on Saturday night. So, we would set there and listen to the Grand Old Opry until late. The kid would go to sleep. Jessie would have to wake him up and get him started to walk home, so he would not have to carry him home. He would end up having to carry him part of the way. That was around '49, because me and the spouse [Henry Faye Bush Hooper] got married in 1953. We got married on 3/8/53. We have been married 67 years.

Paul & Henry Faye Bush Hooper, Courtesy of Henry Faye Hooper

I lived with Ma Parrish, mostly. Well, Mama and Daddy lived just below her, in the old house where the Akridge boy died. I spent the night at Ma's a whole bunch.

Our Neighbors

I can recall the 3 stores in Aiken that you mentioned. Let's see Mrs. Danley's, one across the dirt road directly from her on her side of the highway, was owned by your great-great granddaddy, Charlie Hooper, at one time.

After that, Randall Gray had it. There were several different ones owned it. Anyway, one time Troy Chandler had a barber shop there. Velt and Joyce Warr owned it one time. My friend, Jessie Adkison, used to live in the house back behind it at one time.

Every fall Daddy would get a bunch of families together and go out to West Texas to pull cotton. We would start out early, get out to the Waco area where we had to pick cotton. You couldn't get the bur and all. After that, we'd move on up further west, after we'd been there a month or two. We'd get out in Lubbock, Plain View, Amarillo and Crosby, kind of in that area. Out there in that area, they had converted the gins to separate the cotton from the burs. So we would get bur and all. It took 2000 lbs. of cotton to make bale. Me and Ed Hudspeth, Shine Hooper and Carter Hooper would put 4 bales a day on Daddy's pickup. The others would get another bale on it.

As workers we would follow the cotton. We loaded all paraphernalia on one vehicle. We all got in the same vehicle. We loaded up on top of the furniture and what-have-you, and we'd go west. We'd get to a certain cotton area and stop. Some farmer would approach Daddy, or Ed, or somebody. They'd find out where the field was, how much he had to do, and if he had a place for us to stay. If he had living quarters on his place, that was where we stayed. If he had to, he would have to come up with some place for us to stay, some house. It didn't matter what it looked like, because we weren't going to be there for very long anyway. We would unload all that mess and get everything set up. We usually had a kerosene stove. It would be just like you going down camping on Sam Rayburn today, without a camper. You would get everything you could together, load it in the back of your truck, haul it down there, and set up camping.

PHA: Did just the men go, and the wives stayed back in East Texas?

Everybody, the wives, the kids, the whole family went. Everybody had a job to do. Everybody that was big enough to pick cotton, picked cotton, except Mama, Ethyl, and Mavis. They did the cooking. They usually did it individually. Mama cooked for her family. Ed's wife cooked for hers.

Anyhow, that's the way we did it. We worked, until it got so wet, or it got so cold that we couldn't stand it. We loaded up all of our junk and come back to East Texas. We did that every year for a bunch of years, I guess, until after we married.

[Henry Faye Hooper joined in the narrative.]

Paul speaking to Henry Faye: If I'm not mistaken, let's see, we got married in '53. Didn't we go? Didn't you go cotton picking the first time?

Henry Faye: We got married, and left that same night...

Paul: Oh no, no, no...That's the time I worked in the oil field and worked for Stewart Brothers and Parker in Monahans. Didn't you go cotton picking the first time that you went?

Henry Faye: The first time I went. I remember going cotton picking, but when we went out there...

Paul: We went to stay. It was in the oil field. We went to Monahans. Rented a house in Wicket.

Henry Faye: We decided one night.... He asked me to go with him. We had gone to the movies. He asked me to go back with him.

I said, "Well, we'll have to get married first."

Our Neighbors

We went to Ma Pearline, or did we go to Ma Parrish first?

Paul: I don't know who first. We sought Mama and Daddy, and Riley and Burlie [Bush], that we wanted to get married. They didn't object and we got their blessings. That was a Saturday night. Sunday morning I went to Frank Campbell's house. He was County Clerk at that time. He met me at the courthouse to write us up some license. We had Lee Warren in Aiken to marry us that afternoon. That same day, evening, we loaded up, went to Monahans. I was working for Stewart Brothers and Parker doodle bugging.

Doodle bugging is where you dig a shot hole. You dig a hole with a rig 60 to 80 to 150 to 200 ft., drop a charge of dynamite in it. A crew comes behind you, designating these charges to give a picture of the earth underground. I was working for Stewart Brothers and Parker, and Daddy was, too. I don't remember how long we lived out there. Do you, Mama?

Henry Faye: I don't know. I know it was a long time to be away from my Mama!

Paul: I worked for Roy Stewart, hauling chickens. I worked for Harold McDonald, hauling chickens. I worked in Harold's feed mill for a while. I hauled chickens for Hugh Armstreet, and seems like, the man's name was W.E. Bennifield. I hauled logs for J.C. McSwain. I worked for Hollis [Adkison] in the log woods. Hollis was the driller, when I worked for Stewart Brothers and Parker. I hauled chicken feed for Ralston Purina in '68 and '69. We bought this grocery store and house down here in Martinsville and moved out of Shelby County. Been here ever since.

I worked for Texas Highway Department in 1972. I retired from the department the last of August in '96. I bought an 18-wheeler in '97. I hauled lumber, brick, fence post, landscape timbers, and whatever could be put on a flatbed trailer. I sold it in '98 to Troy Chandler.

Days Gone By

[This is the second interview with Paul. Henry Faye, his wife, and Ann Crain Hooper, my mother are present].

On the eighth day of March in 1953. We, my wife and I, made a giant step and we got married. On the eighth of March which is coming up next month will be 68 years ago.

I worked for Claude Sanford at the Magnolia service station right behind the jail house of that time for quite a while. I worked for Roy Stewart hauling live chickens. He had a feed store, and I would deliver feed to those who were feeding out chickens.

Being paid by the week, it's kinda like a man has a chain 'round you. He could do what he wants to with you. If he didn't have any work for me, he would loan me out every once in a while. He loaned me out to Roy Herder to haul chicken feed. It was one of those days that Ma Parrish had a birthday party at her house. The whole family was there. It so happened that I had a load to deliver to the Aiken Community. I stopped on the side of that hill and went and had dinner with Ma and the rest of the bunch.

He loaned me out to Hugh Armstreet to deliver a load of live chickens to Frank Smith and Sons, a processing plant, out in Waco. When I got there the plant was down. I waited all day to unload. About 6 pm a call come in for me. I had just gotten unloaded and had tied my coops down. I went to the office to take the call. He wanted to know what the problem was. I told him about the plant. He talked to me like I was the one that broke the plant down. He talked to me like I was a stepchild.

"I'll be there before you get the phone hung up," I said.

It is two hundred miles from Waco to Center. I made it in three hours and forty-five minutes. When I pulled upon the scales in East Center, he was standing there in the door. I had done burnt that truck up. I mean, you could hear the valves, rods, and everything just a clattering.

"Here's your truck," I said.

He said, "Pull it over there and park it. It ain't no good no more."

Well, I got his truck back to him.

Anyway, that's kinda how things went. I was loaned out to different ones, but I was getting paid by Uncle Roy. It all worked out.

I hauled logs for J.C. McSwain and I hauled chickens for Harold McDonald. Then we got into the big rigs. Me and your daddy run up and down the road trying to make a living, while your mother and my wife raised you kids.

I had lots of partners: Buford Estes, Billy Hooper, a boy named Hardy. I made a trip with Fate Adams a time or two, Billy Joe Walls, he changed his name to Lester B Wall.

Anyhow, I've done lots of traveling, seen lots of miles, seen quite a bit of country, and wasted lots of time.

On my first trip with Fate Adams, we loaded in the Los Angeles area. When we started out we had to go over the mountain and go over the White Water scales. To avoid the scales we could detour by going to San Diego and cut across Sheep Mountain. As we were going up the hill out of LA, California, there was a parking area with a café. There was a patrolman's car sitting there. He was inside the café drinking coffee and watching traffic. Before we got to the forks in the road, he came out and followed us. When we got to the top of the hill, he pulled us over.

He got out and said, "I know you are trying to miss the scales at White Water. If you will go back and cross the scales without being overweight, I'll let you go. Otherwise, if you are going down this way, there is a feed mill that has a set of scales, and I will weigh you down there."

Well, we knew that we were overloaded. We told him that we were going down this way to hit a certain highway to go over Sheep Mountain to see that part of the country, because we hadn't been that way.

"Yeah, I know, you hadn't been that way, because you are trying to dodge those scales," he said.

We went on down to the feed mill. He pulled us in on the scales, and we weighed. Sure enough, we were over. I don't remember what it cost us, but he wrote us a ticket, and we paid the fine.

We left and took the highway that goes up, over, and down Sheep Mountain. We started down through there. All of a sudden our brakes got hot. The smoke was just a-boiling from my right, rear wheels. We finally got it stopped. We pulled over on the side of that rocky mountain. Partially over. We couldn't get completely off the road, because the edge was right there. It was probably one thousand feet to the bottom. We finally got enough of rocks and sand together to put out the fire on the wheel. It had burnt that brake shield completely up. It had melted the grease in the axle. We took the brake arm loose, and tied it up with a coat hanger, so it wouldn't work. The right, rear section of the trailer didn't have but one brake working on that side. We drove it all the way in, but we missed the White Water scales. We had gone around them, but it cost us in the long run.

There is a lot of open country between here and there. There wasn't such a thing as an interstate. The speed limit for trucks was 45 miles per hour. Every crossroad had one red-light. It took forever to get anywhere.

I've always wanted to get a truck that had enough horsepower to run. I finally got one that would do that, but didn't catch a load going from coast to coast. I always wanted to see how fast someone could take a load from one side of the states to the other, since the interstate highway system was completed. I had a truck that would run, but I never caught that kind of load.

Now, you can drive only so many hours, then you have to shut down for so many hours. You could do it, but you would have to have a pocket full of pills. You just keep driving.

I picked up a load of flat steel at the Houston shipping channel one day and left for Little Rock, Arkansas. The only stop that I made was at Corrigan, Texas. I got to Nacogdoches, hit the loop, went on around, and the next time I had to stop was at the scales in Arkansas. I didn't have to stop then. I rolled across the scales. The next time I stopped was in Little Rock. That is non-stop driving, and it is not forbidden.

I picked up a load of lumber at Russellville, Arkansas. I came down Highway 7, which is like a bad snake road. It is terrible to drive down. I went from there to Crockett, Texas, non-stop. There were no red lights in the way, so I kept driving.

After I retired from the highway department, I sat around here for 3 or 4 months. Then me and Mama bought a truck and trailer. We drove around for a year and a half.

We run up and down the highway. We hauled lumber, metal roofing, anything we could tie down and put a tarp on.

Days Gone By

My wife, Henry Faye, didn't try to drive any. She could handle it, though. One time we were at a fuel stop in Florida. We put in a hundred gallons of fuel. She kicked it in gear, released the brake, and pull it out from the diesel pumps, while I went in, got the ticket, and paid the bill. She backed it up and parked it.

We went from the lower end of Florida up to North Carolina, across to Colorado, and on up into Idaho, and the states in between. I have pictures of the arch in Missouri. I took a load of lumber up there.

The only time I was in Illinois. I brought PVC pipe back to Carthage, Texas. Never got into Michigan in that area. Today you can't walk up there, because the snow is so deep.

Since I retired I sold my truck. We started staying at home. We bought goats. We had quite a few of them. Bought some cows. Sold all of them, but two. Bought a bull. Now we got three cows and a bull. That's the only thing that I have to take care of every morning. It takes about thirty minutes. I feed my cows, and then go over to feed Debbie's birds and squirrels.

Henry Faye: Critters. That is what she calls them, her critters.

Paul: I was feeding Debbie's birds one morning, when I counted fifteen of those red birds as they were feeding. As I come from behind the house and saw them, I stood still, so they wouldn't fly. I put some of the feed out between the corner there and Brenda's house. I also put some feed out behind the house and on the side toward the Family Dollar Store. It is no telling how many were there. I didn't bother to count those.

Henry Faye: Debbie called over here one day and wanted me to ask Daddy, "What should I do with a baby armadillo?"

Our Neighbors

"Knock it in the head," he said.

She had a fit! (Laughing)

Paul: It was about the size of a good-sized rat. You could tell it was an armadillo. The telling difference was the armor plates on its back. The thing is doing well, because I see signs every morning where it had disturbed the ground where I feed the birds.

Henry Faye: It's no telling how much she spends on feed. She has the money, so let her. She is something else about her critters, but she won't take these cats over there. She is afraid they will catch her critters.

Paul: We have a black cat that's as black as an ace of spades. Brenda has one the same. I went out one morning to feed, and when I got to the back gate there was a black cat lying out near the shop. She watched and never took her eyes off of me. I had seen ours in the front door when I left the house. I got in the truck and went over to Brenda's. Hers was home. There is another black cat in the neighborhood. There is not a white spot on it.

Henry Faye: We have one that is solid white. Someone left them out in front of the store. Debbie brought them in and wouldn't get rid of them. The other one is the ugliest thing you have ever seen. When Debbie would leave for work, I would grab her up and put her outside.

One morning I couldn't find her. She had hidden in the back closet. I reached down to pick her up and out fell a little black kitten. She had had one, not a litter of four or five like most cats. Paul built a little pen for her in the closet. Then later on, she hid under the cabinet and had another litter of just one. That one died right away. She only had one cat at a time.

[A white cat comes into the room].

Henry Faye: There's the white one. She is scary. You can look at her one time, and she will have blue eyes. You can see her another time, and she will have red.

Paul: The cat is strange. She can't stand still. She has a [motor] tick and jerks her head sideways.

I don't remember the date or year when Ma Hooper died, but you can look on her tomb stone. On that date, me and Billy were in Pocatello, Idaho. Billy went down to call in.

He come back and said, "Ma Hooper passed away."

Ann: She is buried at White Rock?

Paul: She is buried past where Billy is buried on the left, on the opposite side of the road. Rube and Willie Mae Parrish are buried before Billy on the same side of that road. Raymond, Mike, and Harlan are right below. I'm not exactly sure where Ma and Pa Hooper are, but just past where we're all buried.

(We all laughed. He meant where we have our plots picked out. Paul excused himself and left the room for a few minutes. Henry Faye began telling her story.)

Henry Faye: He was in West Texas. They came in and decided to move to West Texas. All of them. We went to the movie that night. Paul asked me to go back with him. I told him that we would have to get married first.

"Okay," he said.

He didn't ask me. (Laughing)

We went down to Ma Pearline's and asked. They were moving out there. She told us that it would be all right, and we would have to go to the courthouse to get the marriage license. Mr. Willie didn't say anything. Someone called the judge and he met us there. It was Paul and me, Mama and Mrs. Pearline. The judge fixed the papers up. Then, we went over to Lee Warren's and he married us.

Riley and Burlie Bush are my parents. She was originally from Houston. She was a Courtney. I don't know how they met. She was born and raised down there. We lived on every hill down highway seven from Aiken to where Mary Sproul lives now. Then, we moved up to where Rachel and Jack Fountain lived across from White Rock Church. Rube Bush owned it when we lived there.

Then, we went to Nacogdoches. When I was in the fifth grade, I went to school there. I went to school in Aiken at Excelsior and in Garrison. Daddy was a farmer. He farmed wherever anyone needed help. That is where we lived.

From Jack's and Rachel's place we moved to William McCary's place. Mother raised chickens for him. Mrs. Hatton lived across the road.

Paul: That is where you were living when we got married.

Henry Faye: (addressing Ann) Do you remember when Paul first came out West to see Billy?

Ann: (Laughing) Yeah, he was a little bitty guy with a huge cowboy hat. Your hat was bigger than you were.

Paul: I don't remember that.

Henry Faye: A lot of things he doesn't want me to remind him. Do you remember, when I called out there that night wanting to talk to Paul? You told me that he and Billy were down at the bar. When they came back, he called me.

He told me, "Don't call me no more, unless it is an emergency."

Paul: (Laughing) I can't remember that. She said that I said it. I guess I did.

Henry Faye: You did say that. I hung up on you! It wouldn't have mattered what had happened, he wouldn't have heard it from me. I wasn't going to call out there for anything. I don't let him forget it either.

Fate Adams was out there with a load. Paul hitched a ride back home with him. He was home the next day. (Laughing)

Paul: You remind me at least twice a week.

PHA: It's a good thing that you came back for her.

Henry Faye: (Laughing) He was there by daylight the next morning.

[Paul and Henry Faye celebrated their 70th anniversary in 2023...PHA]

Randy Soape: WOW. Reading the names was just like hearing Pa Hooper [Carter Hooper] talking about the same.

One story Pa Hooper told. Everyone got setup like Paul Hooper was saying. They started picking cotton the first morning. Uncle Travis Hooper, Uncle Verlon Hooper, Pa Hooper, and several others encountered rattlesnakes. Everybody loaded up and left, headed for safer "pickin's."

Momma (Essie Hooper Soape) told a story about catching a baby jackrabbit, bringing it to East Texas and turning it loose. It hung around for a good while.

<u>Nina Jo Hudspeth Walker</u>: WOW. Paul, what memories! I remember going with Mom & Daddy and a bunch of y'all to West Texas. I was not old enough for school, about 4, I think. I don't remember a lot, but I remember bits & pieces like, riding on Mom's or Daddy's cotton sack while they picked cotton until their sack got too full & heavy. Then I had to wait at the end of the row, or 'till they emptied their sack. I also remember us stopping on the side of road & camping one night. Have no idea where we were. Then we ran across Earnest & Lid Warr. I guess, they were living out there, or maybe just working there. Also, being just a kid I had no idea where we were, just in West Texas. LOL I remember, Mrs. Warr had one mean turkey and fast too. Man, a road runner had nothing on that mean gobbler. If you could make it from her gate to her front door without that gobbler catching you, you were lucky... needless to say I wasn't lucky! Thanks Paul, for jogging my memories (except, for the "turkey part." I think that turkey gave me a complex.). LOL

Days Gone By

Cotton Picking Trips

By Joyce Wilson Bright

I liked Paul's story about the cotton picking trips. Mama loved to tell people about going to Lubbock with the Hoopers to pick cotton. It was so much fun, I was only about 5, and Velma would have been 11. I think Billy Wayne was her age. Anyway, I have a picture that Velma took of me with Billy Wayne. It had to have been cold, I had on a little, long coat, and the wind was really blowing. He had on a straw hat. In the evenings all the kids jumped rope. That was a big thing back then.

I'm not sure if that was a cotton patch or not. I don't remember a lot about the trip out there, but I know we went in the back of Mr. Willie's truck, and there were several that went. I'm not sure how many kids went, but there were several because we had a big rope and all the kids jumped rope in the evenings. I was looking at the picture and your Dad had a suit on and I don't think that was a straw hat. He was such a likable person.

Be sure and show it to Paul. I'm not sure if he went or not. I just remember there being several kids. I looked at it again and couldn't tell if that was a cotton patch. It may have been. I think the bushes would be dead, and they picked the bolls. It was different from picking cotton. I know they had metal buildings separate that the families stayed in, and remember eating pork and beans, and peaches. There were a lot of jackrabbits, and you could see them from far away; also groundhogs.

I wish I could remember the guy's name where Mr. Willie took all of us to pick the cotton bolls. I know it was in Lubbock. Velma and I only went that one time. Mama and Daddy went another time.

Mama loved it and loved to tell people about going on those trips. Of course to the kids, it was a lot of fun. Those were some good memories.

Hi Pam, I talked to Velma and she said that was the cotton patch.

N. Joyce Wilson Bright & Billy Wayne Hooper, Courtesy of Joyce Wilson Bright

Delano Warr

<u>Eldora Gilchrist</u>: Does anyone remember when Delano Warr had a radio station in the shed behind Aunt Donnie's house?

<u>Barbara J. Scates</u>: I think the FCC came out and shut him down, because his broadcast was interfering with other radio stations. Pretty smart for an old country boy to put together the electronics to be as powerful as a radio station. Not long after a tornado came thru and

scattered his equipment all over the pasture...45 RPM records were everywhere.

Russell Andrews: He had enough antennas on that car of his he could talk to someone in Europe.

Eldora Gilchrist: Dickie has his old car. It's a 1954 Mercury Comet two door hardtop. It had 2 whip Ariels with Motorola police band radio still in it when Dickie bought it. He paid Aunt Donnie $50 for it years ago.

Wrinkled Memories

By Barbara Scates

We sometimes wonder just when a child starts to remember things that happen around them. At what age does the brain start to have those wrinkles experts say happen when the brain stores memory? Everything is computerized this day and time, but humans still rely on what God gave us to store memory...the brain. Most children are probably three to five years old before they start to remember things and then it seems like it's not long 'till we start to forget everything again. We forget things that happened yesterday, but remember what happened 40 years ago. The brain is a strange thing and is not easily upgraded.

I wrote a record of my growing-up years for my family and am sharing a few of these things with you. This record of happenings and events is to the best of my memory, but not necessarily accurate. I am simply relying on my wrinkled brain to try to recapture those long ago years.

In The Beginning

I guess my first memory of anything was being shuffled off to Grandmother's and Papaw Luman's house in what I think was the middle of the night. I was probably about 3 years old. The only thing I really remember is crying when someone, perhaps my daddy, John Thomas Williams, Jr., put me in the bed with grandmother, Eunice Luman. All that was going through my mind was that I wanted my mother, Vaudine Luman Williams. I had no idea that my brain most likely was getting its first wrinkle. My guess is that my mother was going to the hospital to give birth to my younger sister, Gay Nell. That first wrinkle must have been quite a shocker because I do not remember Mamma coming home from the hospital with a baby.

Our house was about ten miles west of Center on Highway 7. We lived in the Mt. Herman Community. There were five of us kids; Glenn Williams, Billy Williams, Wanda Williams, Barbara Williams (me) and Gay Nell Williams.

Our Momma was Elizabeth Vaudine Luman Williams and Daddy was John Thomas Williams, Jr.

Daddy was a Baptist preacher known as "Brother Junior". He had a good speaking voice, one that made you set up and pay attention. On Sunday mornings, he would go to the local radio station, KDET, in Center and preach on the air. We would listen from our old wooden box radio.

Daddy could play the guitar and sing too. He actually made a record at one time at the radio station. I remember him singing a song to us called "Penny Candy".

Charlie Fountain was our neighbor. He and his wife Delva were good people. They had chicken houses. One year their well was unable to furnish enough water for their chickens and Charlie came and ask Momma if he could put a pump in our well to pump water to his chickens. Since we didn't have running water in the house, he offered to run water to our house in exchange for using our water for his chickens. So Momma agreed and that's how we came to have running water in our house.

School Daze

Most of our friends and neighbors attended school at Excelsior. But not us. We rode the school bus into Center each day. Our bus driver was Mr. T.J. Smith. Most of the time he was a pretty nice guy, although he hardly ever had much to say. If we got loud on the bus, he would glance up in the mirror and we knew to get quieter. Every year at Christmas time, Mr. Smith would give us one of those little New Testament Bibles. Sometimes he would also give us apples or oranges.

We all remember our teachers. One that really sticks in my mind is Mr. J.B. Taylor. He and his family lived near us in Mt. Herman or maybe just on the outskirts. Mr. Taylor was the arithmetic teacher...we didn't call it Math back then. A student would ask him how to work a problem.

He always answered the same answer with a smile, "You work it with a pencil and piece of paper."

He always called me "Little Williams", since I was the fourth one from the same Williams family, and he taught all of us. Guess he didn't know there was one more coming his way in a couple of years.

Friends & Neighbors

Don Lovell was a neighbor and he was about the same age as my sister, Wanda. Don's parents owned the store in Mt Herman. It was called "Tony's" at one time and then became "Ura's." Tony and Ura Lovell were Don's parents. Don came to our house and hung out with us almost every day. Wanda, Gay, and I would follow Don around wherever he went. We usually ended up on the bank of a creek or stream. He would cut a limb and fix up fishing poles for all of us. He also baited our hooks and took off all the perch we caught. We would take them home. My mother would give us a skillet, grease, and corn meal, so we could cook them outside. Don would clean the fish and build a fire, and we cooked up the best tasting fish you could ever ask for. For some reason there was a ladder standing at the back of our house, and we would climb on top of the house and eat our fish. It was all Don's idea! We did whatever Don did!

Don had a BB gun and he would shoot birds. Again we cooked the birds and climbed the ladder to the top of the house and feasted on those birds. I would not eat a bird now, but those were delicious!

Momma would take us to Caney Creek to set out hooks. We would hand fish all day, and then go back and check the hooks the next morning. If you have ever been on a creek and heard something that sounded like a panther screaming, never fear. It is probably just Don Lovell letting everybody in the county know he caught a fish. He would get so excited when he caught a fish and he would holler to let us all know…I would love to hear him holler that he caught a fish just one more time! Momma always said he scared all the fish away with his hollering. But we loved him. He was so happy when he was fishing or hunting. We had the best fun growing up with him!!!

Jamie Warr was another neighbor. We rode the bus with him and his brother Delano. I usually sat with Jamie in the seat that has the hump in the floor. Don Lovell sat in the seat in front of us. We always had a good time laughing and joking. I remember one night Jamie carried several of us to the Rio Theater. We were all sitting quietly during a really scary part of the movie. Well, Jamie sneezed…and if you never heard a Jamie Warr sneeze, then you don't know what you missed. It was extremely loud, and he could make it last forever. A couple of girls were sitting in front of us, and his sneeze scared them really bad. They got up and left! The truth is, it scared me too, but after the scare was over, it was really funny!

The Big Pressure Cooker Blow Up in Mt. Herman

I have one more story I have to tell. My sisters, Wanda, Gay Nell, and I learned to cook at an early age. We could cook a meal as good as our mother could. Our mother worked and most days when we got home from school, we put on a pot of beans to cook. Momma had this pressure cooker that would cook the beans real fast. We were pretty good at cooking in it, even though I was a little afraid of it, because if you didn't watch it closely and turn the burner down when it heated up, it would blow the plug out of the lid and scare you half to death.

I remember one summer day, we put on a pot of beans late in the afternoon. We went outside to play and forgot about the pressure cooker. Wanda remembered it, and we took off running to the backdoor. We had a screen door, so we peeped in to see what the pressure cooker was doing. Well, as we expected it was making all kinds of noise and steam was coming out of the little, jiggler thing on the top. We knew it was getting ready to blow. Wanda started to go in and turn the burner off, but decided it was not a good idea. So we stood there on the back steps peeping through that old screen door waiting for it to blow up. It didn't take long. It blew up and we ran away from that back step as quickly as we could. When we realized all was quiet, we slowly walked back to peer inside that screen door. Pinto beans were dripping from the ceiling and all over the kitchen floor. If you have never seen your supper dripping from the ceiling, then you have no idea how we were feeling. We went inside and began the process of cleaning up the mess. Wanda stood in a chair and wiped beans off the ceiling. Gay and I attempted to clean beans from the floor. I don't think I told you that Wanda was probably 9 or 10 years old, and I was 7 or 8 years old, and little sister was 5 or 6 years old. I am not sure that kids this day and time even know how to cook, much less take on a cleaning job as big as a blown-up pressure cooker. I have been afraid of pressure cookers ever since that day. But...that was the good ole days!!!

Some of our other friends and neighbors:

Jimmie Nell Adkison, Kathy Adkison, Edward Adkison, Tommy Adkison, Ronny Adkison, David Adkison (David and I have the same birthday), Donna Adkison, EllaRay Choate, Lonnie Choate, Donnie Choate, Loretta Choate, Larry Choate, Jimmy Ray Choate, Larry Russell, Dudley Russell, Ferrell Russell, Joye Taylor Hodges, Peggy Taylor, Bob Wilson, Janice Wilson, Royce Wilson, Tommy Emanis, Gary Bruce Emanis, Charlotte Parker, Mattie Parker.

Just for fun...see if you remember any of these!

Floorboard - the floor of a car

Footfeed - the gas pedal

Hubcap - a bowl for the cats to eat out of...LOL

Pocket - the glove compartment of a car

Rat - a verb meaning tangling your hair with a ratting comb then smoothing it out for that big hair look

Sears & Roebuck Catalog - toilet paper

Sunday-go-to-meeting clothes - clothes worn to church (only)

Turtle Hull - trunk of a car

Remember: Tom Walkers, Black Draught, Cigar Boxes, Top Cola, Party Lines, Peacock Lake, picking up Coke bottles, Arthur D. Youngblood (bus driver), Pearl Lake, and Jess Warren's Store.

Jan Cruse: Good memories. Don was a part of our home growing up also. I always thought, because he was an only child that he enjoyed all the noise of siblings.

Gwen Taylor Stewart: I just love your stories—they bring back so many wonderful memories of the people who grew up in our "neighborhood". (I guess the wrinkles are still there—but they just have a few wrinkles!). And thank you for sharing your sweet memories of my dad-JB Taylor.

Nina Jo Hudspeth Walker: Good stories Barbara, I'm with you on the pressure cooker incident, except mine was chicken hanging from the ceiling. No excuse for me though, I was an adult. LOL

Gaye T L: Gay Nell and I were in the same grade. She was always called by her first and middle names. They never got us confused!

Debbie B H: I remember Gaye Nell well. We were in the same grade.

A Tribute to My Hero

By Jana Adams Ivy

As I am relaxing here in Dundee, Michigan, feeling the gentle, cool breeze, a phone call from my brother, Mike, takes me back to my special, treasured memories of my childhood. He informed me with sadness that one of my favorite teachers, mentor, and hero had

Our Neighbors

passed, Mr. Bo Barbe. Not only was he the tallest man in stature that I had ever known, he stood just as tall in his values of honesty, hard work, kindness, and his love for impacting others to be the best they could be.

During Excelsior Elementary, life was filled with fun, simple times, and lots of love and laughter, thanks to Mr. Bo Barbe.

When Mrs. Linda caught me devouring Cheetos in Reading class, she quietly asked, "Are you eating Cheetos in class?"

My immediate response was, "No Ma'am!"

As Mrs. Linda strolled slowly over to my desk, staring at my orange-crusted fingers and tongue, she whispered, "Do I need to talk to your best buddy, Mr. Barbe about this?"

As she gave me something to wipe my orange fingers with, I immediately, handed over my unfinished Cheetos with a shameful nod, because I simply could not disappoint Mr. Barbe.

On my birthday, each year, I recall anxiously awaiting for Mr. Barbe to lift me high into the sky to give me my Gentle Birthday Pats, as he held me by my homemade corduroys, while swirling me around in the air as I listened to his wonderful laughter. Routinely, he made all of us kids feel special with his kindness. He always took the time to build your confidence, while giving you great advice about being a role model for others.

In high school, I ran track with Mr. Barbe's daughter, Deb, who was also a great friend. At the starting line, you could always glance up to the stands, and there his smiling face would be. He was our greatest fan, constantly encouraging and cheering us on. Before each race, he issued us the "PEP TALK", which included sharing with us the advantages that

Deb and I had over the other participants. After each meet, he always provided me dinner and made sure that he delivered me home safely.

Applying for scholarships for college was very competitive. The essay topic was to write about your hero and what influence he had on your life. Of course, I chose Mr. Bo Barbe, and I won the scholarship, which helped me further my education at Stephen F. Austin. I chose Education as my major with an emphasis in Special Education, since that was the route my hero studied. When I graduated from college, I used Mr. Barbe as my reference for my first job interview at the American International Charolais Association, just behind the Astrodome in Houston, Texas. The ad listed in the paper quoted, "Must have knowledge of "bells, " but Mr. Barbe assured me it was a misprint and should have said, "Bulls". With his advice, I was hired as the Assistant to the Breed Director of Charolais cattle. I didn't apply for a teaching position, since it was in the middle of the year. But, a year later, I received a call from a familiar voice, Mr. Barbe.

He asked, "How are you doing? And would you like a job in Center, Texas, as a Special Education teacher?"

I replied, "Where do I go for an interview?"

His reply was, "Well, this is your interview, young lady; you are hired; I will be your Director of Special Education." Of course, we had an initial formal interview and I was immediately hired. I taught Elementary School for 31 years and attribute my success in the teaching field to Mr. Bo Barbe, my hero.

He will always be remembered as the Gentle Giant whose values stood as tall as his lofty height. Thank you, Mr. Bo Barbe, for impacting my life and enriching the lives of countless others. You will be greatly missed, but always a hero in my eyes.

With loving memories, Jana Adams Ivy, Dundee, Michigan.

Grit in Your Spit

By Howell Adkison

One particular day at Excelsior, Charles Wheeler and I were chasing each other around the old well house. One of us reversed his direction and we ran right smack into each other and collided. He fell out on the grass. I fell against the corner of the shed and busted my left eyebrow open. Mr. Billy Bo came and checked me out, stopped the bleeding, and hauled me to the doctor. I got about six or eight stitches.

Later that year, or maybe it was the next, someone had given the school stalks of sugarcane for the kids. I was cutting on my piece with my sharp knife and sliced right through my left forefinger. Mr. Billy Bo hauled me to the doctor again. This time I got about thirteen stitches. I still have that scar today.

What I remember most about Mr. Billy Bo is that he was, at that time, trying out for a major league baseball team. I don't recall which team. He had Charles Wheeler to catch for him as he practiced. Charles would get his back against the old white school building. Mr. Billy Bo would throw ball after ball to him. Charles would catch them. Now, you had to have "grit in your spit" to keep standing there catching balls coming at you faster than today's speed limit.

Over the years when we would see each other, Mr. Billy Bo always had a smile on his face and a kind word.

John B: My dad always had a smile on his face. I sure do miss him!!!Thank you for sharing your stories.

<u>Joy Tarver</u>: I remember him in the woman-less wedding play at Excelsior. He was hilarious.

<u>Theresa Bush Bradshaw</u>: My dad, Travis Bush, was the groom. Such fun memories.

<u>Erma Bush Parrish</u>: Theresa, He would only be in it if he could be the groom. Said he wasn't wearing a dress.

<u>Jimmie Nell Adkison Lee</u>: Through 12 years of school Mr. Barbe was the teacher I loved the most. I remember when he lived across the highway from the school in this tiny house. It broke my heart when he passed away.

Where Do I Start

By Ann Crain Hooper

As told to Pamila Hooper Adkison

Back then, I was working as a car hop at a drive through restaurant in Andrews. Billy Wayne [Hooper] and WH [Adkison] were in Andrews working in the oil fields. I met him at the drive through. He would come get something to eat. We just got to talking and he asked to take me out. I told him he would have to go to my house to get it Okayed. He did. He talked to Mom. I don't remember if he talked to Dad or not. He talked to Mom, and she Okayed it. So we started dating.

Billy had a black Buick with birds on the fenders. He thought he was a cool cat. I guess he was, because he caught a lot of girls, I'm sure.

The oil crew that Billy worked with moved to Monahans. He moved with them, but he would come back to Andrews to see me. It was on a Friday, when we decided to get married. The reason I remember that is; it was ball game night. (Laughing) Every preacher in Andrews was at the ball game. So we couldn't do it that night. A few days later he came over, and we were going to New Mexico. Well that didn't work out. Mama was with us. When it started getting late, she made us turn around and go back home. We didn't get married that night. So another week went by, before he came over again. We were going to a Church of Christ. Everybody was gone that night. We finally found a Baptist preacher that would marry us. We got married and went to Monahans that night. He worked in the oil fields, and I kept house. We were married on October the 24th, '52.

Anna Crain Hooper 1952, Courtesy Ann Hooper

Billy Wayne Hooper 1952, Courtesy of Ann Hooper

Our Neighbors

We lived in a little motel-like room. It had a couch that made out into a bed. It was one big room. It had a kitchen, a bathroom and bedroom. All combined.

When we lived in Monahans, Pa Willie came out there to work in the oil fields. He came by himself. The rest of the family didn't come out, because Ma Pearline was expecting.

Billy and Pa Willie were working and got their clothes dirty. So they decided they needed to wash them. The laundry building was right behind where we lived.

"Okay, I'll wash your clothes for you," I said.

I had never washed clothes. Mother took care of that before I got married. Starch came in a box. You had to mix it up, boil the water and make it yourself. I had never made starch. I used a whole box to make the starch for a couple pair of pants. Pa Willie was wearing khaki pants at that time. I put his pants in the whole box of starch. I had to rewash them. He said that they were so stiff that they could stand up by themselves. That was a mess.

Paul came out right after his daddy did. We lived in the end building of a motel. Right next to the motel was a paved road. He come walking down that road. Paul was a young guy and thought he was handsome. We thought he was handsome, too. He had a cowboy hat that was bigger than he was. Pa Willie had a place in the same motel, and Paul stayed with him.

The rest of the family finally moved out west after Becky was born. Well, she was born in January. It was in March or later, when they came out to live. They moved to a little place called Wicket, which was on the other side of Monahans. At that time we still lived in Monahans.

Pa Willie's father had gotten sick and was in bad shape. This was before Pam was born. He and Ma Pearline had used our car to go back home. They got near a little town on the other side of Nacogdoches, and wrecked, and tore the Buick up completely. Paul was out there, so we came home in Paul's car.

We stayed two weeks, so we could get all of the insurance and things on Billy's car taken care of.

After two years, Pa Willie and Ma Pearline decided to move back home to East Texas. We followed them.

They had rented a place on Highway 7 when we came back. Billy got a job hauling chickens. Paul did, too. Then I met Foy G and Selvie [Bradshaw]. That's one of Billy's cousins. They lived in Ft. Worth and would come in every once in a while. They talked Billy and me into moving there, and Billy hauled across country. He drove for O.L. Boydston. I don't remember what he hauled at first, but he would come here and get chickens in Center and carry them to California. He did that, and he'd be gone for weeks at a time.

When we came home this time, we stayed at Ma Parrish's. The Pentecostal Church was a little ways from Ma's house. All of us, on Sundays, would sit out on the porch and listen to their service. Some of Billy's aunts were Pentecostal people on his mama's side, and his daddy's side too.

When we moved back to Center from Ft Worth, we found an apartment in town. Pa Willie and Ma Pearline lived at Jericho.

Billy didn't like living in town, so we kept looking until we found the Elsie Dean house in Aiken, and moved in. It's across from the Pentecostal Church. We lived there for a little while. We traded that place for one near the school house. We bought that house from Jack and Rachel Fountain. We lived there for several years.

I worked at Sand Hills Nursery. It's down the road from here. I worked there probably about a year, maybe two. I liked working at the flower shop. Then I worked at Walmart.

I work at a plastic plant for Sug Jones, then I worked in Nacogdoches at Sun Terrace, a lawn chair place.

We were still in Aiken, when I went to beauty school. My next door neighbor was going to beauty school. She talked me into it. I got my license, but I haven't kept them up. That was interesting: how to fix hair, how to cut hair, and how to do perms.

At Excelsior I drove the school bus, and I was a teacher's aide. I would help the teachers with all the kids. I helped in the cafeteria. They had to cook a lot.

Billy had a horse. I took care of his animal. While he was off on his truck, I took care of his animals. He wanted me to be a rancher. When he was at home, he was asleep. He didn't get enough rest.

We bought groceries from Mrs. Danley. She was a very good person. A lot of the time, it would be weeks before I would pay her. I had the money, but she never dunned me.

We moved into this house in '68. The reason I said that is because Ginia was born in '67. She was about one or younger. We bought it from D.L. and Lavern Battles. We had chicken houses here, too. I wouldn't feed chickens.

I told Billy, "Buy it, if you want to, but I'm not feeding chickens."

The reason that I wouldn't was because, everyone who had them, couldn't go anywhere or do anything. They had to stay right there.

So he hired his daddy. I don't know what we paid him. It was not too much. Back then, you didn't get much. We had two big houses. They were laying houses, but when we bought the place there were no chickens in it. We didn't want laying houses. That's the reason that little building is down there. It was for the eggs, where they washed them up and put them in the boxes.

I'll be 82 in November. I was busy, wasn't I? [Laughing]. Now I'm retired and keeping the road hot.

Jimmie Nell Adkison Lee: I remember the smell of Faultless (I think that was the name) Starch to this day!! I bet his pants were stiff.

Alec C: I can remember my momma flicking the starch on Daddy's pants as she hit them with a hot iron. I can still smell it. She took great pride in my daddy's appearance when he was a Houston Fire Chief. She gave up when he took up farming and broilers!!

Jerry H: Does anyone remember the metal inserts used in pants legs to reduce wrinkles. Mom would use these when she hung pants on clothes line.

Pam Adkison: Mother used them on Daddy's pants. Supposedly, they aided in the ironing, and putting the crease in the pants. A woman's house-keeping abilities were evaluated on those creases. I wouldn't pass that test today.

Jerry H: Pam, wrinkles are in style.

Our Neighbors

Ann Crain Hooper (Annie-Go-Go), Courtesy of Cherry Murphree

Annie-Go-Go

By Pamila Hooper Adkison

(Allow me to tell you the story of Annie-Go-Go. Her early years are family stories that I heard in the living room at Ma and Pa Crain's. As stories are being told there is no order to them. Most begin with, 'Do you remember when......?' Before Ann moved to East Texas, I become a part of her life and had a front row seat to the events. Let me share some of these stories with you.)

Once upon a time in a land far, far west of Ft Worth in a small town called Gordon, a handsome young man, Dorsey Crain, and a beautiful young woman, Willie McAllister, fell in love and got married. It was during the years between the two world wars. Life was not easy, but the couple decided to have children to share in their love. Derrell was their first child. Then in late 1938 the small family welcomed Anna Lou Crain into its circle.

Being a child she did not realize that the world was in such turmoil; that another war was coming.

Mr. Crain said, "I am moving to Wheeling, Illinois, to build airplanes for the war effort."

He and Mrs. Crain loaded up the car with Derrell and little Anna and off they went to the north. That winter while Mr. Crain built airplanes, and Mrs. Crain made a home, Anna and Derrell played in the snow. The snow turned the country side into a wonderland. Anna had never seen such beauty.

Excitedly, she woke up each winter morning anticipating another day playing games in the snow. Also, in 1943, a new baby sister was born. She wanted Dolores to come out to play.

Mrs. Crain said, "When Dolores gets bigger, she may go out to play."

After five years in Illinois Mr. and Mrs. Crain moved back to the arid lands around Gordon. They moved in with her grandmother, into the house where Anna was born. Anna, her brother, and sister had not forgotten the snow, but they became curious about their new surroundings. They climbed the trees in the mesquite groves. In the cool of the evenings, Mr. and Mrs. Crain would sit on the porch and watch them play in the unpaved streets of Gordon with their cousins. On the weekends Mr. Crain would walk the children to the movies.

West Texas saw an oil boom develop. In the 1950s, with people buying more cars, and more roads were paved for travel, there became a need for increased oil production. Mr. Crain saw another opportunity to provide for his family. He and Mrs. Crain moved their family one last time to their forever home in Andrews, which is far, far west of Gordon. Anna grew and grew until she became a teenager. She liked skating at the roller rink and going to the movies. These activities required an entrance fee. As you may guess, she was always in need of extra cash. She decided to get a job. She worked as an usher at the local movie house.

The automobile changed many things of the American life. Drive-in movies sprang up around the country. Motorists could watch a movie and not leave their cars. Drive-up diners became popular with car owners. One could pull into the parking lot of a diner, turn his headlights on, and blow his horn. A carhop would come out to the car and take his order for any item on the menu. With a smile, she would return with his meal and a soda pop.

The Mustang had been an established diner in Andrews. The added service of a drive-up feature made it attractive to the oilfield men who appreciated the curb service, and the teenagers who would stop by for a quick Coke as they cruised Broadway and Main streets.

Anna became a carhop on roller skates. She worked at the Mustang, which was only a few blocks from home. She was punctual and efficient at her job. She was kind to everyone and her engaging personality brought many back to the business.

Anna never could have imagined that this job would lead to a major change in her life. It soon became obvious that the oilfield man, that drove the Buick with the eagle ornaments on the front fenders, was stopping by just because of Anna. She thought he was charming, but he was from East Texas and would probably go back. He did go back, but Billy Wayne Hooper took Anna with him as his new wife.

All that Anna knew about East Texas was that it was far, far east of Ft. Worth. She was familiar with the desert landscape of the southwest with stretches of flatland. The trees in Andrews were about as high as the roof of the house. East Texas was different with gently, rolling hills and pine trees. When Anna saw the tall majestic pines in East Texas she was mesmerized by their beauty.

"Why, the water tank for the city of Andrews isn't as tall as these pines," she said.

Another thing Anna had to adjust to was the size of her new family. Most of her aunts and uncles had three or four children. Mr. and Mrs. Hooper had nine children at home. They welcomed her and treated her as one of their daughters. Mrs. Hooper even taught her to sew, which in a rural family was an economic asset. Mr. Hooper called her 'Ms. Ann' until he passed away.

When Anna moved east she changed her name to Ann.

Every couple of years Ann would travel back to Andrews to visit her parents. On the alternate years they would drive to Center, Texas, to visit Ann and her family. Yes, the drive was hard, but letters and phone calls are not the same as seeing one's parents in person. This small practice lasted for decades, until her parents could not make the 500 mile drive. Ann would still make the trip. She would pack up her children and grandchildren to go see Ma and Pa Crain. A few times she managed to have her great, granddaughter, the 5th generation to Ma Crain, make the trip to Ma's house.

Ann and Billy Wayne raised four children. They had two girls and two boys. The boys were sandwiched between the girls in birth order. Pam and Jimmy came first. Then eight years later Cole and Ginia came along. The age gap between the boys made it seem like they were raising two different families, but her family wouldn't have been complete otherwise.

*Cole, Pam, Billy Wayne, Ginia (the baby), & Jimmy Hooper,
Courtesy of Pamila Hooper Adkison*

Ann became renowned for her chicken dumplings. There were friends who would pay her to make dumplings on special occasions for their own families.

For the main holidays of each year Ann would prepare dinner at her home. Anyone was welcome. She had one rule. She started serving at 12 noon. If you arrived late, chances are that the meal would be cold and the dumplings would be gone.

Ann put great effort in keeping the family together. As the hostess, she made the arrangements for the Hooper Reunion. She kept up with everyone's addresses and informed them with announcements of the time and place.

Ann worked at different places during her life. One place was at Sug Jones' Plastic Plant in Center. In Nacogdoches she worked at Sun Terrace Furniture factory. She spent 4 or 5 years employed at Walmart in Center. Before she retired she worked for the Excelsior School District as a teacher's aide, cafeteria server, and bus driver.

Years later it was not unusual, when she was out in public, for adult

Days Gone By

men or women to hug her and say, "When I went to Excelsior you drove my school bus."

With great joy she would reply, "O yes, I remember you."

Ann joined the Red Hat Ladies of Center. This energetic group would don red hats and scarves and would have lunch once a month. As they walked around town, people would smile, wave, or blow their car horn. They enlivened downtown and were always welcome. One year Ann and the Red Hat Ladies took a cruise around the Hawaiian Islands.

(This spirited group must have been the talk of the ship.)

After Ann retired, Mrs. Arlene LeFever persuaded her to join the Golden Harvest Singers from First Baptist Church. The singers would visit Old Folks Homes and serenade the residents. They would participate in singing competitions of East Texas and take trips to other parts of the USA. Mackinac Island, MN; Niagara Falls, and Amish country in Indiana are some of the places she has been with the Singers. Ann has also visited: Branson, MO; Eureka Springs, AK; Mesa Verdi and Phoenix in Arizona, and Pikes Peak, CO. She has also been to Paris, France.

(You must keep this a secret from her pastor. When Ann and Mrs. LeFever would get bored, they would sneak over to Shreveport and go to the "boats". Her limit was $20 and that had to cover lunch, too.)

As of this writing, Ann goes to the Senior Citizen Site on the days that the Golden Harvest Singers do not meet. Having lunch there is a bonus. She mainly goes there to play cards or bingo. When the bingo lady doesn't show up, Ann does the calling of the numbers.

Ann enjoys telling about her trips. She has friends who say that they would like to travel some.

She tells them, "Give me a call. I have my bag packed by the front door. I'll go with you."

(That is the story of Annie-Go-Go. Right this minute I know she is planning another trip to Andrews for a reunion with her sister, and nieces and nephews. God speed. I love you Mother, Pam.)

(P.S. We took the trip to Andrews. We had a flat in Abilene, and drove on the donut tire the rest of the way. The flat happened about 5 pm. It was midnight when we made it to Andrews. We shared pictures with Dolores, and Mark and Shelly, Derrell's kids. Mother taught us how to play Head and Foot, a game using five decks of cards. We made it home safely.

Ura Lovell

<u>Jimmie Nell Adkison Lee</u>: I remember Ura was the first woman I ever saw pump gas…she always had perfectly painted nails, hair done perfectly and dressed up every day. She had a pair of brown gloves that she put on before pumping the gas. The front of the store was paved with soda water bottle caps (we never said "Coke", all of them were "sodie waters.")

*Howell Adkison & Ura Lovell, Mar 1968,
Courtesy of Pamila Hooper Adkison*

Earl Campbell

By Pamila Hooper Adkison

Vivian and Earl Campbell started running the store at Mt. Herman when my sons were babies. We were by the store two or three times a week. The boys played hide-n-seek behind the bread counter. They checked out the candy display and used the watermelons for stools.

They were about two and four when everything changed. As children they liked popcorn, Captain Kangaroo, and Kool Aid. On that particular day, Earl wasn't there at first. He had been checking on his cattle. He came in through the back door slapping the dust off his clothes (army-green, khaki pants and shirt) with his western hat. Both boys stopped their playing and stood still. Looking up with big eyes, they watched him as he crossed the room going into the feed room.

After he had passed them, they ran over to me excitedly and said,

"Look. Look. That's Mr. Green Jeans!"

Mr. Green Jeans is a character on the Captain Kangaroo show.

After that they were always hoping to see Mr. Green Jeans, aka Earl Campbell, at the store.

Vivian Campbell (middle), Clint & Heath Adkison (L-R) about 5 years after this story, Photograph by Pamila Hooper Adkison

Days Gone By

The Akridge Boys

By Barbara Scates

We lived just off the main highway in Mt Herman. The dirt road we lived on made a split right after you turned off the highway...so if you went straight, our house was the first house on that road. If you took the right at the "Y" in the road, the first house on that road was Mrs. Fannie Mae Adkison. So Mrs. Fannie Mae's house was almost in our back door. She was a fine lady and a good neighbor. You would see her on Sunday mornings and most Sunday evenings walking to and from church at Mt Herman Church of Christ. A pretty good little walk, but her faith was strong and she seemed to enjoy her walk. Never too cold nor too hot for her...just like the Pony Express... neither wind, rain, sleet, nor snow stopped her.

Many Sunday afternoons, her children and grandchildren would visit. Since Mrs. Fannie Mae's house was practically in our back yard, we always noticed when the Akridge family would visit. They would sit on the back porch and visit. We could hear them laugh and talk. We always noticed the Akridge boys and they were about the same age as Wanda and me...Billy, Gene, and Jimmy (Jimbo). There were a couple of younger boys and a little curly haired girl. The older boys were out playing one day, so we got real brave and walked over in that direction to watch them climbing a tree. They were good climbers, so up and down the tree they went...sometimes swinging from the limbs. I don't really know what happened, but the oldest boy, Billy, all of a sudden fell out of the tree. It scared us half to death, but we waited around to see what happened. We heard the boys saying he had broken his arm. Mr. Akridge got him in the car and took him to the hospital. It was broken! I always felt bad about that and felt like if we had not walked over to watch, maybe it wouldn't have happened. Years later he was turned down by the army (draft) because of that broke arm...guess it didn't heal quite right. Both his brothers, Gene and Jimbo, served in the Army and defended our country, so a big "Thank You" to them for their service!

Jess Warren

By Howell Adkison

Mr. Jess' old store was a place you could get food, feed, and hardware. He usually had what you needed, if you could get him to look for it long enough. It's not that he didn't want to make a sale, but if he was in the middle of a game of dominoes, he didn't have time. Grudgingly, he would get up to do so.

If you needed feed, he would hand you the keys to the barn and say, "Get what you need."

He usually opened early for the farmers and loggers. The store had a big front porch, high off the ground, because of the hill it was built on. On the east side it had a side door going out to the feed barn across the lot. As a kid out of school and on weekends, I got to work with Dad. We were regulars at Mr. Jess'. If we got in early, I would get a Topp Cola and a Baby Ruth. Man, I had it made.

As you go in the front door, the store had a big, long counter on the left side. Further down the store aisle was the old wood heater and domino table. Right past that was the side door to the feed barn.

If it was raining the county work crew would be playing dominoes, sometimes even if it wasn't.

I remember, two of the men were Grover Anthony and Jamie Warr. One day I was watching them play, when Grover got up and slammed down his dominoes. Half of them bounced off the table. The other half went when he kicked the table over. He went outside to cool off. Jamie and Mr. Jess straightened things back up. Grover came back in. They resumed playing like nothing had happened. I realized that they took their game very seriously.

Against the back wall on the right Mr. Jess had a big ole safe. I don't think he believed in banks. I always wondered how much money was in it.

Jess Warren's Store in Mt Herman, 2022, Photograph by Pamila Hooper Adkison

Jess Warren's front steps. The porch was higher back then. Mr. Jess had it filled in with dirt. Photograph by Pamila Hooper Adkison

Royce Lynn Johnson: 22 shells went up to 75 cents a box back in the '60s. Jess Warren didn't notice they went up and continued selling them for 60 cents a box. People were coming from Center to buy them. Probably went on for six months...

Jerry H: My dad played dominoes at Mr. Warren's store. I remember the old Coke cooler, as you walk in from the front porch, was filled [with] cold water. You had to slide and pull the bottle out. What was the poster on the back wall?

Rhonda Chandler: Kerri Wiggins, I remember picking peas at y'all's old place across from the lake road. I still remember your dad.

Alec C: It's sad that the way of life we had is gone. Children aren't raised like we were anymore. Working and playing hard, like we all did, would kill 'em!!

Our Neighbors

<u>Mitchell Anthony</u>: Was her name Ethel or Evillia? I can't remember for sure.

<u>Jimmie Nell Adkison Lee</u>: Mitchell, I think it was Ella. We called her "Ms. Eller".

<u>Mitchell Anthony</u>: Jerry, It's a crying shame we didn't have a camera back then. Those pictures would be like solid gold today. There might have been 4-5 lights in the place, if that! Men would be standing around, just itching for somebody to get up, so they could play dominoes!

Yeah, Daddy (Grover Anthony) was dead serious about dominoes. He could tell you what you had in your hand by the way you played. If you were playing doubles, his partner was expected to play off his hand, and vice versa!

I remember sitting on the nail and staple kegs, watching them play, and buying Big RC Colas, 22 bullets, and shotgun shells. Mr. Jess had horse collars, and just about every kind of "Georgia Stock and Plow and Sweep" you needed! You didn't want to be in the way when Mrs. Ella was coming home. Let's just say she brought that car to the house. Cherished times indeed!

<u>Alec C</u>: I can remember getting a baby Coke out of Mr. Jess' old Coke box for .15 cents and drinking it on that big ole' porch with my Daddy (P.R. Cline). We would ride Daddy's big old Walker stud up there like Kings!!

Howell, I hadn't thought of Mr. Jamie Warr in years. He took care of Daddy's cows when we still lived in Houston and came up when Daddy was off. My daddy cried for a while when he passed. I did much longer. My daddy treasured his friend and his advice. Jamie Warr was, hands down, the funniest guy without saying very much. I hope they saved his truck, because I can't think of him without [thinking of] that truck! I was about 8 years old. I was fidgety and goofing off in the truck bed, while Daddy and Jaime were talking farming, like always. I didn't listen when Daddy told me to sit down, so I ended up falling head over heels out the tailgate.

They paused for a second, then Jaime said to my pop, "I usually let the tailgate down to get out, Russell."

Then they laughed so hard. They had to put it down to sit on, because they were out of breath!

Man, I was mad as H3#@! For a second.

John B: I grew up right across the road. Awesome memories watching those domino games sitting on a nail keg or wooden Coke crate. We used to take Coke bottles there for money.

Delores Harris Brown: I remember Jess Warren's Store too. On Saturday after my grandpa had worked that morning, he would clean up and put on his khaki pants & shirt and drive to Jess Warren's store for domino games all Saturday afternoon. Sometimes he would let me go with him, as long as I sat on a Coke Cola crate and stayed quiet & still. I loved those afternoons!

Mary Dell Windham: I have the old door and the keys to the old feed house.

Ms. Eller

By Jimmie Nell Adkison Lee

I remember that beautiful black Ford of Ms. Eller's. Her name may have been Ella, but we called her "Ms. Eller." (I heard she won it at the Center City Fair). We lived on that dirt road right off Hwy 7 in Mt Herman. There was a sand bed right there by the road in front of our house that we played in.

When we heard Ms. Eller's Ford coming, one of us would yell, "Get out of the road. Ms. Eller is coming!!!"

With the windows down and her bonnet flapping in the wind, she knew one speed. FAST. Some of our chickens didn't have a chance. We had fried chicken for supper some nights. Bless her heart, she was born with a Cleft Palate that I'm sure, was not repairable when she was born in that day and time, but we all could understand her.

When I graduated from high school in 1965, she made me a cotton dress without a pattern and it fit perfectly.

Karen Bittick: Jimmie Nell, I remember going to Jess Warren's store with my daddy when I was little. I always got to get me a big cookie out of one of the large jars sitting on the big long counter. It was dark in the store. I don't remember it having many windows.

Jimmie Nell Adkison Lee: Karen, I don't think there were windows, just light from the huge front door and the door by the domino table. I remember one lone light bulb swinging from the ceiling AND he gave change from his pocket.

<u>Relissa B</u>: I remember her handmade bonnets at the Warren's store across the road from Earl and Vivian Campbell.

<u>Pam Adkison</u>: I bought one, a bonnet, from her for a Christmas present for my mawmaw (Willie Parrish).

<u>Joe Hayter:</u> Jess Warren's store had just about anything you would need. One of my best memories of Jess's store was the domino games. I witnessed many epic domino battles between some true champion players there when I was a kid growing up!

They would be playing dominoes in the back of the store, while Mrs. Ella Warren would be sitting in a rocking chair on the covered porch of the store sewing. She was the best seamstress I knew of. I remember I had a FFA jacket that the sleeves needed to be shortened on. I wouldn't let my mother [Maxine Hayter] touch it! Only Miss Ella was worthy of and capable of fixing that for me! And she did a perfect job, the seams looked better after she fixed it, than it did brand new. I miss those day.

<u>Joyce Bright</u>: I heard that Mr. Jess would be so busy playing dominoes, he would let people make their own change, if they bought something.

Carter Hooper

<u>Eldora Gilchrist:</u> Who remembers the old man that dug snake root for a living? I think his last name may have been Hooper. At one time he lived in Mr. Jesse's rent house, which was between our house at the end of the road and my grandparents' house further up the road.

Joy Tarver: He was my Uncle Carter Hooper. He dug that root and supported his family on it. I carried it to the post office to ship it. It was bringing $300.00 a pound back then. He never let anybody know where his patch was neither. He was the sweetest man, and Aunt Vernise was his wife.

Kerri L W: What is snake root?

Jan Akridge: They make a medicine out of it. Billy knows what the plant looks like. You dry the roots of it and send it off to this company. They paid good money for it. It just took a lot to make a pound.

Eldora Gilchrist: Jan, do you think he may have mailed it to Sears? Daddy used to trap mink up and down Little Iron Ore Creek when I was a kid. He cured the hides and sold them to Sears.

Jan Akridge: Billy's Mom and Dad (Edna and Bill Akridge) dug snake root.

Delores Harris Brown: Isn't it like Ginseng? The roots looked like the form of a human body?

Zaundra W: That was my grandfather and grandmother.

Leta Lucas

By Joyce Wilson Bright

My grandma, Leta Lucas, lived on the hill just past Lillie Mae's store. Back then, the store wasn't there. We lived across the field. I would walk thru the field to Grandma's. She still had to milk the cows in the morning. In the afternoons, I would help her shell corn to feed the chickens. She always had fresh peanuts stored in the barn. We would pick them off and she would make peanut candy with ribbon cane syrup. It sure was good. I wish I had some now. We picked blackberries, grapes, and muscadines. The last thing I can remember doing with her was much later. Billy Fountain had given her 25 chickens that were left when he sold chickens. I helped her clean them.

That was a big job, and I said, "Never again."

I hated to see Grandma's ole house burn. Such good memories I have of the things I did with her.

Barbara Scates

By Jan Akridge

On a lighter side, the first post I did was about the older neighbors I had when we first got married. This is about one of the younger ones. Barbara Williams Scates! I first met Barbara when my uncle, Joe Adams married her mother Vaudine. That made us first cousins by marriage. Later when Billy and I were dating, we spent all our dates at their house, or Homer and Wanda Fountain's in Mt. Herman. Barbara was friends to so many. She helped so many young ones back then that had nowhere to go or stay. We had so much fun, sadness, laughter and tears together. What are best friends for!!!! I tell this all the time about when I first married. I would take my chicken down to Barbara's, so she could cut it up for me (I sure didn't know how). One day I took that chicken down there, and she wasn't there. Needless to say Billy got 2 wings, and 2 legs for supper that night.

Kimberly S P: Kara Osborne and I would go to Barbara J. Scates' house before going to town on the weekends. Jerry and Barbara Scates always welcomed us kids. Billy & Jan Akridge would be there lots of times, playing cards. That is some of my favorite times with them. Thanks for putting up with us.

Jill Fountain Parker: Kimberly, I too stayed at their house a lot growing up. Sometimes there were 10 or 15 kids there. We slept on floor, couch, chair, beds...Don't know how Barbara and Jerry Scates put up with us all, but thank God they did. Some good memories made there!

Angie S S: Our house was always full!!!! I look back and realize now how wonderful it was! Mama always seemed to have time for anyone who needed to come by and visit, vent, or whatever. My best memories are from those times!

Jan Akridge: Mine too, Angie! She never ask for anything in return!

Angie S S: Jan, no, she loved doing for everyone else! I think that's what made her happy to be available to anyone who came by! I always wanted to be that mother like her to have a house full of kids and friends anytime! I do have all the great memories of my childhood home full of all of y'all and it was so good.

Jan Akridge: Best times!

Cindy Scates Eubank: I have so many memories at Barbara J. Scates' house. She is like a second mother. Not only did the kids hang out there. I remember Mom and Dad, Billy and Jan Akridge, and a few other adults that would get together sometimes. Randy Scates and Phillip Holt would stop by on their way home. She always had something to eat and time to listen. I have sat for hours pouring my feelings out, and she always listens.

Jan Akridge: Cindy, she makes the best tuna fish. I've seen her make 4 hamburger patties feed 8 people. LOL.

Cindy Scates Eubank: Jan, she is amazing. She made me some clothes one time. She can do anything. I have seen her tear down a wall to make more room, and then put it back up again.

Barbara J. Scates: Thanks to everyone for all the kind words. I have always loved helping anyone in need. The local teenagers always came by for a visit on their way for their Friday night out and most nights, they would stop back by on their way home. We had a pool table and a quick game usually finished off their night. I tried to give a little friendly advice to some of the teens. I remember the night they stopped for their usual Friday night visit, and I was sick in the bed. They all checked on me several times while they were there. I could hear them downstairs playing their usual game of pool. I ended up in the hospital with appendicitis! I teased them later about shooting pool while I was upstairs dying! I looked forward to those visits and hope I provided a safe place for them to gather on Friday nights!

Mila Justice Smith: Barbara, you're still that great friend and "go to" for kids now, along with so many other family and friends. You have the most loving heart that attracts people to you. I'm so proud to call you both family and friend.

Barbara J. Scates: Jan, you finally learned to cut up a chicken! Glad I was there to help you until you learned...sorry I was not there the day you needed me! LOL

Jan Akridge: You're the one that made me finally learn to cut it up. STEP BY STEP. LOL. Even the pulley bone!

Wayne Powdrill

By Pamila Hooper Adkison

With his Elvis looks and gentle nature, Wayne was movie-star handsome. To an eight year old girl, he was perfect. That's about how old I was when I met him. Among the young girls my age on the school bus, Wayne was voted the most handsome. We had a list which included Dexter Davis, Jesse Hudspeth and Jerryl Adam. We didn't count the Hooper boys, Fred and Jerry. They didn't get a vote. They were kin. But Wayne... Wayne was always Number One on each of our lists.

Wayne was a hugger.

Phyllis has called before and said," Rocky is in. We're having a cookout."

Wayne greeted you with a hug. Before the night was over, if you were lucky, you got another hug from Wayne.

One night Wayne was sitting at the kitchen table when Rance was going to bed. Rance bent over and kissed Wayne on top of his head. You don't see many teenagers doing that. Wayne was a good dad.

Kayla was daddy's little girl.

In high school Phyllis and Wayne were the ideal couple. He carried her books at the bus stop. They shared a Coke at Mrs. Danley's store before the Excelsior bus came by. He opened the car door for her when they went on a date. She did his book reports.

Wayne was not a sports fan. It was too much trouble to keep up with the number of strikes the quarterback got or the touchdowns the pitcher made.

He did like to hunt and fish though. He went on a hunting trip with Howell one year. At the time we were logging in the Angelina River bottom. The dry summer had stretched into fall. The drought had left the Angelina low enough that the timber on a river island could be accessed. With help from boxcars and cross logs, the crew crossed over to the island. Because of its remoteness, it had not been hunted in years. Howell got permission for the whole crew to hunt on the tract that season. About midmorning everyone is back at the camp telling their stories and counting their squirrels. Everyone but Wayne. A few of them head back to the island to find him.

Daddy or Don said, "Wayne is the only man who can get lost on an island."

Wayne could be selective about his food, but if it was caught on a hook, he would eat it.

That was Wayne.

Wayne took a lot of ribbing throughout his life. His good nature would not allow him to hold a grudge. He loved his family and friends.

Wayne was not an angel. He had his problems. One clear decision he made was to make the Lord, Jesus, his Savior.

Today he is a saint.

Today he is not lost.

Today he has a report for all of us.

Today Wayne is fishing with Peter, James, and John.

Our Neighbors

Jan Akridge: I love this Pam, so sweet! He was a good man and as you say, good looking too!

Johnny W: I thought a lot of Wayne. All of us drivers knew him as "Wine". When you heard that name, you knew who they were talking about.

Gaye T L: I remember all those boys on the school bus the short time I rode it. Mr. Arthur D, right. And to a little girl they did all look like Elvis.

Pam Adkison: Gaye, Mr. Arthur D, right! The boys had that Elvis haircut.

Adam J: Hi! Pam I knew Wayne well. I'd run into him on one of these dirt roads. We'd stop and shoot the bull 'till another vehicle came down the road.

Terri Lacher: Beautifully written. Love your stories from the heart. Although I didn't grow up here in Shelby County, reading your stories combined with the warmth and acceptance I've received since I moved here 30 years ago, makes me feel like one of y'all. Love hearing your stories of early Shelby County days! Makes my heart smile!

Cindy Scates Eubank: Wayne, my dad [Jimmy Scates] and Cecil Wilson were best friends and they love to hunt and fish together. Lots of camping trips. He was a gentle giant. Loved by all.

Shane Fenley: I honestly don't think I knew his name was Wayne, until I was close to grown. He was always Uncle Wine

Angie S S: He was definitely a good man! Great tribute!

Phyllis Powdrill: Thanks Pam it was good to hear these words again.

Days Gone By

And thanks to everyone for remembering Wine. He was my first and only love and I still miss him every day. May he Rest in Peace.

The George Adams Family

By Jana Adams Ivy

George and Bernice bought their first home in Houston in 1954. After a few years, George and Bernice moved to Pasadena, where Wanda, (1957), was born. Mother always said she had dreamed of having only one child, a girl with many curls and blue eyes. After having four boys, when Wanda was born, George and Bernice decided that their family was complete. So, since Mother got the girl she had always dreamed of, she visited the doctor to make sure there wouldn't be any more children.

*George and Bernice Adams with Jerryl, Mike and Steve,
Courtesy of Jana Adams Ivy*

Each of the first five children had professional portraits made in a studio in the Houston area around the age of two to three years. Admiring the portraits on the wall, this was Bernice's pride and joy. But, to their surprise, almost two years later in 1959, Jana was born. Mother just decided that it was meant to be, so she let nature take its course.

With six children, money was tight, but George just had an eye for the finer things in life. George and Bernice moved several more times, and by the time Jerryl had finished Elementary School, he had been enrolled in seven different schools.

George loved buying Chevrolet cars, and spending more extravagantly than he could afford. After working for the Sherriff Department as a Deputy, George's new passion was sirens, blinking red and blue lights, antennae, and CB radios. He would accessorize the family car with as many gadgets as he could salvage off of wrecked police cars.

Eventually, the family moved to Buna, and then Silsbee, where George worked for Permian Oil. Shortly, Mark, (1961), the seventh child was born. Repossession of a vehicle, and debtors knocking on the door seemed to follow the Adams Family. Mother could make a dollar squeak, while George always felt money was burning a hole in his pocket, so he spent quicker than he could make it.

While George was working for Permian Oil, he became injured at a valve station in Silsbee that wrenched his back. It was during the winter, driving on plank roads in the middle of nowhere. He climbed out of his tanker truck, slipping on the running board, which had iced up due to the sleet and snow. After several attempts to loosen the valve, he tried one last time with a large wrench. As he tugged on the valve, it suddenly worked itself loose, and slung George about thirty yards across the road, into a frozen drainage ditch. Almost passing out from the pain, he realized he couldn't move his legs, and pain was shooting up and down his back.

The pain that wrenched through his body felt like an explosion inside his body. He felt as if every bone in his back was broken. As the sleet covered his soaked coveralls, and he lay moaning in the icy ditch, he realized he must get help, but his lifeless body would not cooperate. He was miles from nowhere. Crawling fifty yards, in excruciating pain, which seemed to take hours, he finally reached his truck, drenched from head to toe and freezing. The injury had left George disabled and unable to continue to work fulltime. His demeanor had changed due to his injury, and the pain spoke louder on some days, louder than any words. His pain medications increased his irradiate moodiness.

By this time, Bernice was expecting their eighth child, and money was tight. They moved several more times, as rent was due from the previous house they had lived in. Workman's Compensation was running out, and George was still was unable to hold a full time job. He could work for two days, and couldn't even get out of bed on the third day due to the pain. He was waiting on insurance to approve of the badly needed surgery for his broken back. The doctor said he would be paralyzed from the waist down if he had surgery, and would never bear any more children, which turned out to be false.

I remember moving back to the Aiken Community with our family (George Adams Family), when I was only three and a half years old in 1962. The Adams family consisted of eight kids: Jerryl, (15), Mike (13), Steve (11), Randy (7), Wanda (5), me (Jana, 3,), Mark (1 ½), and Dana, who was a newborn. We were moving because Daddy had been injured in an oil field accident while working for Permian Oil in Silsbee, Texas, and we wanted a house of our own. So, after a year of moving from county to county, we decided to settle in Aiken, Texas. We purchased an acre of land from Aunt Ruby and Uncle Lewis Fountain, who lived just down the road on Highway 7, paying month to month.

Aunt Ruby was Daddy's older sister. They owned Fountain's Liquor store, which was just across the highway from Jack and Shirley Berg and their children, Toni and Larry. Jackie was born later. Aunt Ruby and Uncle Lewis lived behind the store with their only son, Billy Rex Fountain. They also were in the business of chicken farming with multiple chicken houses. The smell of ammonia was torture to your nostrils, especially on a foggy morning, as the pungent smell lingered for hours.

Great Aunt Viola Smith, a widow who lived next to us, was the only house between Fountain's Liquor and us. She had 3 children, Thelma, Flossie and Winston Smith.

Across the road from us lived Charles and Shirley Brown and their children, Deborah, Richard and Karen. Later, there was Randy, Keith and Bradley. Mrs. Brown was a 1st grade teacher at Excelsior.

Down the little dirt road behind Aunt Ruby's house lived Paul Hooper and Henry Faye. They had Brenda, Raymond, Beverly, and Deborah Hooper. On down at the end of the road lived the Lucas Family, Doc, Mrs. Vivian, Becky, William and Elizabeth. On the west side of our house lived Mr. and Mrs. Guy Shipley, who had a large farm. They always shared their colored eggs that the hens laid with us.

Daddy, Jerryl, Mike, and Steve, and volunteer neighbors built our house while our Grandpa Adams (Dolphus), supervised the project. Never known for using a level, Grandpa would size up each window just by eyeballing it. Not one window was level in that house. Some of the lumber was new, yet most of it was salvaged from other home places that had been torn down. Finally, the house was finished, except for the bathroom, and our new address was Route 2, Box 156, Center, Texas. Grandpa had built a two-seater outhouse for use while the house was under construction, so we could make use of it until the bathtub, lavatory, and toilet that we had ordered came in.

Aunt Viola, who we considered a witch doctor of sort, brought her dowsing rod, which was a forked branch cut from a live tree to search for water underground in order to build a well for water. When the ends of the stick began trembling, that's where there was water underground. So, we dug a well. It dried up shortly, so we dug another one. The Adams Family had many exciting adventures. Silas, who was helping dig the well, was hit with a bucket full of dirt when the rope was accidentally released. The boys pulled him out of the well with a ladder, and his head was bleeding profusely. Aunt Viola came over and doctored his head with a bandage as she shouted gargled words for his healing like a witch doctor. She soaked the bandage in stump water before placing it on his head. Silas never went to the doctor, laid in the shade, and rested for a while, then continued working that afternoon.

Mother always made sure we were in church every Sunday morning and night at White Rock Missionary Baptist Church. She taught Sunday School there. Since Mother couldn't drive, we walked to church on many Sundays, that Daddy didn't drive us. The benches were too hard on Daddy's back, so he always listened to gospel music from home. Theresa Danley used to come home from church with us, and stay until we returned to church that evening. We spent many days sneaking off from the house, exploring our favorite creek or swimming hole in the woods behind our house. Many of us were baptized in Pearl Lake during the summer months when it was warm. Brother Pat Windham was preaching at White Rock revival when I was saved. I was baptized in the baptistery at his church in Sardis, since White Rock didn't have a baptistery at the time.

Daddy finally had surgery at the Veteran's Hospital in Shreveport, Louisiana. He was brought home in a hospital bed, which was set up in the living room, and in traction for many months. We all took turns being naughty and running around inside the house, fighting over the black and white TV, while Daddy was just lying there. We were just out of his reach so he used to throw a broom, or whatever he could at us to break up a fight. Mother was always busy washing, hanging out laundry, or in the kitchen cooking vegetables from our garden. It took Daddy almost a year to recovery, so that he could walk.

His back resembled an old TV antenna down his spine where his scars were. It covered the entire length of his back.

Jerryl, Mike, and Steve used to hide in the woods from Grandpa Adams, who was mean as a two headed snake, and watched him drink his whiskey he had hidden in a hollow stump. After he swigged it down, and went on his way, the boys poured most of the whiskey out, took turns "spoiling" the bottle, and returned it to the stump. Later, when he returned for his next gulp, Jerryl, Mike, and Steve were hiding in the bushes, laughing, as he drank from the bottle.

Grandpa never liked my mom because she wouldn't let him come to our house when he had been heavily drinking.

While bailing hay, Mike and Steve ran over a skunk, and it sprayed them with stench. Mother bathed them outside in a washtub filled with tomato juice. They still stunk too badly to come in the house, so she doused them with vinegar. When they went to school the next day at Excelsior, they smelled so badly that Mrs. Lawson snuck home and got her husband's aftershave and rubbed it all over them for several days. Finally the smell went, dissipated.

Jerryl and Mike bought a 1955 Chevrolet together. Mike, with no driver's license took me to Lillie Mae's grocery before church one morning. When leaving Lillie Mae's, Mike floored the old car, while I was hanging onto the silver handle of the door. As he turned onto the highway, the front passenger door flew open in front of Mrs. Berg's house, but I hung on. By the time he had stopped, Mike had drug me about 30 yards, and I was screaming and dirty. To stop me from crying, he consoled me and took me back to Lillie Mae's and got me the biggest ice cream cone as a bribe not to tell on him for racing the engine.

Jerryl, Mike, and Steve used to pay for their lunches in high school by working after school. They chopped wood, sold Coke bottles, cut, raked, and bailed hay, worked at the chicken plant, and school cafeteria, picking up odd jobs anywhere. Hand-me-down clothes were all that we had due to Daddy being out of work.

Daddy was very strict on us kids, and we had a 10:00 curfew. One night, Jerryl, Mike, and Steve snuck into town, and were late getting back. Their bedroom window had been nailed shut! So, they climbed through Wanda's and my window. George was waiting behind that curtain and beat the fire out of all three of them with a baseball bat for being late.

Jerryl, Mike, and Steve loved to play rough and fight each other when they were bored. Daddy used to pour a bucket of ice water on them to break up their fights, before anyone got hurt.

Randy always took toys, clocks, bicycles, and whatever else he could find, and disassembled them to figure out how they worked, then put them back together. There were always pieces he couldn't account for. He was the quiet one

Once, when getting off the bus after school, Wanda's foot was run over by a passing motorist that didn't stop for the bus. Jerryl and Mike grabbed her to keep her from walking in front of the speeding vehicle. Of course, George sped off in hot pursuit, whoop aerials swaying, sirens going, and pulled in behind him like "Barney Fife". George scared him to death, giving him the cussing of his life. Wanda was okay, just sore, thanks to her big brothers.

I, (Jana), was always adventurous and mischievous. When the older boys were playing washers, I wouldn't get out of the way. Mike and Steve kept warning me to move out of the way.

Our Neighbors

Mike threw a washer, and Steve hollered, "Watch out, Jana!"

But it was too late, and that washer knocked my two front teeth down my throat, and I swallowed them. I was only four.

When Jerryl and Phyllis got married by Mr. Johnson in Salem, we ate watermelon on the back porch. That night they stayed in Wanda's and my room for their honeymoon. I hid under the headboard to see what a honeymoon was about. Phyllis caught me because I started giggling so loudly.

I learned how to drive in Charles Brown's old flatbed truck that we used to feed the cows when I was ten. It was a stick shift. Karen Brown and I took turns putting out cubes for the cows and knocking each other off the back of the truck when we let out the clutch too fast. I learned how to drive a tractor at age 10. Wanda and I learned how to swim by sneaking down to Shipley's pond with Karen Brown, and swimming all the way across.

We used to walk to Lillie Mae's and buy Daddy's cigarettes, Kool unfiltered, and bring back what was on his list, and nothing extra. We would play a few games of pinball in the game room.

I always visited Uncle Lewis at Fountain's Liquor Store, and no matter how little money I had to spend, he always said it was good for an RC Cola, Tom's Cheetos, and a piece of candy. Most times, I rarely had more than 25 cents, so I made sure Aunt Ruby was working the chicken houses, as she was not as generous as Uncle Lewis.

I used to drive Daddy to the hospital in the middle of the night after Jerryl, Mike, Steve, and Randy had left home, because Mother still didn't have her license. I was only ten, but I sat on two pillows, and drove him to the emergency room in Center, which was fifteen miles away because he had terrible migraine headaches. One night, I backed into a parked garbage truck in the station wagon while leaving the hospital. The security guard at the hospital asked me how old I was, and I told him I was almost old enough to get my license, even though I was only ten. He told me to drive safely!

Mark was very strong, and we were best friends, but we always fought with each other, being so close in age. He could jump a barbed wire fence flat-footed, without a running start. He loved trapping wild animals. Mark and I used to play in the oily dirt from Daddy working on cars, and we would get warts on top of our feet. Aunt Viola would tie a knot in a string for each wart seed and dip it in stump water, then shout words while the string touched each wart. In a day or two, our feet were cleared from warts. We never understood her "magic".

Mother sent me to school to Mrs. Brown's first grade class at Excelsior when I was only five. Even though, I was two years younger than Wanda, we were only one grade apart.

Dana was the curly-headed, blondest one of us all. I was chasing her through the house one time, when she was three, and we ran into Wanda in the kitchen with a pan of hot, boiling water in her hand. Dana had burns all over her left shoulder, and she had to stay in the hospital a few nights. It took a while for her to heal, and she had thick deep scars on that shoulder all her life. I still remember the strong smell of that yellow burn cream and the bandages she wore for weeks.

Dana, Mark, and I used to sneak down to Aunt Rubie's gravel pit in the winter and slide across the icy surface on an old chicken coop. One time, the ice was too thin, and we fell in and were soaked. We always took Dana on our adventures, because she never got in trouble, being Daddy's favorite. We didn't get a whipping if Dana was involved.

Kip was born on June 14, 1967, the ninth Adams child. Daddy was supposed to be impotent, so he was the miracle child. He was already an uncle when he was born, because Jerryl and Phyllis already had Jennifer who was born almost three months before him. Everyone spoiled him, especially Cathy Danley (Mike's wife) and Jean Russell (Steve's wife). He always cried when it thundered or lightning, and would get sick at his stomach because he was scared. Every summer, all of us picked peas for Uncle Lowell Russell and Kermit McSwain to earn extra money. I remember riding to Shreveport with Uncle Lowell and Karen Brown on occasion to sell his peas.

Dean, the tenth and final Adams child was born on April 26, 1972. He was the smallest one of us all. Since, Mother had delivered the previous nine naturally, Dean was born by cesarean birth. While she was still in the hospital, Phyllis, her daughter-in-law, went into labor two days later and Melinda Sue was born. Mother and Phyllis were roommates for a day at the hospital.

Back at home, Daddy took us all to Lillie Mae's Grocery and we picked out enough Swanson TV dinners to last a couple of days for us at home while Mother was recovering. We bought twenty-two dinners on credit, and cooked one for each of us for the next few days. This was a treat, because we rarely ate store bought dinners.

Dean was our cherished one, since he was definitely the last to be born, and Mother had a hysterectomy. When Dean was only nine months old, he almost died of pneumonia that winter.

The Adams Family spent many summers traveling to the beach and driving over the Orange City Bridge in Orange, Texas. We would all be piled into the back of a cab-over camper on the Ford truck. Most of the time, the Brown kids, or the Battles kids were with us. I guess George and Bernice just didn't have enough kids. Ha.

All the Adams children attended Excelsior School, except for Jerryl, who was in high school when we moved to Aiken.

George and Bernice Adams. Courtesy of Jana Adams Ivy

Idell, Johnnie, and Yvonne Fults

<u>Linda Winder</u>: Shelby, Idell was a character like no other! She thought the world of you. I can barely play 42, so I could not play with her. She would take a hand no one would even bid on and win every time. I never knew what the trump was! I think you learned how to play from her.

<u>Shelby Johnson</u>: Linda, she was even better at Moon than Dominoes. We hardly had enough for 42, but we played Moon with Johnnie or OG Jones. After one play Idell knew what was in everybody's hand.

Mila Justice Smith: She was so much fun to be around and visit. I sure miss her.

Miranda M Y: She was so sweet! When I worked at Pine Grove for a short time she was one of my favorites up there. She always asked, "How is Mr. James Lee doing?" Happy Heavenly Birthday Ms. Idell!

Allen M: Shelby, I remember her riding that ole Honda to the cabin with you. And us eating dinner with her.

Fannie Mae Adkison

By Jan Akridge

One of the strongest women I have ever met in my life time so far was Fannie Mae Adkison. She was my husband's grandmother. When we married we moved next door to her. I'm going to tell you some stories she told me. This story is about how she got burned when she was little. It was wash day and her mother and some others had the fire burning around the old black wash pot. That day she had a kerchief tied around her neck. Just like a three year old she was running around the pot and playing. Somehow she got to close to the flames and her kerchief caught on fire. Her mother grabbed a blanket they were washing and wrapped it around her. As she was healing her parents let her do something that she would try and do to copy her mother. They let her have her first dip of snuff. And that is how she started to dipping her snuff. She started at 3 and dipped until she was 99. I'm so proud I got to know and love this lady.

Royce Lynn Johnson: Almost all women born around the turn of the century (1900) started dipping snuff at a young age (12- 14) and continued all their lives. Most lived to be very old. I never heard of them having any problems with it. Black women of that age all dipped also. Snuff is very addictive, putting ten times the nicotine into your system than cigarettes. Hence the saying "she's out of snuff."

Jan Akridge: I don't know of any women that dips now. LOL.

Royce Lynn Johnson: Jan, I know some that seemed to always be "out of snuff."

Delores Harris Brown: I remember my grandmother Luman dipping snuff, but quit when I was about 5 or 6 yrs. old. I knew another older woman that chewed tobacco.

Mila Justice Smith: Gene Edward's great Aunt Lid Warr dipped snuff. She always had a Planters peanut spit can with her.

Delores Harris Brown: Mila, yes Aunt Lid did!!

Rodger McLane: Mila, my dad has her spit cup, one of her spoons, and a handkerchief of Maw Warr's.

Mila Justice Smith: Rodger, those are sweet memories to have. I thought a lot of Lid and Earnest. He and my father-in-law, Jack Smith, could get wound up telling stories from their young days and keep us all laughing. Lid would sit there with her spit can and add a little to the story. She was as funny as he was.

Jason Adkison: I remember granny taking a butter knife and getting some Garret snuff.

Gaye T L: We loved Mrs. Fannie Mae.

Royce Lynn Johnson: Do I remember this correctly that some of them used a chewed black gum twig to rub it on their gums?

Delores Harris Brown: Royce Lynn, yes! I know Ma did & Aunt Ellie Walker (her sister). Aunt Ivy Dell Rudd was the first woman I ever saw smoke cigarettes. Ma's oldest sister.

Gwen Taylor Stewart: Miss Fannie Mae is one of my earliest, fondest memories. When my brothers and I were young, and Mom was working, she would come babysit us. We loved her.

Taja Adkison Harvey: That's one thing I'll never forget about Grandma Adkison. I didn't know the story behind it.

Jason Adkison: Taja, sweetest lady ever was.

Taja Adkison Harvey: Jason, yes. My dad took us over there a lot when we were growing up.

Bridgette H: Taja, but when it was bedtime, she would run us off.

Royce Lynn Johnson: Bridgette, "I'm gonna have to go to bed, so you-all can go home."

Shannon A C: I went to church with Mrs. Fannie Mae, when I was younger. I remember her. She was a sweetheart.

Relissa B: That's Mama Adkison!

Days Gone By

Fred Borders: My mother had 4 sisters that never married and stayed on the home place until their deaths. Both my grandmothers were gone years before I was born, so they served as my grandmothers. I loved them very much. They all dipped snuff and spit into the fire place when it was burning. I always considered it an old woman's habit, so there was no danger in me ever trying Skoal or any kind of snuff.

Eldora Gilchrist: Jerry H's grandparents are mine too. Our mothers were sisters. Mamaw would have us get about a 6-in stick or a little limb off of a certain kind of tree, when we walked home from school, for her to make a brush to use snuff on her gums. Wish I could remember what kind of tree it was.

Charlotte N H: Eldora, Black gum?

Jan Akridge: When I was a little girl we would take Hershey's cocoa and mix some sugar in it and act like we were dipping snuff.

Delores Harris Brown: Jan, did that too.

Gaye T L: Jan, us too. We also smoked grape vines.

Jan Akridge: Gaye, I never smoked a grapevine. I remember chewing on some weed in the field that was real, real sour.

Delores Harris Brown: Rabbit Tobacco? I remember that for some reason. I do know about smoking grape vine though.

Gaye T L: Delores, it's a Luman thing I guess.

Delores Harris Brown: Gaye, my thoughts as well.

Gwen Taylor Stewart: Jan, we did that too!

Royce Lynn Johnson: Gaye, Blister your tongue.

Nina Jo Hudspeth Walker: Jan, sour dock.

Merle Howard: My grandmother dipped snuff and my father did. Thankful my mother never did dip it, that I know of. I was never curious about snuff. I remember getting stung while playing as a child with Mattie Borders at her grandmothers (Ma Hughes) home. They put snuff on my sting and it worked. Fond memory.

Mila Justice Smith: Merle, as far as I'm concerned, the only good thing about tobacco and snuff is that it's great for treating stings!

LaResa L: Our ma, Vada Anthony, dipped snuff. We had to bring her peach tree limbs for her to use to dip. Didn't hurt her, she lived to be 92.

Royce Lynn Johnson: Maybe snuff was why these women lived so long! Every one of them lived to a ripe old age that I can think of!

Delores Harris Brown: Royce Lynn, yes! My grandma was 94 and had a garden every year until she was 92.

Nina Jo Hudspeth Walker: Jan, my Grandmaw, Ada Hooper, dipped snuff ever since I could remember & did so 'till she died...I think we still have a few of those old brown bottles around here.

Jan Akridge, Nina Jo, I have one of Grandma Adkison's jars.

Royce Lynn Johnson: In Greer Town (on 711 below Ironosa) some of the old women lined their walkways with 100's of the empty snuff bottles.

Eldora Gilchrist: Pam, it was fall and the garden was already grown over with dead weeds & grass. R E and I decided we would build us a grass hut, so we did at the back of the garden. We put some tow sacks down for the floor. We decided we would smoke some grapevine so we got some matches and caught our hut on fire. Mother was hanging out clothes, as she had been washing that day. She came and we finally got the fire out, all of us working on it. Then she gave us both a whooping.

Pam Adkison: My brother, Jimmy Hooper, rolled corn silk in newspaper. He lit it on the stove burner and smoked it. Mama would run him outside because it smelled so bad.

Linda Winder: When I was cleaning at my mother's house recently, I found two small silver canisters on a small shelf on an old Grandfather's Clock. Aunt Chris Mahan told me they were used to carrying small amounts of snuff in a pocket or purse. Mama never dipped snuff, but her mother, Ethel McSwain, did all her life, so I am sure they belonged to Ma Swain.

She said her father-in-law taught her to dip when she was first married and "I did what I had a mind to do."

I sneaked a taste of her snuff once and only once. Horrible, horrible stuff.

Jimmie Nell Adkison Lee: Ma Adkison would walk down on wash day and help Mama wash. I still remember the day (I was about 4 maybe) that Ma had a big fire under the wash pot, and I was playing all around it. She was stirring the clothes in the pot (I still remember the lye soap floating in the pot). I had on a dress and at some point I got to close to the fire. Ma had me jerked away so fast and I got a good switching. I'm sure she had a flash back of what had had happened to her as a little girl. I never knew how Ma got burned until it was posted. Thanks for that. Can y'all imagine the pain she endured back then!!

Does anyone know how Pa Adkison died? I heard that he lit a bunch of rags, doused in kerosene, on a pole to burn down a wasp nest. The wind blew the fire back in his face, and he breathed in the fire. That's all I ever knew and I don't know if that is what happened.

Jan Akridge: Jimmie Nell, that's what she told me. I think he lived a few days after. She had some bad times with fire in her life

Jimmie Nell Adkison Lee: Jan, yes, she did. Can you imagine her life without a husband to help and children? No welfare back then or any assistance. They all had a hard time and had to quit school to help feed each other. Neighbors and family did all they could to help. This morning Uncle Jesse's death certificate came up under my *Ancestry.com* and it showed he died of Congestive Heart Failure. He was 56yr old. Daddy was only 54. His was Liver Cancer.

Mattie Warr, Ruby Warr and Mary Warr Scates

Helen Windham: I called her Old Grandma Warr, because I called Dad's mom, Lid, Grandma Warr. I remember that she was a little lady who wore her hair in a bun. She was always nice to me, and I liked visiting her. She lived with my grandparents for a while, and then she lived with her daughter and son-in-law, Essie and Ernest Stanfield until she passed away.

Her casket was brought to my Aunt Essie Stanfield's house and placed in a small bedroom for the wake. I believe that was the only time I was at a wake in a home, which had been very common before that time.

Rodger McLane: Helen, Daddy remembers her dying at Aunt Essie's. She had a moment where she said, "Look at that black man with the hat on the donkey." A man had a straw hat on his donkey and she must have been remembering it.

Helen Windham: Rodger, It is strange what people see or talk about when they are passing. Grandpa Warr talked about seeing a beautiful garden with exotic flowers that he had never seen before that were vibrant colors!

Rodger McLane: Helen, how interesting! Heaven.

Karen Bittick: Helen, I remember going to Aunt Essie's with my Mamma and Ma McSwain to see Grandma Warr. She was so tiny and died later on. I also remember going to her funeral at Old Salem. This was 1966.

Rodger McLane: Steve Tomlin, Dobbler, told me some great stories about my grandmother.

Russell Andrews: Who was your grandmother?

Rodger McLane: Ruby Warr.

Russell Andrews: Rodger, I knew her. Her mother's name was Liddy. She lived on 711 back then. I knew her sisters, Mary and Shirley, and brother, Billy. Mary was supposed to marry my brother, William L Andrews, whom went by Shorty, but he was killed in Vietnam on Feb 16 1967. She went on to marry a very nice man by the name Bubba Scates. Mrs. Warr was called Lid.

Rodger McLane: Russell, Oh I'm sorry to hear about your brother. I'll mention this to my dad.

Delores Harris Brown: Russell, I was thinking you were Shorty's brother.

I remember when he was killed and how devastated the family and Mary was. Mary & her husband have the farm I grew up on. I went by to see her in October, but she wasn't home.

Russell Andrews: Delores, did you grow up in the little house besides the road?

Delores Harris Brown: Russell, yep! Sure did.

Russell Andrews: Delores, Mary hasn't been doing real well of lately. She may have been in the hospital. I believe, she had a stroke.

Delores Harris Brown: Russell, oh no! I knew she had been sick, right before I came home, and had been in the hospital. I hope she is doing better.

Delores Harris Brown: Russell, I had ridden out to see Gene Edward & Mila. Gene is a cousin on my Luman side, and I stopped to see Mary.

Russell Andrews: Delores, I believe she's doing a little better.

Delores Harris Brown: I truly hope so.

Rodger McLane: Russell and Delores, I saw Aunt Mary earlier this year and she was doing alright. We talk to Larry and April every now and then. Larry let me have the old Warr family pictures copied.

Delores Harris Brown: Roger, that's great! I'm friends with April on FB, but I haven't seen anything about Mary. I try to ask about her as often as I can. I know she has health problems.

Russell Andrews: Roger, your grandma, Miss Ruby was the toughest woman I ever knew. I had rather fight a grizzly than her.

Rodger McLane: Russell, I read this comment to my sister, and we cackled. Thank you for sharing that thought with us. We loved her, but we knew she was tough.

Delores Harris Brown: Roger, she was that! I always thought Ruby was so pretty, and didn't put up with any nonsense!

Russell, my middle sister, Lacie, and her youngest daughter look identical to Ruby. They're mean as she was, too!

Mae Lee Vandygriff Goodman Taylor

By Joye Taylor Hodges

My precious mother, or Mama as I called her, was a very pretty woman with almost black hair and green eyes. The first time my daddy saw her, she had a red ribbon in her hair. He said he thought she was the most beautiful woman he'd ever seen and he determined to meet her. My mama only had a fourth grade education, because of her family's home situation – her father had a job following mill work where they moved often. Of course, the children were also moved from school to school. Mama was the oldest of five children. Just before her eleventh birthday, her daddy became ill and passed away. Her Mother was left with five young children to provide for and see that they got their schooling. My Mom had to help take on a large part of the care of her siblings and her schooling suffered for it. Regardless, she was blessed with plenty of common sense, and was smart and level-headed as well.

When she reached the age of 13 years and 3 months, she married her first husband, Luther Goodman from Black Jack. That was on February 14, 1926. Mr. Goodman was a bachelor, had never been married and was 8 yrs. and a few months older than Mama. I learned later that he had been coming over to their home looking for a wife. Even though my Mama was just a child at 13, I don't know why my grandma would let her marry him at that age. I can't imagine that Mama would have known what real love was. Perhaps my grandma felt the need to have one less mouth to feed. Mama never said one way or another whether she loved him or not, but I'm sure if she didn't when she married him, she loved him later on. He was a kind man, treated Mama with love, and provided well for his family. She didn't have her first child until she was 16. My first half-sister Laverne Goodman, was born Nov. 2, 1928. My second half-sister Loyce Goodman, was born July 21, 1932. My grandma lived down around Camp Worth. Mama and Luther, and the girls, lived at Black Jack. In April of 1937, Luther got sick with pneumonia and died at the age of 32 and Mama was 24. They had had eleven years together, but it was a sad and difficult time for Mama with two small children to raise alone. Laverne was 8 and Loyce was 4.

Mama took whatever kinds of work she could find, such as working in the woods using a crosscut saw with her on one end and a man on the other end. She took in washing and ironing and waitressing. That's what she was doing when she met my daddy in 1939. She had been invited to a country dance down in Fountain Town in San Augustine County, and caught a ride with a friend. The dance was at the home of a friend who lived back down in the area where she came from. It just so happened that my daddy was helping play the fiddle music. When he got a break, he went over and introduced himself to the "beautiful lady wearing a red ribbon tied in her dark hair". From that night on, they became an item. Every time they could get a ride, they tried to see each other. Neither of them had a car and had to bum a ride with someone else. Since Daddy lived at Mt. Herman, that was pretty far from Black Jack. Mama was renting a small cottage behind the main house belonging to a nice lady who often kept the kids when she worked or went to the dances. Maybe she felt sorry for Mama being a young widow trying to work and make a living for the kids. Mama and Daddy weren't able to get ways to see each other often, or if one could, the other couldn't, but they were finally able to get married on August 28, 1940, and he moved them over to Mt. Herman. They had to live with his parents for a while, but he and Mama built their own home together on Daddy's land next door to his parents as soon as possible.

I was born in November, 1941, and my Grandma Taylor died of cancer when I was 4 months old. She'd had part of one leg removed years earlier because of it, but it came back and killed her this time. She was another story unto herself for she was a gutsy lady. They had removed her leg on her kitchen table. Daddy wasn't very old. He said they made him go out and walk up and down the road while they cut it off, but he said the deadening medicine didn't work too well. He could hear her screaming all the while he was walking, and he couldn't imagine the pain she must be in.

Another time, she was complaining that the stump of her leg was just on fire, stinging unbearably. Someone told them they'd heard that if ants or something got on the limb they had buried, they would sting and burn like that. So they went over to Mt. Pleasant and dug up the box and sure enough, the leg was covered in fire ants. So they cleaned them all out and killed them and reburied the leg and she was fine after that.

She did all her work thumping across the floor in an old straight chair. When she needed to do her gardening, they cut the handle of her hoe a little shorter and they carried her a pad to sit on. She would hoe all around her as far as she could reach. Daddy would be working another spot and when she needed to move, he'd come pick her up and move her over to a new area. For sure, she was no slacker. If my Grandpa didn't do something she liked, she'd hit him over the back with the

Our Neighbors

broom. She was tiny, but she could put the fear into those sons of hers, and probably Aunt Letha too, the only girl. Mama said she just loved her when she lived there.

After Mama moved over here, she easily made friends with all the neighbors and got along well with everyone. The ladies would get together once a week and quilt. I have Mama's friendship quilt. They all made themselves one and each one made a square and embroidered their names and the date on it for the other ladies. Mrs. Fannie Mae Adkison had one on it. Many of the women who lived on my road, possibly Mrs. Verna Mills, Mrs. Tommie Eddins, Mrs. Florine Ellington, Mrs. Clara Holder, Mrs. Annie Parker, my Aunt Annice, and Aunt Letha,(all the ones who didn't work outside the home), and of course, my Mama had one on it. It's hard to remember who all lived on this road and maybe some who lived down the other roads at that time, such as Mrs. Ella Warren and Mrs. Jewel Adkison. But I'm all the more proud of it because they're all gone now, and I thought the world of each of those sweet ladies.

Mama and Daddy both worked a cotton patch which was a higher paying crop back then, and they had a garden for family use. Laverne and Loyce went two years at Mt. Herman before going on to Center High, but neither of them finished. I loved my sisters and I wanted to go wherever they went, but they had other plans. Laverne was 13 years older than me, and she got married when she was 18 and I lacked 3 months being 5. She married D L Battles and they moved to Nebraska, because he had a sister and brother-in-law who lived there. After a good cold snap with all the ice and snow, they decided to head back to East Texas. D L moved them about every two or three years. He was always chasing rainbows. They had six children, two girls and four boys.

One day when Mama was out hoeing in the garden, she said she heard me just screaming like someone was killing me. She threw down her hoe and came running into the house. Laverne and Loyce had me down combing the tangles out of my hair. I had really thick hair and being pretty young, when I combed it, I would just slick over the top. It would get matted underneath, and it would hurt to pull a comb through that, so I didn't. That's what they were doing, trying to comb out those matted tangles. I did think I was dying. Ha.

Mama said she used to try to lay down and take a little short nap after lunch, because she was tired.

Every time she closed her eyes, I'd shake her and say, "Mama, are you asleep?"

I would never take a nap myself. Also, when I was little, there used to be clusters of airplanes that would come over, and it would just scare me to death. I don't know what I thought they were gonna do, but I would start crying and screaming "air main, air main" and crawl under the bed. Mama would have to come and calm me down. They used to do that pretty often. It was scary to see so many planes flying together, and not that high in the sky. Those were propeller planes and made a loud noise. Boy, it would really scare me if I saw that many today.

Well, another sad day came when my other sister left home when she got to be 15, and I was gonna be left all alone. At least she was here about 3 years after Laverne left. We were always very close despite the fact that she was 9 years older than me. She moved to Nacogdoches to live with one of my Mama's sisters and got a job in a drug store for a while, and then she got a job as a telephone operator. She eventually moved to Houston and was able to continue working for the telephone company. She married the love of her life, E. J. (Jack) Orgeron, in 1952, when she was 20. They had four children together, three girls and one boy.

Mama and Daddy eventually got jobs in town working at Hayes Laundry & Press Shop. Daddy worked there until he lost his sight to glaucoma and had to quit. Mama had to get a car, learn to drive and get her license, so she could get herself to work. She decided to change jobs and go to work for Eastex Poultry where she worked for 20 years. By that time, she had racked up about 30 years at both places. After retiring from there, she worked part-time at a small plant farm near our home, simply because she enjoyed having something to do. She was always busy. She loved to work in our yard and always had pretty flowers of all kinds. She tried to grow some in my yard, but the ground wasn't very fertile.

All during my growing up, Mama sewed clothes for me. I remember some of my first ones were made from flour sack material, but it was pretty. She would save up enough sacks of the same print until she got enough to make something. She'd make me little short sets, blouses, jumpers, etc. Later on as I got older, she bought beautiful material and made my clothes that I thought were so pretty. She was very talented. She could quilt, crochet, embroider, and all, plus she was a great cook. She was always a hard worker. It seemed to me that she enjoyed being outside more than inside. She could never understand why I didn't take to flower growing and gardening. I told her I was a secretary and did office work, or painting, or craft work. We just weren't cut from the same cloth. Mama loved to go fishing or squirrel hunting with Daddy also.

Daddy always wanted me to be able to play some kind of musical instrument, but that was not to be. On the other hand, I could draw or paint so I was talented in that way, and have never known of another person in my family who does that. Surprisingly, this talent has trickled down to my daughter, my son, two of my granddaughters, and my two grandsons. But before me, I don't know of anyone else who had that talent. However, I can write poetry to some extent. I found out that one of my mama's sisters wrote poetry, and one of my first cousin's boys writes it. So that seems to run in Mama's side of the family.

Life always has a way of bringing surprises. During the course of my work in genealogy, I discovered that one of my first cousins was married to a cousin of mine. Neither of us knew we were related. Thankfully, he wasn't related to his wife. His wife and I were related on the other side. So we've done some extensive research in our line...discovered we were both related to Cynda Hooper Jones. I already knew I was related to her, but my new cousin, Allison, did not know she was. So we were both related to Sister Dolly Hooper and her children. I had known for years that I was related to Joyce Hooper Warr, Velt's wife, Cynda's sister, also a sister to Mildred McSwain, James Lee McSwain's wife, and therefore am related to all of Mildred's children.

My mama was born in Sabine County, but her mama and daddy were married in Shelby County and lived on the border of Shelby and San Augustine, so people from both counties came in touch all the time. As a result, my mama's brother Thomas E. Vandygriff married Florine "Cricket" Warr, older sister of Velt Warr. In my teen years, the Warrs used to live near us and we ran around together and went to parties at their home every Saturday night. We just played records and danced, drank soft drinks and ate chips and such, sometimes played spin the bottle, or just sat around on the porch and talked. It was all good clean fun. Shirley and I were close friends and I sometimes spent the night with her. Didn't get much sleep because of the noise made by Billy's pigeons cooing, or whatever sound they make. It went on all night; not the parties, the pigeon noise. Ha. The parties were usually over around 11:00 p.m., because Mr. and Mrs. Warr had to go to bed.

Since my Daddy played the fiddle, he would often get together with some of his friends to play for a little while. Idell Fults was a good guitar player. Sometimes she and her sister, Johnnie, came to our house, or Daddy, Mama, and I would go to theirs. In the earlier years, they still lived in their old house which had two large rooms in front and the kitchen ran along the back of the house. They played music in the main big old room with the fireplace, two beds and some straight chairs. If it was cold weather, you'd burn your front side and freeze your back side, but you didn't notice it so much while listening to the good music they were playing.

I remember one time I had some warts on my hand and Johnnie said she could take those off. She got a long piece of twine, tied a knot in it over each wart, then she went outside where I couldn't see and buried the twine. She said when the twine rotted, the warts would be gone. Well, my warts went away after not too much longer. I don't know if it was because the twine rotted, or they just went away on their own, but I'd had them a long time.

Another friend Daddy played with was Junior Williams, Barbara Scates' daddy. Sometimes they got together down at the Williams' home and they played a few rounds. I loved to go there because they had the two boys, Glen Alvin and Billy who were old enough for me to play with. I believe Wanda may have been a baby then, but I know Barbara and Gay had not been born yet.

Anyway, it was about to kill us kids when we had to be quiet and couldn't get our playtime juices heated up, but every chance we got when they would stop to rest, we'd start crawling around on the floor chasing each other. Well, it's not that the room wasn't all that large, but with lots of people sitting around in there, it got pretty close, so we were dodging legs right and left and we'd crawl under the kitchen table 'cause the living room and kitchen were all made together. Anyway, I was really traveling and all of a sudden, one of those table legs just hauled off and jumped right out in front of me and caused me to cut my lip open and it bled and bled, so that put a qui-e-tous on the chase for me. I was mortally wounded. Although it wasn't really that bad, I thought I was gonna die, and it left a little scar on the inside of my mouth but not on the outside, so I have that to remind me of those fun times.

Sometimes, they all loaded up in Mr. Williams' flatbed truck, set me and the two boys tightly against the cab on the back of the truck with strict instructions not to move from that spot, and they'd go to someone's home for a dance and to play music with some other musicians, maybe even a little dancing. If any of the kids got sleepy, the hostess had a room fixed for them to be taken back and put down to sleep. I usually conked out before these parties were over and had to be woken up and dragged out in a stupor, 'cause I didn't know where I was since I was still half asleep. Those were all fun years.

Another thing I remember about my mama and her ingenuity is that when my permanent teeth started coming in, I had two big old tushes on the top that came in way up higher than my other teeth. Well, my mama would tell me bedtime stories every night when I went to bed After I got grown, I was amazed that she even knew those children's stories, such as *Goldilocks and The Three Bears*, *The Three Little Pigs*, *Little Red Riding Hood* to name a few. What really amazed me, after I was grown, was that while she was telling the stories, she would hold her finger and thumb on those tushes with a good bit of pressure every single night as she told me my stories. Those old teeth grew on down straight and even with the others. She saved herself and Daddy the expense of getting braces for me. Now I've always wondered, "How did she know to do that, or to be so diligent with it every night?"

She always made lye soap in her big black wash pot, and she was the one who got up first in the winter and would go start up the heater in the living room, then she'd start breakfast in our wood stove in the kitchen. Every day we'd have some kind of meat from the smokehouse; sausages, bacon, or ham. We'd have scrambled eggs for us kids. .Daddy would have his two fried eggs. She always made biscuits, or hoecake and gravy, or spotted gravy. Daddy and Mama drank coffee, and we kids drank milk from our cow.

We had chickens running free in the yard, so we had plenty of eggs.

Our Neighbors

I remember taking eggs to Jess Warren's Store to get me a soft drink and candy bar, or peanuts. I found eggs everywhere 'cause those old hens would lay their eggs under bushes, or the edge of the house.

Mama raised tame black berries along the back fence, and she'd make jelly so we had jelly. She made fig preserves from our fig tree.

I remember we had an ice box, and we'd go to Center to the ice house, and they'd bring us a big old block of ice and set it on a burlap bag in the back of our car. We'd bring it home and put it in the ice box. It would last a pretty good while. We just chipped off what we needed with an ice pick, and the block of ice kept the box cool for our milk and butter, etc.

We always had a hog when I was a kid, and I can remember a little bit when the neighbors would all get together for the hog killings. I was more interested in playing with the other kids. We'd always raise a hog until Mama and Daddy started working in town.

I had first cousins who would come visit, and they would climb our trees, so I thought I should be able to do whatever they did. The only bad thing was, I fell out of them more than once and knocked the breath out of myself, just knocked myself cold. I know Daddy cut down at least one of his trees to keep me from killing myself climbing it. I was just the clumsiest child ever born.

Another time when we were at the Big Bud Fenley's home, the boy cousins and Gene Fenley were walking across the top of a board fence that had a board nailed flat along the top of it, so they were just like little cat squirrels scooting across that fence. I got up there and started walking and hadn't gone two or three feet before I lost my balance. Unfortunately, there was a piece of tin, with a corner sticking straight up, leaning against the fence right where I fell. I landed on it with my knee and cut it to the bone. Oh, it hurt terribly and bled like crazy.

They got it stopped and wrapped it good and didn't take me to get stitches. It got well pretty fast, but I have always had a huge scar above my knee.

Gene Fenley's parents were good friends with my parents and my Mama's sisters, so Gene was always playing with my cousins. I had all those boy cousins, four to be exact, and only one girl cousin on Mama's side. We were terribly outnumbered. We all visited back and forth fairly often. Mr. Big Bud was another musician Daddy played with.

Well, like I said, my Mama was a wonderful Mama to me. She was always right with me every time I got sick and stayed with me in the hospital or at home. After I had Tamara, I got pregnant with a second baby and had a miscarriage in my first trimester. When I got pregnant with my third child, for the first three months of the pregnancy, I smothered. I was hyperventilating, but I didn't figure it out until later. My doctors didn't either, but as soon as the three months were over, it stopped immediately. That was when I had lost the other baby. In my mind I guess I was afraid I was going to lose this baby too, so I would smother. Johnny worked nights. My Mama was so good. She came out and stayed with me every night 'till he got home about 2:30 in the morning, because I couldn't sleep. I was so miserable, couldn't lie down, gasping for air, and couldn't catch my breath. It was awful. She tried having me breathe into a paper sack and everything, but nothing worked. Oh, glorious day, when three months passed, it all just vanished and I could breathe. I knew immediately I'd hyperventilated 'till that time passed. Mama was there for me. She wasn't getting any sleep, bless her heart. She went with me to my doctor appointments, and let me sit in the car because I looked like some kind of idiot with my mouth wide open, gasping for air. She would sit in the waiting room until they called me.

I had an ulcer and was in the hospital once, and she stayed with me during that, and another time when I had my gallbladder attack and surgery. A week after I went home, I had another attack. I had a stone in my bile duct, and they did more surgery and couldn't find it, said it must've passed. During that same summer, I had half of my stomach removed. She was there for that. She was there for the birth of both of my babies. She went above and beyond the call of duty, and believe me, she was a precious Mama to me whom I dearly loved and appreciated.

Mama and Daddy took us to the drive-in movie every Saturday night and many times, I invited my first cousin Peggy to go with us. The first car I remember Daddy owning was a little 1932 Ford 2-seater which also had a rumble seat, so Peggy and I sat in the back seat although we didn't have a lot of room, but that didn't matter when we were going to the movies.

My grandpa used to take me to an outdoor movie that Mr. Fred Williams put on at his home. It was located where Barbara and Jerry Scates' new home is now. He had a sawmill, so he had split some logs for the seats and laid the boards on some pieces of logs. He threw some sheets over wires to make screens, and then he had movie nights. The movies were usually Zombie movies. At my young age, after I got back home and went to bed, I had trouble sleeping or would have nightmares about those creepy Zombies, but I would be ready to go again the next week. I dare say, Mr. Williams didn't get rich with his picture show business. I don't think it cost but a nickel for me. I don't know what Grandpa's admission was. Not much, I'm sure.

Another thing I remember. The origin of Jess Warren's Store. Well, that store was a blessing to all of us who lived near it. We, kids who caught the school bus down there every morning, had a time playing. It had that real high porch. We could walk under the porch, or run across it and down the steps. We played Fox and Dogs a lot. Don't you know we were a smelly bunch when we got on that bus and got to school?

Back to the origin of Mr. Jess' store. I don't know if you remember there used to be a small building out to the side in which Mr. Jess kept his feed and seeds that he sold. That was his first store, and it was my grandpa's store first. My grandpa, John Franklin Taylor, built the store out here on his land and stayed in business about two years before he went bankrupt. People kept begging him to let them have stuff on credit with a promise to pay. He was so soft-hearted that he kept doing it until he didn't have anything left in his store to sell. With no money to pay for his goods, he had to file bankruptcy. So, Mr. Jess Warren wound up buying the store at a bargain. He moved the building across the highway by rolling it across on poles pulled by horses or oxen. It first sat in the spot where his building is now. When they built the new store, they moved the little store over to the side to use for the feed store and built the much bigger store. That's the story of how Jess Warren's Store came to be.

Another thing that Mama always did was cut and perm my hair. When I got grown, I began cutting and perming her hair. My daddy had always cut his brothers' hair. Many of his friends would drop by and want a haircut. Mama would also put in Laverne's perms. I have cut my own hair as well as Johnny's, Tamara's, Mark's, and Beth's for years. Then Mark started cutting his own hair and his boys' hair. Tamara used to go get hers cut at the beauty shop, but then she started letting me cut it. Beth initially went to a beauty shop in town to get that beautiful long hair cut off for the first time, but since then I've kept it cut until recently. Tamara started trying her hand at it and she's been cutting Beth's. It seems that hair-cutting also runs in our family. My cousin, Mavis Williams, even came out and asked me to cut her hair. None of us have been to a beauty shop in years. Of course, people might think we should go. Ha.

All in all, I guess my parents saw that I had a fairly full childhood of fun and lots of good times with cousins and friends.

Well, this by no means covers all the things about my mama, how she always cooked and had us out for dinner every Sunday. It was a real treat we always looked forward to. It was really great when my sisters and their families and me and my family all got to get together for Christmas dinner enjoying the good company at Mama's and Daddy's for this didn't happen every Christmas.

There was one activity we always got together for and that was an annual visit to Crystal Lake in Joaquin, and both my sisters and families, my family and Mama all went and took picnic dinners, and everyone who wanted to would swim. The rest of us sat and visited in the shade and caught up on the family news since we'd last seen each other. Of course, Daddy didn't go because he couldn't see or hear that well by then and didn't get any pleasure out of it. He really hated to have to miss out too for he loved his family very much. After Crystal Lake closed down its activities, we began meeting at Lake Livingston which was pretty centrally located between all of us, and we did the same thing... carried food, visited and the young folks swam, but it was our sort of family reunion. Every year, Mama would have more great-grandkids to meet for the first time. She and Daddy died before they got to see any of Mark's four children.

It was terribly sad that in a sense, I lost both of my parents twice. I couldn't communicate with Daddy anymore after he went both deaf and blind. Then Mama got Alzheimer, and that was the most horrible thing I believe that can happen. You look into their eyes that were once so bright and intelligent, and you suddenly see absolutely nothing staring back at you. There's no more comprehension, no recognition. It's all just been whisked away leaving a wide expanse of nothingness. It just broke my heart. She changed completely. Some days she was so sweet and caring; the next, she was combative and angry, thinking we were laughing at her. She got out of the house at night once. Tamara found her out at her house. She had her suitcase. She said she was going to find Monroe (my daddy).

Tam told her, "Now Big Mama, you know where Pa Taylor is."

And she said "Oh yeah, I know where he's at. He's over there in that cemetery."

So she let Tamara bring her back. Johnny had to install some locks high up on the door so she couldn't reach them and get out. It got so bad we had to place Mama in the nursing home, and she was so far gone, it didn't upset her. Of course, it did me. I would never have done that if it hadn't been necessary, but my doctor told me it was for the sake of my own health; that I was heading for a stroke or heart attack if I didn't get out from under the stress. All she did was walk, walk, walk, and she didn't know us when we went. She'd leave us sitting there and go off down the hall. Then one night near Christmas, they called us and said she had fallen while walking, and broke her hip, and that they had taken her to Nacogdoches Medical Center. They said we'd better gather up all the family because at her age, they usually didn't make it through that kind of surgery, (she was 88). We called my sister in Houston. She and her girls came. Laverne and her girls and some of the boys, and me and my family all went. We were in the waiting room, and a nurse came and told us to come look, and we looked down the hall. They were rolling her to recovery, but she was sitting up on the bed looking around. They said it probably wouldn't be long before they put her in a room, because she most definitely was awake, and they would let us know. Anyway, it wasn't long, and they put her in a room with a woman, whose family was visiting. Some of them had the flu. Of course, my sister, Loyce, and I both caught the flu. Anyway, the hospital sent Mama back to the nursing home soon after. Since it was Christmas time, all their main people were off for the holidays and only a few aides were on staff. I was sick with the flu and couldn't go see Mama, but Laverne went a couple of times and she said Mama was just curled up in a fetal position, and never would even raise her head or anything, just kept lying there. She said there were plates of food there uneaten. Apparently Mama hadn't been fed or hadn't eaten. I don't believe, the aides tried too hard to get her to eat, and she just died. She developed double pneumonia and heart failure and died on January 2, 2001. She was one of a kind. I still miss her and my daddy. I was lucky to have them for my parents, and I loved them so very much.

Sisters Lily Fountain Kitchen and Mattie Fountain Warr

Lily Fountain Kitchen and Mattie Fountain Warr are the daughters of Noah Shadmarc Fountain and Sarah Elizabeth Snell, who came to Texas from Alabama in the 1870s and settled in Ironosa in northwestern San Augustine County, near the Shelby County line. (Information from Christine Mahan.)

<u>Helen Windham</u>: I have never seen a picture of my great grandmother, Mattie Warr, when she was that young! I don't remember her sister.

<u>Linda Winder</u>: Lillie was the youngest of the children of Noah Fountain, born in Ironosa. She and her husband lived in California and this photo was taken on a visit to Texas.

<u>Rodger McLane</u>: Linda, I just asked Delores Harris Brown if she knew if anyone kept up with the sister who went to California. Did she have a big family? I wonder if anyone knows her grandkids, or are friends with her descendants.

<u>Linda Winder:</u> Chris, Do you know the answer to Rodger McLane's question? You mentioned a daughter in the Fountain book.

Chris M: Linda, Aunt Lilly only had one daughter, Aunt Essie, who would correspondent with her family, occasionally. After Aunt Essie passed. I know of no one that kept in touch.

Rodger McLane: Chris, sweet Aunt Essie. She and Uncle Ernest were too good. I remember Mamaw Ruby telling her how rough I talked to the satellite people, when they tried charging Ruby extra to fix her TV. Aunt Essie told me I told them just right. I was maybe 11 or 12. LOL.

Linda Winder: Rodger, According to the Warr notes (collected by Chris Mahan) Lillie Holland Fountain Kitchen had one daughter, Mary, who married Doc Shrock. Lillie Kitchen lived in Lancaster, California when she died January 30, 1979. Her funeral program notes that she was born in "Arnocie, Texas" August 20, 1887.

Chris M: Grandma Warr was a gentle soul, always greeted you with a hug and a pat on the back, even tempered, until someone said something bad about a Fountain. She once said there is not a bad one in the whole group.

Jack & Rachel Fountain

Jill Fountain Parker: Does anyone remember my grandparents (Jack and Rachel Fountain) having a little gas station in Aiken? I know they did but we never really talked about it much. It was located where Bryan Sumstine lives now. There used to be an old house there, and the station was attached to it. That little house was a Camp Worth house that Jack and Rachel bought from Frost Lumber when they closed the sawmill town down. I remember the little house being there when I was young. I had friends that lived there and actually stayed there with them a lot.

Pam Adkison: Jill, I remember their gas station. Mrs. Rachel had a box of eight crayons in stock. I pitched a tantrum until Mother bought them for me. LOL. It wasn't long after that, when Mother and Daddy bought the place from Jack and Rachel. Your grandparents moved the gas station building off the property, when we moved in. This was the last half of 1960. I was in the middle of second grade. We moved from Elsie Deans' house (Mrs. White's house. It is for sale now), which we had rented. I knew that they had moved the front of the house there, but didn't know where they got it. That part had two large rooms with high ceilings. Jack then added the dining room, kitchen, a bedroom, bathroom, and a detached garage. Jack later added another bedroom that had a separate entrance with a porch. I'm not clear about this, but this bedroom was for one of their kinfolk that had started living with them. Years later, Daddy had Jack to expand the kitchen and one of the bedrooms. I'm not giving enough credit to Rachel. She was a hard worker, and made every step Jack made.

She probably told him, "Hold my ladder, Jack, while I finish this."

Howell Adkison: My dad (Hollis) and mother (Myrtle) were friends with Mr. Jack and Mrs. Rachel. Back in the late sixties, Mr. Jack had problems with his back and was not able to work. Mrs. Rachel tried to get him to go to the doctor, but he refused.

Dad found out and told Mother, "I am going over and get D.L. Battles to help me. We will get him some help." They got there and Mr. Jack still refused to go.

Dad told him, "Jack, you are going to the doctor."

Dad and Mr. D.L. cradled him up, put him in the car, and off they went. I think, later he had surgery and got well enough to go back to work. My dad cared for his friends and would help them however he could.

The Fenleys

<u>Sharon Fenley Prince</u>: My Great Grandparents Fenley. They are buried at Spring Ridge and lived in that area. Most of my Fenley ancestors live in Lufkin, TX. How Norris and Sarah Fenley ended up in Shelby County, I do not know. If you notice, Big Bud's (my grandfather) face is dirty. They say he rubbed smut on his face just for this picture. He loved the attention. Big Bud and Little Bud were twins. This is how they got their nicknames. LOL.

<u>Royce Lynn Johnson</u>: "Big Bud and Little Bud". Heard so much about them.

<u>Shane Fenley</u>: For not ever knowing them when I was growing up, I was always called Bud.

L-R: Sarah Ellen Fenley (Granny), Marline Hendricks (Aunt Ronnie's daughter), Old Scott (dog) Viola Gertrude (Aunt Cotton), Elvin Norris Fenley (Grandpa) Behind: Ira (Big Bud), Ila (Little Bud), Courtesy of Sharon Fenley Prince

The Four Mints

<u>Joyce Bright:</u> Pam, I thought of something else, but can't remember their name. They were a great Quartet from the area. One was a McSwain, One was a Wilson, who married Lola Houston. Lola Houston and her mom and dad lived in a house that was where Shirley and Charles Brown lived. It was in the 1950s. If you will add my cousin, Sulane McSwain Mayer, she will know. She is Mama's sister's daughter. She was Vircle and Clarence McSwain's daughter. I called and told her about West Shelby County and Outer Bank, but don't know if she got signed up. Also, Linda, Royce Lynn's sister could give you information about the Quartet. Hope all is going good.

<u>Eldora Gilchrist:</u> They were The Four Mints, got real famous in Las Vegas. Some movie company even came to Center and made a movie about their life. Jamie Warr played one of them as a small boy growing up. They were very good. I posted some info about them earlier. There's a movie about them?

<u>Delores Harris Brown</u>: I think I have a clipping from the newspaper that Mama or Ma saved about them and maybe a picture. I will have to look.

<u>Helen Windham</u>: Delores, I have heard about a movie! I sure would like to see it. If you can find the clipping, we might be able to track down the movie!

<u>Delores Harris Brown</u>: Helen, I will look thru their scrapbooks and pictures they saved. Maybe I can find it.

<u>Eldora Gilchrist</u>: The Four Mints, the Wilson boys, Charles and James Paul. I don't know if the movie ever got produced or not. Noah Gene lives in Biloxi, Mississippi, but he does have a home on the Pearl Lake Road just across from Aunt Donnie's house. It's a very nice large house

sitting up off of the road. The other two were Noah Gene Warr and his brother, Alton. As far as I know, Noah and Jana are still living. I've seen him a couple of times in the past few years here in town, but I think the other three are all deceased. James Paul was married to Lola Houston.

Terri Lacher: Helen, the movie was never completed, but not sure why. I think they called it, "Born to Swing." And I believe Jimmy Jones was also in it.

Terri Lacher: Just saw this. I wrote an article earlier this year about the Four Mints in the *Around the Town* paper. I've been researching them for a project and have access to newspaper clippings, if anyone would like to know more about them. You can also go to YouTube and listen to a couple of their hit songs. It is my opinion that if the British invasion had not happen in the early '60s, they easily could have gone on even farther in their careers. Shelby County's own very talented musicians!

That Kid That Got Lost That Time

By Fred Borders

This story will probably be boring and maybe a bit lengthy, but I got nothing else to do tonight.

As most of you know, I grew up in the Sandhills between Jericho and Brady. I have one brother, Mack, about 22 months older than me. We had a dog named Tyke that was a great squirrel dog. Since there were woods all around us Tyke would often hunt alone. During squirrel season we would hear him barking off in the woods and our mother or dad would go kill the squirrel. That's right, my mother was a dead eye with a Mossberg automatic 22 with a peep site. One evening when I was seven and Mack was nine we heard Tyke barking off in the woods in front of the house. Daddy wasn't home from work and Mama was busy cooking supper. Mack and I didn't have guns yet, but we figured we needed to go to Tyke anyway. We got to the tree he was barking up and were trying to find the squirrel. Mack gave up and said we should go home. Me, being a big seven year old, I told him I was going to look a while longer. A few minutes later when I decided to go home, I realized I had no idea which way home was. After tracing through the woods for a while it got dark. I made the decision that I would sleep until day light, and then find my way out. It was late fall, but I don't remember being cold. I heard a car, so thought I should lay facing that direction, and I would know which direction to go come daylight, because there was the county road on one side and a pig trail road on the other side leading to an abandoned home site. It wasn't long before I heard a car on the other side, so I turned over to face the other way. Sometime later in the night, I heard a woman calling. I answered, and it turned out to be one of Bob Powdrill's daughters. Mr. Bob owned the store at the crossroads at Jericho. She and Mr. Bob had found me. They put me in Mr. Bob's old Dodge pickup, and we drove the half mile or so to our house. When we turned into our driveway, I remember seeing the yard full of cars and pickups. I was wondering what was going on, because we had never had that much company at one time. My mother was so glad to see me. She didn't even consider whipping my butt.

At least once or twice per year, until I was about 30 years old, I would meet someone and when they would get my name they would say, "Oh, you're that boy that got lost that time."

I hadn't heard that in many years, until a few years ago. We were eating at the Dairy Queen one night with Connie and Joe Bill. Connie was talking to William Rudd. Although I grew up only a mile or so from William, he was several years older and left this area for college and didn't come back to Jericho, so we had never met. I took the opportunity to introduce myself.

Then I heard it again, "You were that kid that got lost." He told me their farm hand, Jack Smith borrowed his horse to help hunt for me.

There's one other detail I remember worth mentioning. After the commotion settled, I remember seeing half cooked chicken in cold grease on the stove. When my mother suddenly realized I wasn't around, nothing else mattered. She turned the fires off and concentrated on me.

Jimmie Nell Adkison Lee: Wonderful story!!! These are stories that if not told and written down, will die with us. Oh how I wish children today could live what we lived, but it most likely would be boring to them.

William Rudd: I have shared that story many times over the years. The news spread rapidly and the whole community mobilized in the search for Fred. I never saw a lot of deep emotion ever coming from Jack, except in this case. He was almost in tears, as we saddled my horse about 8 o'clock that evening for the ride to the Border's home in our cattle trailer. Warm emotional memories Fred.

Fred Borders: William, when we drove up, another car wouldn't have fit in the yard. It looked like a church homecoming. It honestly didn't occur to me at the time that they were there for me. Incredibly, I was never scared nor thought I was in danger. I knew that once I got to a road I would come out someplace.

Our Neighbors

Catherine L: I cried and smiled. So precious. Our boys would roam the woods. We would honk the horns until they showed up. All children are so precious. I can see y'all as little boys. Raised from the heart of East Texas. With wonderful, loving parents and community. God is good. Thank you for the story.

Tammy Fenley: Not boring at all. I enjoyed every word of it! I have been thinking about videoing different people telling such short stories to keep and share. I would love to hear more of your stories.

Fred Borders: Tammy, I'm better at writing than talking. I can take my time to think of the words I want to use.

Tammy Fenley: I know what you mean. I prefer to write over talking as well. It would be better & more interesting to future generations (they are more likely to watch something, than read about it) to have the actual person telling the story themselves. Don't you?

Mack Borders: I remember that night well. I didn't know Fred hadn't come home, until Mama sent me outside to tell him to come into the house. When I didn't find him, I came back in and told her that he must still be in the woods with Tyke.

She said, "It'll be dark soon, you go get him right now."

When I couldn't find him and came back alone, Mama became very upset and said to Daddy, "Fred's lost in the woods."

I went with Daddy when he went for help, while Mama stayed at home in case Fred returned. I remember we stopped at Uncle Stokley Andrews' house, and one or two more, and the word began to spread. A couple of people, almost, beat us back home. Before long there was a large crowd. People came from miles around. Some people brought horses, one man brought a couple of hound dogs. Everybody had flashlights or lanterns. It was the most exciting thing a 9 year old boy had ever seen in the Sandhills.

Thanks to a multitude of good people, people who dropped their night time chores, their evening meals, everything to help a lost kid, things turned out well for our family that night.

I didn't know, until I read Fred's post, that Jack Smith was one of the people on horseback, though I'm not surprised. Jack was a good man and he would have done anything for one of the neighborhood kids, if they had needed help.

<u>Fred Borders</u>: Mack, I don't want to sound unappreciative, because I appreciate what they did very much. But it really wasn't necessary, because I had a plan. I would have been home the next day by mid-morning. There was really no cause for alarm.

I didn't know about Mr. Jack Smith being there either, until William told me. When Mr. Roy Rudd had our place leased for farming and Mr. Jack was running a tractor, Mama would let me carry him a Coke or a pear, after we got home from school. I would also carry one for myself. He would shut down long enough for us eat, or drink, and talk.

<u>Mack Borders</u>: Fred, I knew you would find your way home after daylight. Other than being tired, hungry, and thirsty you would not have been any worse for wear. Mama would've suffered a lot more than you. I was mostly thinking of the helpful and unselfish nature of people back in that time. Not to say, there aren't lots of those people today, but they are a much smaller percentage of the population.

<u>Fred Borders</u>: Mack, my comments about "no reason for alarm" was meant to be humorous. I know, when a small child is lost in the woods that there's going to be alarm. In those days neighbors really pulled together. However, there's little doubt in my mind, that I would have

found my way home. I also know, as parents Momma and Daddy couldn't count on that. I knew I was between the county road and that pig trail that made that loop around by the McDonald place and came out in front of our house. I'm sure you and I had walked it, and probably, rode bicycles around it. As long as I didn't cross a road, I was surrounded. You never know, when one is disoriented he's likely to do anything. I do remember that when we pulled up to our house, it was on the wrong side of the road.

Mack Borders: Fred, I've done that after being turned around in those woods for a while. Took me a while to get my mind straight after getting home.

William Rudd: Mack, on a cloudy autumn day when I was 13, I decided to go squirrel hunting in the woods just northwest of the Jericho crossroads. As the afternoon progressed, I heard a thunderstorm in the distance and decided it was time to go home. Like Fred, I knew that there was a road on all four sides of the heavily wooded area, and that I was not hopelessly lost. At the same time I was lost, became disoriented, and wasn't sure which direction I needed to go. So, I picked one and finally came to a road, wasn't sure which side of the area I was on, looked both directions, didn't recognize anything, then decided, yes I knew which road I was on and headed out in the direction that would take me home. As I passed over a hill I recognized some familiar landmarks as the storm began to move in. I was not on the road I thought I was on and I took the wrong end of the road for getting home. Thankfully, just as the storm arrived Royce Lynn Johnson's dad came by and gave me a ride. It's very disconcerting and creates weird anxieties when one is disoriented and totally confused about where one is. I did not recover my senses, until we arrived at the grocery store at the crossroads.

Fred Borders, William, my parents always called that section of woods the Big Woods.

William Rudd, Fred, It was always Big Woods at my house too. I just didn't know if I should call it that in the write-up.

Barry R: My dad, William, has told me this story a few times over the years. Also, he talked about you bringing pears to Jack. Thanks for sharing all the particulars of the story here, Fred. I spent a lot of time down there over the years and appreciate hearing the history, stories etc. from the area there around Jericho crossroads.

Fred Borders: Barry, they're good memories and I'm blessed with a good memory. The pears were those big old fall pears that we gathered for preserves. When they sit for a while they would mellow and turn yellow. I loved them like that and so did Jack. I still like them.

Karen Bittick: For some reason I don't remember Fred being lost, but you can bet the Jericho party line was buzzing faster than the Internet. It felt good to know our Dad (Royce Johnson) gave you a ride home William Rudd.

Fred Borders: Karen, it was the fall of '56. As Mack was saying, he and daddy drove out to spread the word, because we didn't have a phone.

William Rudd: Fred, I was a senior in high school that fall. At Christmas break I had accumulated enough credits to graduate so my dad decided I needed to stay home during the spring semester to help with the crops. His idea was that it would be good practical experience and that I needed to help earn money for college. I wasn't happy about any of that. We planted a big crop of melons and peas. The peas did well. In the third week of June, we had a bumper crop of melons almost ready to start ripening on beautiful healthy vines. In the fourth week Hurricane Audrey showed up and spent several days dumping rain on the fields. As the skies cleared and the sun returned, all of the vines, every one of them, were wilted down and lying flat on the ground. None of them recovered. It was a sad sight to look across the fields and see thousands of melons, not ripe, but ready to ripen and nothing else but dead vines. We didn't harvest any, not one good melon, that year. My dad offered Bert McSwain an option to peddle on shares any melons he wanted to take from the field. After two loads Burt told my dad he was through. He was scared to go back and face the backlash from selling melons that were not good. ... A lot of lessons learned that spring. Mainly, Mother Nature does whatever she wants to do, whenever she wants to do it. I did participate in the spring graduation exercise at school, but I missed associating with fellow graduates during the semester. And my parents still paid my college expenses.

My sisters and I picked a lot of peas over the years. My dad and mom provided all of our food, clothing, shelter and entertainment needs, so we were never paid a penny a pound directly like the rest of the pickers. One day when I was 13, we had finished picking for the day when Foy Bradshaw came by looking for additional pickers. I was a good pea picker and saw an opportunity to make some real cash. So, I volunteered. When we got to his field he put me in the butter bean patch. If you've ever picked butter beans, you know that it takes a lot of butter beans to make a pound. It's more difficult to identify levels of maturity than with peas. These are really demotivating issues for a 13 year old. I was extremely disgusted. It was a dismal afternoon. I never volunteered again to pick peas for Foy.

<u>Royce Lynn Johnson</u>: William, People ask why I don't plant butterbeans. I tell them it would cost me 50 dollars a bushel to get them picked. And they wouldn't pay that.

<u>Fred Borders</u>: Royce, I wouldn't make at 50 cents per pound. It was a good morning for me to pick 100 pounds and make a dollar. Bruce Gregg would pick 300 to my 100 and didn't seem to be working any harder than me. A few years later working on Bell Egg Farm I could beat him

Days Gone By

Buster and Era Fountain

<u>Jill Fountain</u>: I think Buster (Jack's brother) and Era Fountain had a little store somewhere in Aiken or Mt. Herman. I remember at a young age a bunch of us my age and older picking peas for him. I can't remember what he paid?

I'm not even sure where Uncle Buster lived back in them days. I only remember them living in town, but it was somewhere in Aiken

<u>Randy F</u>: Buster's store was across the dirt road from Mrs. Danley's on same side of highway

<u>Pam Adkison</u>: Jill, Could they have lived in the house where Benny and Thelma live now?

<u>Benny Russell</u>: Yes, they did live where Thelma and I live today.

Gathering Eggs

By Lori Goodwin

Here lately, I find myself contemplating home and what home truly means. I was so incredibly blessed to be raised in a beautiful house on 20 acres with a natural spring fed lake. It is a piece of land that can only be described as beautiful and blessed. My brother and I explored every single inch of that land. We had carefree adventure hikes, swam in the lake, fished, rode go carts, played with our dogs...pretty much anything our little souls could imagine, we did. As a kid, I didn't fully appreciate the somewhat charmed life I was given.

As I wander through my parents' [Richard and Shirley Goodwin] home now, with all of its beautiful doohickeys and whatnots, my eyes notice instead the full celebration of our family. In every room, in seemingly every corner, there is something that reminds me that we were celebrated, we were wanted, and we were loved. For my parents, it has never been about the stuff. The stuff was just icing. It has always been about God and family. Their life has been defined by the incredible love that they have shown to others, a love that can be felt in every nook and cranny of that house. That love turned a beautiful house and plot of land into a home. That sacrificial, relentless, unconditional love...it's that love that turned those 4 walls and some dirt into one of the most special places on earth. It's that love that built our family and our home. Gathering eggs.

3

Excelsior School

Kathleen Fenley: I remember going over to Excelsior to ring the bell. They had it out front facing the highway. We would go over there on weekends to play on the seesaw and merry go round. This was before they put the fence around it.

Excelsior School Bell 2022, Photograph by Pamila Hooper Adkison

Mila Justice Smith: I may not have gotten to grow up in Aiken, but I got there as fast as I could! Teaching at Excelsior was such a wonderful experience and the best of blessings, because I got to know so many wonderful people. I had the pleasure of teaching truly wonderful kids, many of whom I now consider friends and I'm extremely proud of every one of them. (My children also got a great start on their education at Excelsior. I certainly could not have asked for a better school for them to attend.) Thank you for letting me share in the memories of such a wonderful and loving community.

Nina Jo Hudspeth Walker: Mila, you along with many others, are the kind of people that make this a wonderful and caring community. We're very proud to have had many good teachers, such as yourself, that teach or at one time or another taught us, our children, and in my case also my grandchildren at Excelsior school.

Mila Justice Smith: Nina Jo, you're so sweet!! Thank you for those kind words. My years of teaching at Excelsior were absolutely wonderful! It's been said by many, and I agree completely, that Excelsior is more than just school. It's family. And all my students have been so much more—they're my kids! And I consider them my friends as well. There's no better place to teach than Excelsior, and no better community to be a part of. Thank you for giving me that honor.

Kimberly P: I remember my first day of school. I rode the wrong bus home. I fell asleep and the bus driver found me when he got back.

Eldora Gilchrist: When I was going to school at Excelsior, "Humpie" Tyler & his family lived one house down pass the school. Someone build an A-frame ladder across the fence behind Mrs. Eddins' & Mrs. Lawson's rooms. That was so the Tyler kids could just cross the fence & be at school instead of going the long way around. I think I have the name right, but not sure.

Who's Who of Excelsior, Courtesy of Barbara Scates

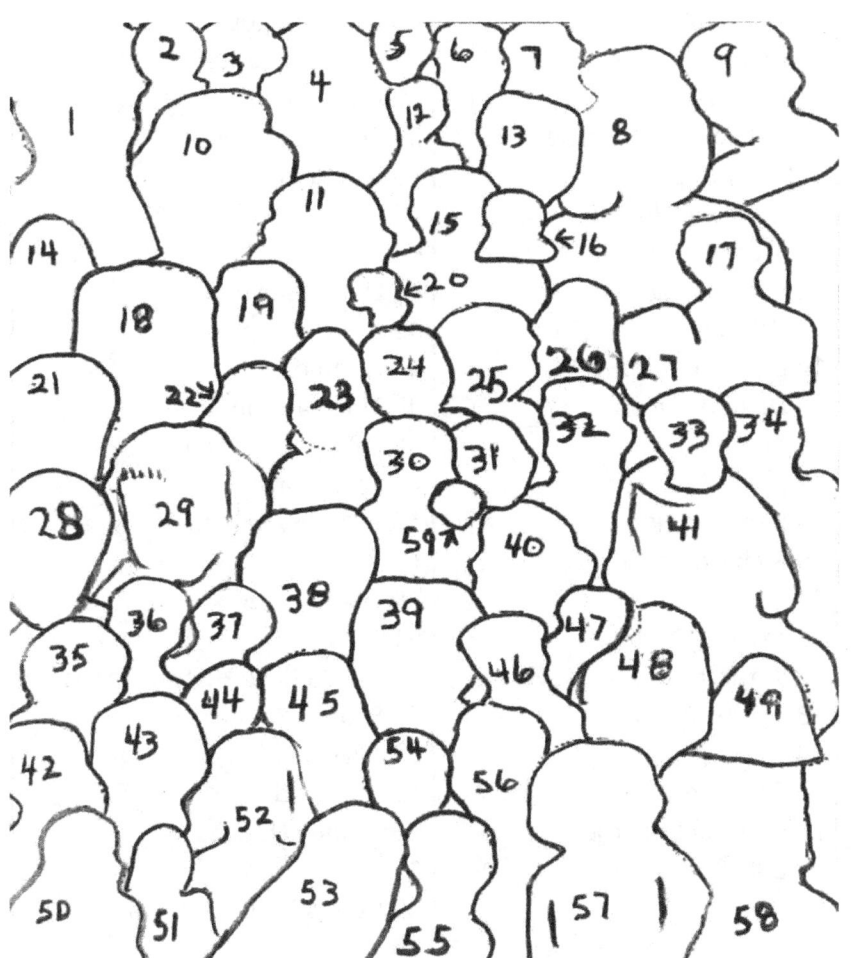

Map of Who's Who

Days Gone By

1 Jackie Lee Fountain	31 Gene Fenley
2 Ricky White	32
3 Janet Danley Watson	33 Rowdy Danley
4 Billy Akridge	34 Jimmy Jernigan
5 James Fults	35 Joye Hodges
6 Kristi Rains DeRise	36 Homer Fountain
7 Ricky White	37 Melinda Adams
8 Claudia Faye Hudspeth	38 Cornelia Lawson
9 Benny Russell	39 Rex Rains
10 Charlsie Wheeler	40
11 Mary Ann Williams	41
12 Mark Hodges	42 Linda. Barbe
13 Rex Davis	43
14 Evelyn Eddins	44 Donnie Cline
15 Dean Adams	45 Tina Lawson Brown
16 Adam J	46 Earline Drennan
17	47 Keith Davis
18 Kenneth Hooper	48 Billy Rex Fountain
19 Richard Brown?	49
20	50 Lea Osborn
21 Jeanine Porter	51
22 Kathryn Hooper Davis	52 Cynda Kaye Hooper Jones
23 Shirley Brown	53 Sharon Sanders Stringer
24	54 Alice West
25 Ella Palmar	55 Mrs. Eddins
26 Rhonda Chandler	56 Johnny Hodges
27 Billy Bo Barbe	57
28 Robert Bright	58 Cathy Danley Adams
29 Jean Russell Adams,	59
30 Dexter Davis	

Corresponding names of Who's Who

The Old White Building at Excelsior School

Debbie S A: I remember when we had lunch in the old white building.

Shannon A C: Old lunch room is where the haunted house was. I never had lunch in there, but did have music. Christopher was in that building for Kindergarten.

Janette M: We had Girl Scout meetings in the old white building, too. Holly Barbee's mom was the scout leader.

Toni Berg Ford: I remember lunches, music recitals, plays and Concerts in the White Building. The Calvary Boys held a concert there. The original Calvary Boys. I have had some very good times in the White Building.

Nina Jo Hudspeth Walker: I started my first year of school in the old lunchroom. The old, old school building was still out back. The older kids were in it. I think it was the next year that they built the front long building & tore down the old, old building out back. If memory serves, I think it had a bell tower with a rope to ring it, & I'm thinking, it is the same bell that's out front now!

Karen Brown-Fallon: I remember practicing for the Sadie Hawkins dance in the old building! Mrs. Wheeler told me I couldn't "dance" & had 2 left feet (not much has changed). Also, I took piano lessons in that building with Mrs. Hughes!

Greg N Shannon S: I didn't go to the old white building, but I remember the haunted house and Alice West teaching music in there.

Joyce Bright: Mrs. Lawson was my teacher, when I went to school there. She was such a sweet lady. They used to play volley ball at the old Excelsior school on the weekends.

Gene Akridge: Does anyone remember Mr. and Mrs. Holt that lived behind Mrs. Danley's store? If I remember right, she was a teacher at Excelsior. Mr. Holt had missing fingers, and maybe, part of his arm. He used sticks to build ships inside small neck jugs. People said he had them all over the country. I never understood how he did it.

Cynda Jones: Gene, Mr. Chester Holt taught my brother, Kenneth, how to do it. Kenneth made little straight back chairs in a bottle and made one for me several years before he passed away. I have no idea how he did it, because he wouldn't tell me. LOL.

Erma Bush Parrish: Mrs. Holt was my first and second grade teacher at Excelsior. I still have a Valentine card she gave me in 1960. I framed it and have it displayed in my curio cabinet. I have a picture somewhere of the Easter egg-hunts she would have at her house.

Shirley Di Verdi: Erma, Mrs. Holt taught me also in first and second grade. I remember one Christmas we drew names at school. The person that got my name brought me a box of 8 crayons. Mrs. Holt felt bad I guess. I remember she gave me a dollar. She was definitely a good teacher, which everyone liked. Hearing these stories are a good thing, they bring back memories that I haven't thought about in years.

Jean R A: Cynda, Kenneth made Steve one as well.

Jean R A: Erma, such a special memory... Remember those Easter Egg Hunts.

Jean R A: Shirley, Mrs. Holt was a good teacher.

Eldora Gilchrist: Was his name Chester? If so he was an excellent shot. The local men always ganged around at the county fairgrounds to watch him shoot the moving ducks. I always wanted Daddy to let me shoot. So finally, he did one year and I made him proud.

He asked me, "Where did you learn to shoot like that?"

I said, "I've been practicing."

I forgot to tell you. I had been practicing my shooting with R.E.'s marbles, by lining them up in a crack in the swing seat, swinging it gently. Then I'd run back to the water shelf on the front porch & shoot.

The Old White building was built in 1916, Courtesy of Laura Harris

Excelsior Old White Schoolhouse 2022, Photograph by Pamila Hooper Adkison

Days Gone By

*The kitchen in the Old White Building. 2022.
Photograph by Pamila Hooper Adkison*

Pam Adkison: Barbara, do you know who nailed the license plates to the floor in the old white building?

Barbara Scates: I nailed them on the floor! It was to cover holes in the worn out flooring. The linoleum was torn and sticking up, so I didn't want anyone to trip and fall...just thought it would add a little conversation to the floor to cover the flaws with license plates! Bet you never thought that was the reason!!! Hahaha!

Pam Adkison: LOL. That's one of those "nice to know" things that makes this area so rich. Where did you get them?

Barbara Scates: Clark Paul Williams, Jr...It's no telling what the plates came off. I told him I needed some, and he came thru with them!

Excelsior/World History Since 1895

By Laura Wheeler Harris

[I recommend getting the interesting booklet that Laura Harris has publish. It has much more about Excelsior. For our book, I have included many of her comments pertaining to Excelsior School and left out some of those about world events.....PHA]

Excerpts from Laura Wheeler Harris in a pamphlet she published: Dedication of a Historical Marker for the Excelsior Common School No. 47.

> People have been coming to school since before 1895. Every day children have been educated to pursue the goal of leaving Excelsior to attend high school. The children have prayed, saluted the flag, sat in class, and had good clean fun. This is by no means a complete historical list, either for the world or for Excelsior.
>
> Before 1895, families began to gather in the community of Aiken to form a school. R. Wheeler is listed as authority at the school in the History of Early Shelby County, Texas Schools by J.B. Sanders.
>
> 1900: A category 4 hurricane killed 8000 people in Galveston, Texas. This is still the most deadly disaster in American history. Meanwhile, back in Aiken, the first school building was built. Everyone in the community worked on it. According to my Grandfather, Euel Hopkins, his father was among those who built it. The building had two mud chimneys.
>
> 1901: The first major oil discovery in Texas was made near Spindletop in Beaumont. Meanwhile, back in Aiken, William and Allie Wheeler donated one acre of land to Walnut Grove #47 school.

1909: In a deed dated November 23, 1909, Walnut Grove School #47 acquired one acre of land from William Henry Wheeler and his wife, Allie, for $22.

1910: The Boy Scouts of America was founded. Meanwhile, back in Aiken, the trustee for Excelsior were: W.E. Chandler of Waterman, J.M. Windham, and J.H. Beck.

1911: The teachers at Excelsior were W.S. Wheeler and Thomas Covington.

1912: The Girl Scouts formed in Savanah, Georgia. Meanwhile, back in Aiken, C.C. Hooper was listed as a trustee for Excelsior.

1913: The 19th Amendment to the US Constitution is ratified allowing the Federal Government to impose an income tax. Meanwhile, back in Aiken, P.C. Stokes was listed as a teacher at Excelsior with 61 pupils.

1914: WWI starts and the USA stays neutral.

1916: Woodrow Wilson is president. Meanwhile, back in Aiken, another building was erected on the Excelsior School grounds. Earliest referred to as a school classroom, then, the lunchroom, and now "the white building."

1917: The USA declares war on Germany and enters WWI. Meanwhile, back in Aiken, Addie Mae Shipp and Corine Hughes were listed as teachers at Excelsior. J.F. Hopkins, C.B. Harrell, and J.H. Windham were listed as trustees.

1918 The US military had over one million troops in Europe fighting WWI.

1919: The Treaty of Versailles ends WWI.

1920: Women were given the right to vote with the 19th amendment.

1929: The stock market crashed causing the worst American depression in US history. Meanwhile, back in Aiken, we were all poor so the crash went pretty much unnoticed.

1933: Hitler became the German chancellor. Meanwhile, back in Aiken, White Rock School consolidated with Excelsior School.

1940: The US Congress enacted the first peace time draft…. The first McDonald's restaurant opened. Meanwhile, back in Aiken, while making a phone call at the clerk's office in Aiken, Euel Hopkins happened to see the deed to the acre of land sold by William Henry Wheeler to Excelsior School lying on the desk. Being about lunch time Hopkins took the judge to his father's house (James Franklin Hopkins) for lunch where he arranged for not only his business to be done, but also for the 1909 deed to be registered on September 24, 1940.

1941: The Japanese attacked Pearl Harbor, which brought the US into WWII. Meanwhile, back in Aiken, the trustees were E.L. Hopkins, C.N. Barbee, L.B. Dillard, P.R. Adkison, H.S. Stephen, and Jo Fancher. They discussed repairing the toilets or having to move them. It is now a state requirement to have running water to the building. The Halloween Carnival cleared $21.30. So they bought a 20 foot piece of tin for $2 to make a slide.

1942: The US develops the first atomic bomb and Excelsior made $43.50 on the cake walk.

1944: The Normandy Invasion – D-Day took place. Meanwhile, back in Aiken, the school board said that they would hire Mrs. Eula Russell for principle if they could not find a MAN for the job.

1945: Roosevelt dies suddenly and Vice President Harry Truman assumes the presidency. President Truman authorizes the atomic bomb for Hiroshima. Three days later, Nagasaki was bombed and Japan surrendered.

Courtesy of Cecilia McSwain Boles, Bottom row, l-r, Coatsie Youngblood, Janell Linthicum, Patsy Linthicum, Ivis Mae Fenley, Troy Franklin Yarbrough, Billy Wayne Hooper, Charlie Powdrill, and Guy Lynch. Top Row, Shirley Head, Troy Chandler, Billy Bo Barbe, Mrs. Eula Russell, Eva Dale Bush, Verna Sue Stephens, Steve Stephens

1947: In Aiken, the trustees talked about building a girls' toilet and paying the hand to do it. They began work on the newest building.

1948: President Truman ended segregation in the US military. Meanwhile, back in Aiken, Eula Russell was the Principal, apparently they could not find a man for the job. The teachers were Fernella Eddins, Cornelia Lawson, and Ella Holt.

1950: The Korean War began.

1953 The Korean War fighting ceases.

1954: the first large scale vaccination of children against polio was done, practically wiping out the disease in the US. Racial segregation of public schools was declared unconstitutional.

1955: Meanwhile, back in Aiken, the original 1900 Excelsior school building was sold to L.T Graves and moved off the property. Excelsior moved into the new school building.

1957: Charlsie Wheeler was hired to teach at Excelsior, bringing along her four children, including 4 year old Susan. With no daycare, she wandered about the school at will. The four year old pops up in group pictures and was a favorite of the older girls at school. Most students finished Excelsior in 8 years but it took Susan 10.

1958: Meanwhile, back in Aiken, at Excelsior, the teachers this year were Ella Holt (1-2), Charlsie Wheeler (3-4), Cornelia Lawson (5-6 teacher/principal), and Bo Barbe (7-8). With the addition of Bo Barbe, the 4th teacher, the cafeteria was moved from the new building to the old white building where we not only got good meals but we also performed plays and learned music from Mrs. Nara Hughes.

1959: [Alaska and Hawaii joined the USA as the 49th and 50th states, respectively] Castro becomes the premier of Cuba. Grigsby School consolidated with Excelsior.

1960: The 50 star flag was unveiled.

1961 The Berlin Wall was erected.

1962: [The Vietnam engagement began], and the Cuban missile crisis starts – this is the closes the Cold War came into breaking into an armed conflict.

1963: President Kennedy was assassinated and VP Johnson assumed office. The Supreme Court ruled that the recitation of the Lord's Prayer or Bible verses in public schools is unconstitutional. Center High School burned as a result of students playing with fireworks in the auditorium which caught the stage curtains on fire. Martin Luther King delivers his "I Have a Dream" speech.

1964: The Beatles arrived in the US.

1966: Medicare for citizens over 65 began.

1968: Martin Luther King was assassinated.

1969: Neil Armstrong was the first man on the moon, and the internet was invented.

1973: The Arab oil embargo happened.

1974: Richard Nixon resigned as President, admitting his role in Watergate.

1975: Back in Aiken, Alva and Beula Head leased to Excelsior School 1.65 acres for $25 a year for so long as the public school is operated on the adjoining property known as Excelsior.

1976: Meanwhile back in Aiken, the 560 acre Pinkston Lake was completed.

1977: Elvis Presley died. Meanwhile back in Aiken, a small plane crashed into a tree in front of Mr. Bobby and Mrs. Cleo Russell's house.

1978: The trustees of Excelsior School #47 voted to change from the status of being a common school to an independent school district and be under the control of the Texas Educational Agency in Austin. Excelsior was the last common school in the county out of the 90 common schools that had existed in the county in 1880. Cornelia Lawson was promoted from principal to superintendent of Excelsior ISD following this ruling. At the time, she was one of only a few women superintendents in Texas. Most of Excelsior's older records were lost in a fire after 80 plus years. They had been moved to Center and housed in the Co-op building.

1980: Mt. St Helens erupted. Ronald Reagan beat Carter for president.

1981 Reagan survives an assassination attempt. The IBM personal computer is produced. Meanwhile back in Aiken, a plane crashes in Joy Chandler's mother's [Jewel Hooper Chandler Brown] pasture.

1985: Ginger Russell graduated the 8th grade at Excelsior and enrolled in Lon Morris College the next year as a 14 year old freshmen.

1986: The Challenger Space Shuttle exploded 73 seconds into its flight killing all aboard while everyone watched it on TV.

1990: Operation Desert Storm begins. This is the start of the Gulf War. Meanwhile back in Aiken, Charlsie Wheeler retired, after a 36 year carrier at Excelsior.

1993: The World Trade Center is bombed by the Islamic terrorists. Meanwhile back in Aiken, a car crashes into Mrs. Cleo Russell.

1997: Princess Diana died in a car crash.

1998: Mr. Johnny Lewis became superintendent of Excelsior.

1999: Meanwhile back in Aiken, a tornado hit Aiken completely destroying Evelyn Russell Eddins' house and scaring the daylights out of the students and teachers at the school.

2001: September 11, the World Trade Center, the Pentagon, and a downed plane in Pennsylvania starts the Gulf War. 3000 Americans killed at one time. The day that changed the world.

2003: the Space Shuttle Columbia explodes strewing shuttle debris all over East Texas. Saddam Hussein was captured and executed.

2004: Facebook was founded by Mark Zuckerberg. The tsunami disaster happened in the Indian Ocean.

2005: Hurricane Katrina put 80% of New Orleans under water.

2007: Apple unveils the I-Phone.

2010: Mr. Johnny Lewis retired and became a part-time Superintendent/Principal. Mr. Wayne Mason joined the Excelsior administration as a part-time Superintendent/Principal.

2011: Osama Bin Laden - The man behind the 9/11/01 attacks was killed by US Special Forces. After the body was identified in Afghanistan, he was buried at sea within 24 hours.

2019: Meanwhile back in Aiken, February 23, Excelsior ISD received a historic marker and we held our 125 year reunion. (Harris, 2019)

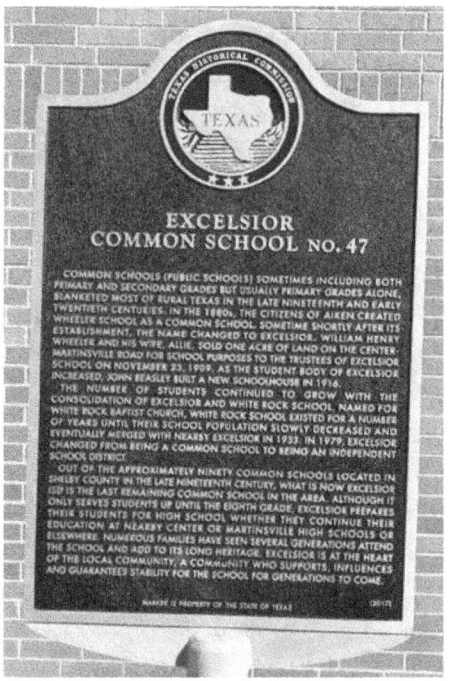

The Texas Historical Commission issued a marker to Excelsior for its 125-year anniversary in 2019

Excelsior Common School No. 47

Common Schools (Public Schools) sometimes included both primary and secondary grades, but usually, primary grades alone blanketed most of rural Texas in the late nineteenth and early twentieth centuries. In the 1880s, the citizens of Aiken created Wheeler School as a common school. Shortly after its establishment, the name changed to Excelsior. William Henry Wheeler and his wife, Allie, sold one acre of land on the Center-Martinsville Road for school purposes to the trustees of Excelsior School on November 23, 1909. As the student body of Excelsior grew, John Beasley built a new schoolhouse in 1916. The number of students continued to grow with the consolidation. (THC) of Excelsior and White Rock School, named for White Rock Baptist Church. White Rock School existed for a number of years until its school population slowly decreased and eventually merged with nearby Excelsior in 1933. In 1979 Excelsior changed from being a common school to an independent school district. Out of the approximately ninety common schools located in Shelby County in the late nineteenth century, what is now Excelsior ISD is the last remaining common school in the area. Although it only serves students up until the eighth grade, Excelsior prepares its students for high school whether they continue their education at nearby Center or Martinsville High Schools or elsewhere. Numerous families have seen several generations attend the school and add to its long heritage, Excelsior is at the heart of the local community. A community that supports, influences, and guarantees stability for the school for generations to come. (THC)

4
Entertainment

Days Gone By

Golden Spur Rodeo Arena

By Jana Ivy

I used to ride our Welch pony to the rodeo to participate in Pole Bending. She was really good at it. When we weren't participating, we were riding round and round outside the arena with friends. When you bought your rodeo ticket, you were put into a drawing for prizes. During the rodeo, winners were announced. Mother (Bernice Adams) won a leather wallet with her initials engraved on it. She was so excited! Allen Earl Fancher always let me leave my horse there until the next morning, so I could ride her home, since we didn't own a horse trailer. For us, we loved the weekly entertainment. It was only about a half mile from our house. If I didn't have the money for entry fees, I would work extra at the arena so we could enter Pole Bending Event. If I stayed too late at the rodeo, Daddy (Fane Adams) would drive up there, make an embarrassing announcement on the intercom that I was to come to the front gate for my ride was there. Good Ole George!! I loved The Golden Spur. Once or twice a year on a Friday, we could ride our horse to school, tie them up out front in the shade, then ride straight to the rodeo, but the rodeo was mostly on Saturday nights.

Tonya McSwain Andrews: My family went to the Golden Spur regularly. My parents and we, four kids, would pile in the single cab pickup to go to the rodeo. We had so much fun. I had a paint Shetland pony and rode in some events.

Randy B: The One-Legged boot races where the Best!!

Relissa B: They had a nice pond back there too. I remember the rodeo arena.

Cecilia Boles: I remember driving up to the entrance gate that was merely an aluminum panel gate leading to a pasture and seems like we had to pay $1 per head to enter. To me we might as well been pulling up to the Houston Livestock Show! LOL. Everyone knew each other and we always had so much fun. No aluminum trailers and expensive trucks! Single cab with six of us packed in the single seat, and not a single word of complaint was uttered. Daddy would not have tolerated any. I remember running barrels, poles, straight away barrels, rescue race, and anything else that was allowed. One time I ran my horse, "Ole Gray", down to the end of the arena to pick up Carolyn Williams Caldwell in the rescue race. Just before we started out the gate while at a dead run, the girth broke and the saddle slid under the horses belly dumping both of us into the dirt and whatever else was on the ground. The main thing that I remember, as I reminisce, is how fond my memories are of families working together and supporting each other. Good clean competition and many Golden Spur Trophies! Who could forget riding around in the arena before the rodeo to the old music playing "Kiss an Angel Good Morning" by Charlie Pride?

My horse loved to rear-up and walk on his hind legs in order to not go inside the arena. I suppose he liked his other job more, that of being a plow horse!! LOL. People would scatter, because he would come down on whomever or whatever was in the way. We never knew to be afraid, because our desire to ride was greater. Such fond memories.

Days Gone By

Respect & Rodeo Days

By Howell Adkison

I'll always remember the first 'whooping'. I got from my Dad. We had just gotten home from Mr. Jess Warren's. Dad asked me did I know what I had done wrong. He explained to me that I had not said "Yes, sir" and "No, sir" to Mr. Jess.

"You will respect your elders." he said.

After that he never had to whoop me again. To this day I catch myself, sometimes, saying, "Yes, sir" or "No, sir" or "Yes, ma'am" or "No, ma'am" to the teenage kids at the drive through window at a fast food diner. Lesson learned.

Later on that year, Dad had gone to the Kirbyville sale barn. He often went with Uncle Jessie or James Lee McSwain. They sold, bought, or traded mules at the auction. On one such trip, he hauled in a horse for us kids to ride. He felt sorry for the horse, because it was in bad shape. It had a pot belly, but skinny. It looked like it was starved. I asked him if the horse was already broken in.

"Yes," he said. "The sellers said that it was already broken."

We unloaded it into the corral. We fed, watered it, and went to the house. Dad told us to let it settle in for a few days, then we will saddle it up and ride. In other words, leave it alone. I couldn't stand it, and snuck down to the lot. I got it out and used the corral fence to climb on. The next thing that I knew, I was getting up off the ground. I thought I had fallen off, because it was supposed to be broken in. So, I climbed back on. Again, I'm getting off the ground. That horse just threw me, which made me mad. I climbed on for the third time, determined to ride that horse. That time I hit the ground hard and it hurt. I tied that horse to a fence post and went to the house.

I told Dad, "That horse won't ride at all. I got on three times and got throwed three times."

"Nah, you just fell off. He's not in good enough shape to throw anyone," he said.

We go down to the corral and Dad climbed on. Well, the rodeo began. He rode it for about one hundred feet before he got bucked off. He looked like he was hurt, so I ran down to check on him.

Dad looked up at me and said, "You're right! He ain't broke in."

For about two weeks Dad was stove-up pretty good. Apparently, the horse wasn't in as bad a shape as we thought. We later got it broken and rode quite often.

Tree Carvings

<u>Jan Akridge</u>: Royce Lynn, I know you have carved yours on a few. What is the oldest you have found?

<u>Royce Lynn Johnson</u>: The oldest tree carving was on the bank of the Attoyac, two bends above Packs Bridge. It was "JE Burgess Sept the 15th, 1896". Exactly like that. Not on a beech, but on a Holly. Beeches don't live that long. Chris Mahan, helped me research. He was 18 when he carved that. Gene Smith and I walked in the bottom Sep 15 1996 and carved it. 100 yrs. later to the day!

<u>Mila Justice Smith</u>: Royce Lynn, Gene Edward has taken each of our

4 grandsons down to the creek behind the house and carved their names and the date on a tree. Reese's name is on the tree too.

<u>Delores Harris Brown</u>: Mila, mine and 3 of my first cousins are on a Holly tree on the farm where I grew up, down near the spring, if the tree is still there, where Mary lives now.

<u>Mila Justice Smith</u>: Delores, it's wonderful to have those visible memories.

Gone Fishing

By Howell Adkison

Now when I was a young boy, trapping and hunting was my big thing. I got to be friends with Royce Wilson. We both hunted a lot. He lived across the creek, I'm guessing, about a mile or so over on the next hill. If I walked behind our shed, I could see his house. I could hear shooting from that direction all the time.

So, one day I decided to hike over to see him. Get there and he had been target practicing. We went inside and were sitting in the kitchen talking to his mother, Mrs. Julie, and his dad, Mr. Buren.

Mr. Buren was kind of a dry fellow, not much nonsense about him. I liked him and got along with him, because he reminded me a little of my Uncle Jessie. Mrs. Julie was as good a person as you would want to meet.

Entertainment

The Wilson house was built on a slope with the back, where the kitchen was, high off the ground and supported by cinder blocks. It had a row of windows across the back wall facing the southwest.

Royce's brother, Bob, was outside doing whatever he was doing. Here we were sitting at the kitchen table talking about our last hunt. All of a sudden this explosion goes off. I'll swear that house raised up several inches off the blocks! Windows rattled, but not a one broke. It scared the fire out of Mrs. Julie. Me too. Royce didn't seem to be concerned, but Mr. Buren was none too pleased.

Bob came walking into the house, chuckling. "I think, I used a little too much."

As a joke, he thought it would be funny to set off a charge of dynamite and rattle his dad a little. Now understand, Royce and Bob liked to shoot things or blow them up. When Mr. Buren and Mrs. Julie got their health back, Bob apologized. At the time, I believe, he was working for a seismic crew, and they had explosives.

Well, when you have fire power, what do you do? Like normal country boys, we went fishing on the Attoyac.

Jess Warren's and the Old Outdoor Theater

By Jimmie Nell Adkison Lee

I wish their house had not gone to ruin. I would love to walk through that old store one more time. Also, I remember when their granddaughter was hit by a car there on Hwy 7 in front of the store...I don't remember the details, but she survived.

That old store holds lots of memories, I still remember the smell and can hear the dominoes clanking together. Also, I remember how dark it seemed in there. After pea picking we would go to Mr. Jess' store for an RC Cola and one of those huge round cookies. We would sit on a nail keg on the huge front porch and watch as an occasional car would come by. Not much traffic then for sure.

I remember the old gas pumps and Daddy (Auvie Adkison) would tell Mr. Jess that he needed 50 cents worth of Ethyl. We would watch the gasoline chug down from the top!! We could drive a long way on 50 cents back then.

Do any of you remember the old outdoor theater?? My very first picture show was right there off Hwy 7. My step-grandmother's sister, Vallie, and her husband, Fred Williams, lived where the road Y's off right as soon as you get off Hwy 7...they would throw up a huge white sheet on a Sat. night and show a western. Sound and all! It cost 10 cents. My Papa Taylor and I would walk from his house to see that movie (I wasn't even old enough for school). People walked and drove from all over and we sat on the ground, no chairs and they served popcorn. My very first movie was at Fred and Vallie's outdoor movie!! Then we had to walk back, and I would be scared to death...it was so dark. My step grandmother, Minnie, told me many stories of Panthers, Wild Cats, and mad Foxes (rabies). I just knew there was one waiting for us! Also Mr. Fred Williams turned his car into a taxi service back then. Wonderful, peaceful, and comforting memories.

I probably could go on and on, but will sign out for now. God Bless and so grateful that we lived in this peaceful time.

Louis and Ruby Fountain

By Nina Jo Hudspeth Walker

I think the first game room was at Louis & Ruby Fountain's liqueur store. It was just past Mrs. Lillie May's store. We just called it "the pool hall." The younger ones on here (Facebook) probably don't remember it. I was only 17 back then, but we were there every weekend, seemed like for years. They would stay open as long as people were there, sometimes most of the night. My oldest son, Vincent, was an infant then & where we went, he went. I don't know how he slept with all the noise of the pinball machines. They were loud, but it didn't bother him. I told him latter that's why he was so hard to wake up. LOL. I remember one night we all stayed there nearly all night. My late husband, Curtis, loved to play the pinball machines. Mrs. Ruby had a prize, if you had the highest score for a week. You would win, I think, a case of Cokes or some such. The last night we stayed up real late, I can't remember who he was playing, he finally got his Cokes. LOL. This would have been about mid and late '60s. I don't remember how long it stayed open, but maybe some of the ones my age might remember and have more stories about being there!

The Fire Tower

<u>Jan Akridge</u>: Well another chapter in the making. I told Billy I have been living out this way for 50 years and never have been to the fire tower. I ask him had he ever climbed it, and he said no, BUT his mother had......I told him she had more courage than me. I'm scared of heights! I love this, who else has climbed it?

Joy Tarver: Tommy Johnson (DZ), Gary Corley, and I climbed it one night. Gary's brand new watch fell off and hit the ground. We went down and tried to find the watch. No luck. We went back next day and never found that watch. The view was wonderful. I would do it again.

Barbara J. Scates: I made it up about 10 feet! I was done...stayed on the ground while everyone else climbed to the top!

Joy Tarver: Barbara, Do you know the silos across from the old International Paper in Nacogdoches. I help build them, 325 ft. tall, all three and the square ones too. I climbed that ladder every day until they were done. I shoveled the concrete into the wall forms.

Karen Bittick: I climbed the fire tower many times. I climbed the water tower on Hwy 7 too. I couldn't even climb a tree now.

Delores Harris Brown: I went up about half way and came back down at the one off 711. I did climb the one out close to the old Center Airport, all the way to the top, at night.

Karen Bittick: Back when the fire tower was used as a lookout for fires, it was in good shape. When International Paper began to sell its properties, they might have sold it too. I am not sure it has been maintained.

Tresa Danley Konderla: I climbed that when I was in high school. Going up was not a problem, but going down took me a loooong time.

Jimmie Nell Adkison Lee: The neat thing is that those who climbed it didn't deface it with nasty graffiti.

Mila Justice Smith: Gene Edward and I lived across the road from the fire tower the first 11 years we were married. I walked up to it lots of times but never climbed it. It wasn't used anymore by the time we married in 1971, and it had a chain link fence around it. The land we lived on belonged to Gene Edward's Uncle Verlon and his grandfather Sel Luman. They let us have an acre there to put a trailer house on.

It was a great place to live, and it was easy to give directions to people on how to find us. "We live across from the Tabernacle Fire Tower.

I understand that there was a good-sized community at Tabernacle at one time. There were a school and a horse racetrack. There's no trace of any of that now, but some of you may know a lot more to share.

Friday Night Volleyball

Jeff Davis: One of my fondest memories was volleyball night at Excelsior. Best I can remember, it was on a Friday evening, and it was some serious competition. I mean, Mom broke her arm on the court.

Phyllis Adams: I remember when your mom broke her arm! And yes, that was some serious volleyball!

Rhonda Chandler: Uncle Tommy almost broke my nose with one of his ball spiking abilities.

Delores Harris Brown: Herbert Langford at the store in Jericho also put up a net for volleyball for all the Jericho area kids.

Mila Justice Smith: Delores, Gene Edward played volleyball there on Friday and Saturday nights during school and any time during the summer. Lots of serious games played then.

Days Gone By

Brandy Adams Stamps: I loved Friday night volleyball!!

Debbie S A: I played every Friday night. I even played with Tommy Chandler, Shirley Berg, Steve Adams, and Jean Russell Adams. We had some good times, and yes, I remember when she broke her arm!!

Vonda B: Good times!! I remember getting spiked on right between the eyes during a tournament somewhere!!

Debbie S A: Vonda, I remember that and think it was San Augustine or Chireno. LOL.

Bobbie Sue Scates: Dusty Sanders spiked it between my eyes one time! It was always hard to rebound one of his spikes. LOL.

Debbie S A: Bobbie Sue, Dusty Sanders could hit that ball!!!

Jerry H: I remember those Friday nights playing volleyball. Many fun times.

Kevin Hughes: Gene spiked one and knocked Mrs. Porter out.

Jana Ivy: I just gave away a shirt the other day that said, "Aikenettes" on the back! I was in college when I played on that team. I remember it was a co-Ed team!

Tammy Fenley: Like Jeff Davis, and others remember playing volleyball at Excelsior, I remember volleyball night at Royce Lynn Johnson's house in South Jericho. As a kid I never got to play volleyball since it was only adults that got to play volleyball, but I remember playing all sorts of other games, like Red Rover, Hide-and-Go-Seek, Red Light Green Light, and all sorts of other games with the other kids. I really remember the night that I busted my head open playing Hide-and-Go-Seek and had to go to the emergency room to get stitches. I remember

Entertainment

taking my cap off and asking Shelby Johnson if my head was bleeding, & then the shocked look on his face told me all I needed to know. I bet I am not the only one who has a ton of memories from those nights?

Seth R: Almost literally, the same thing happened to me when I was little. I busted my lip open, and I asked my friend if I was bleeding. The pain didn't bother me, but when the look on his face told me I was bleeding, that did it!

Tammy Fenley: Seth, LOL, oh how funny ... the crazy twists & turns that life throws at us! The funny things that we remember & how we remember them!!!

Sharon Fenley Prince: I remember those games of volleyball. I would get to play. I was around 13 or 14. I remember one night I was serving and all my serves were going to my dad. Back then I could get a pretty good spin on the ball when I served. He could not return my serves. LOL.

Russell Andrews: I was there just about every time they played. They roasted a coon over an open fire. Somebody said it was Shelby's dog named Georgette, but it was a coon. Tasted good.

Powdrill's Saturday Night Dances

Sharon Fenley Prince: Question: When the Powdrills had the store in Jericho, did they have Saturday night dances in their barn?

William Rudd: Yes. I don't clearly remember how long they did that, but I think, it was at most only a year or 2. It was a little noisy up on the hill where we lived just south of the store.

Karen Bittick: I remember hearing the story of our grandfather Edward Johnson, after a night of square dancing, started home on Ridge Route Road. Every time he passed the Old Sardis Cemetery, it was on the wrong side of the road.

Rodger McLane: Karen, You mention square dancing. I had Linda Scott as a gym teacher in Carthage. She taught us how to square dance. She was kin to my Mamaw Ruby through the Luman side. I guess square dancing was really popular at a time. I heard somewhere, I am not sure, that Edward Johnson (my grandfather) "called the reels" at local square dances. If I am wrong, please correct me.

Pam Adkison: Sharon, I talked to Paul Hooper yesterday. He mentioned that he had been to the dances.

Russell Andrews: Sharon, the barn was moved to town and became Precinct 1 Road and Bridge Barn. I worked out of it for 20 years, until a modern larger building was built. Sadly, it was burnt to the ground.

William Rudd: Russell, I did not know that. Do you know when it was moved?

Russell Andrews: William, no sir, Dad told me about it. He helped take it down, move it, and put it back together. My dad was Talvis Andrews. His dad was Talmadge Andrews.

William Rudd: I knew your family well. Talmadge lived only about a mile from us, all good people. I moved to Dallas in 1962. I think that was before you were old enough for me to remember. My dad and mom built the (barn) building in the early 1940s to house hay, fertilize, and feed to sell in our store. We used it as a community skating rink when the farm product inventories were low. It was surprising to find out that it had a second life before its demise.

<u>Russell Andrews</u>: William, yes I was born 1961. I remember Mrs. Elsie T very well, hard working woman, loved to hunt and very generous. She gave a lot of money to the Mt Pleasant cemetery where I'm the caretaker now.

<u>William Rudd</u>: Do you receive the donations for the cemetery care now? I think Gene Bradshaw did that earlier.

<u>Russell Andrews</u>: William, he still does it. I'm on the committee, but Gene does the money part. He is a very honest and good man.

Deer Season

<u>Jan Akridge:</u> Deer season started today. It's been around for a long time. When Billy and I married they hunted deer with dogs. He had one named Tuffy. I swear he thought more of that dog than he did me. He really was a good deer dog. Billy and friends, Barbara and Jerry Scates, Wanda and Jeff Coats, Tommy Gene and Sharon Emanis, Gene Akridge, Jimmy Scates and families have had deer camps through the years. The first not sure where it was located, Billy could tell me, but he is not here right now. I just remember one night we had this little bitty camper and my youngest J.C. was due pretty soon. Tara and Chad were about 3 and 4 years old. We had spent the night in the camper. When we woke up the next morning, 2 or 3 inches of snow was on the ground. That would have been in '78 or '79. We had one on Cletus Sharpston place. We were there the year the tornado came through

and hit Jesse Dee Johnson's chicken houses on 711. We had one on J.C. McSwain's land. Venorah always sent 1 or 2 pecan pies. She does make the best! Lots of good memories made for the grownups and children. Maybe some of you have memories to add to this post. Barbara Scates is not feeling well, so maybe Jerry Scates or Angie will tell the story about the deer he shot and brought home in his bronco.

<u>Jill Fountain Parker</u>: Momma always made biscuits and gravy for everyone!

<u>Jan Akridge</u>: Jill, she sure did! And it was good too!

<u>Angie S S</u>: I remember the brown bronco, I remember something about that deer and that tale. LOL. I can't remember if it wasn't dead, or what exactly, but I remember the camps, and Venorah bringing those good pies. Some of my best memories growing up was running around at the deer camps!

<u>Royce Lynn Johnson</u>: Tornado in Jericho was November 15, 1987. Started on Big Ironore Creek... went all the way to Missouri. 3rd longest tornado in US history.

<u>Jill Fountain Parker</u>: Royce Lynn, I remember that! Rachel and Jack (my grandparents) were at Camp Worth during that storm!

Entertainment

Pig Latin

Eldora Gilchrist: This may not fit the criteria, here, but who remembers speaking pig Latin? I could a little bit, but my next sister was very good at it.

Michael Scates: I can speak pig Latin and dog Latin. *Ancaggle ouyaggle eakspaggle ogdaggle atinlaggle?*

Eldora Gilchrist: Great, it may have been dog Latin, now that you mention it. I can read what you wrote. So glad someone else remembers. I would have to really work at it to do it again.

Eldora Gilchrist: Michael, do you think it was just a local thing, or was it widespread?

Michael Scates: Eldora, Idk. Barbara J. Scates taught me pig Latin. And I learned the dog Latin from Keith Brown, when I was a teenager.

Jill Fountain Parker: Michael, I can read it, but don't remember that. Pig Latin was taught to me by Momma and listening to y'all!

Mikah Emanis Weems: It's just from them Mt Herman people that went to Excelsior school.

Michael Scates: Mikah, *atsthey ightray.*

Jan Akridge: There was a commercial for a cereal back in the day that used pig Latin. I still sing it sometimes (it stuck in my head).*root fay oops lays* I know what it means. The commercials back then you remember the jingles to them. I couldn't tell you one now for nothing.

Pam Adkison, I read "The Three Little Pigs" to Cole, my brother, in pig Latin. He was about two. I was twelve.

Mila Justice Smith: My sister and I were "fluent" in pig Latin. Our Mom went to work when I was 12 and she was 9 and we stayed with a lady after school 'til my folks got off work. The lady had 2 daughters, and the oldest made a point of giving my sister and me a hard time. We fought back by carrying on all our conversations with each other in pig Latin. She never understood it so we could gripe about her to each other all we wanted to. It really frustrated her, but she couldn't do anything about it.

Tresa Danley Konderla: Kemi Rudd Faulkenbery and I were pretty good at pig Latin. We also made our own way of writing backwards.

No Swimming

By Jan Akridge

Lots of memories have come to mind, since my little sister-in-law Susan Akridge Toomer died the day after Thanksgiving. This memory is about White's pond. It is located kind of behind their house. It was summer and hot that day I went to visit them. I think it was the first year Billy and I were married. The kids (Benny Joe, Danny, and Susie) talked me into walking over to White's pond. We walked through the pasture or field, it was fun at the time. We kind of all got wet, clothes and all. Hair too! Yes indeed it was a fun afternoon. That is, until we started home, and they told me that they were not supposed to go there, because years ago the older children almost drowned there, and the older sister, Carolyn, saved them. As the old song said...*I turned a whiter shade of pale!* There I am and the three younger ones (me being the oldest and supposed to have more sense) dripping wet from head to toe.

My solution.....we walked that field 'till every hair and every piece of clothing was dry. I guess I was so upset to this day I still remember what I was wearing that day. It did make a good memory to laugh about years later. And yes YEARS later I did tell Maw about it.

Brenda H: I remember Momma (Carolyn) telling me about saving all of them. I believe it was God, and she did too, Momma couldn't swim, but she took a leap of Faith and got them all to shore. She told me so many stories, sure miss her.

Pam Adkison: Jan, I have puzzled about where the White's pond is. Then it came to me, it is the same one that I knew as Elsie Dean's pond. Daddy fished there some while we rented from Mr. Dean. Daddy made a small water craft out of a washtub and an inner tube from a 22" truck tire. I remember there being wild blackberry vines nearby.

Jan Akridge: I've only known it as White's pond. It is behind Mrs. White's house that is kind of across from the old church. The raft sounded like a lot of fun. I don't think I've been back to that pond since that day. LOL.

Pam Adkison; I haven't been back either. I was 5 or 6 when we lived there. We weren't allowed to go to the pond without an adult. It seems there was a gravel pit there also.

Jan Akridge: Yes it was, Billy hauled some from there years later.

The Pine Tree Challenge

By Mary Dell Chandler Windham

James, Brooksie, Patsy Hooper, Marie Hooper, Gene Fenley, and I were playing along the pipeline. James challenged us to climb a pine tree that was growing along there. No one took him up on the dare, but he said that he would do it. He climbed that tree so high the top started bending over. He kept going until the top almost touched the ground. Gene grabbed the top and made the tree spring back. It flung James, and he went flying through the air. We all thought it had killed him. He survived though.

Where There is a Will, There is a Way

By Monroe Taylor

Who's going to believe a thing like this? But this is a true story about a part of my younger days and like most folks, we were poor so we had to use our imaginations, but we had fun.

This was in about the year 1923 or '24, or the beginning of the '20s. Someone moved into our community who knew about basketball. It may have been Ashley Beasley, for he was on the first team to play at our Mt. Herman School, and he really had class. I sure did like the game. However, there was a second team between the first and boys like myself, as I was only 12 or 13.

I decided on my own to get something going, but what and how? I looked around and found two rims that had come off of a big wood wagon wheel hub.

I thought, "Well, these will make the goals."

Then the posts and backboards came next, but they were no problem as we had a block of virgin pine timber, so I cut two pine poles and peeled them with a drawing knife. Then I got some scrap lumber we had 'round the place and made the backboards of the lightest weight planks possible. Then, I measured off a court down in our cow pasture, put goals on the backboard and dug some holes.

I figured what was about the right height for us and then set up the poles. But now I don't have a ball. Now what? I never mentioned that the next child was nearly 10 years older than me, so I had to figure many things alone. Here I was, an NBA set up and no ball. Ha. What was I going to use for a ball? I didn't have the money to buy one, even if I'd known where one was, so it had to be something different. My mother always kept a lot of lent cotton for quilt making, so I took a stocking leg which had the foot worn out and stuffed it full of cotton, making a part as round and tight as I could and then I sewed it so that it would stay put.

Then I headed to the court for a workout. It shot really good, but it wouldn't bounce. It was like the Globetrotter's trick ball. But I had a ball, so far so good, and then another idea came to mind. Why not hand dribble? That is, bounce it up and down in my hand as I moved toward the goal for a lay-up shot or while running down court. The same as on the ground.

If anyone failed to dribble enough as he went down court, he was traveling. Don't think we didn't have some fun and have some fast games with a lot of good passing. Why, we looked like the Boston Celtics in action. Our homemade goals had no off-set or space between the goal and the backboard, so we had to be zeroed in to hit it from the outside, but we did. That old cotton ball put us into second season until Christmas when ol' Santa brought two brothers on my team a big rubber ball just made to order. The brothers were Simon and Harvey Russell. Simon Russell owned the Russell Cleaners in Center until he died in 1966. Harvey Russell is a retired school teacher. The last I heard, he lives in Hughes Springs.

Anyway, with the rubber ball, we had to cut down a few weed stumps to make sure we didn't cause a puncture, but we could dribble on the ground now, and the shooting was better. I still wonder if we had as much fun with the new ball as we did the old.

Well, basketball was not all that got underway. Back two or three years earlier. There had been some grown-ups playing baseball about a mile down the road, but it sorta died out the first season, maybe for lack of funds. My friends had been down to watch them play, and like the basketball, we liked the baseball.

Anyway, I got to thinking about a little baseball to go with what we had. Twine thread was easy to get then because all sacks were sewn with it. So I made balls of twine and then I used different kinds of leather to cover them, such as rawhide, tops of old dress boots and shoes. I first cut myself a pattern, then cut my cover. I punched holes in it with an awl, a thing sorta like an ice pick, only smaller. Of course twine was as strong a thread as I had to sew it with, but I pulled my thread through a cake of beeswax to waterproof it and help protect it from us sluggers-to-be. Ha. Then I dampened the cover so it would stretch a little in putting it on, then when it dried, it looked like a factory job. The boys couldn't figure out how I got my cover shaped like a real baseball and tightly sewn on. I made us bats of various woods and I made glove mitts of white duck, mainly worn out cotton sacks, using cotton for padding. The face protector was the biggest problem, but I got one to work and also a breast protector made of part of an

Entertainment

old quilt covered with ducking cloth. If we'd known it, the protectors the other guys used were out here in the store next door. Also, an old-time catcher's mitt as large as a wash pan. We used it, but we had used the homemade stuff for a couple of years or more. We only had six or eight boys in our little league to this time. We rotated around, as we were short in players. The one thing different is the pitcher called his own strikes and balls. That meant we were all to be honest Joes. See.

One day, while we were playing, one of my second cousins about 10 years of age came over. He stopped about 75 feet off to the side of the batter's box, shyly watching. After a bit, a foul ball went out his way, and he picked it up and tossed it back to the pitcher. We noticed he was a southpaw. We asked him to come toss a few and he finally came in. We explained to him the strike zone and what was to be called a ball. So a batter came up and he kicked off that ball like a pro, right down the middle and the batter failed to strike, but my cousin said, "Strike! And a beauty."

We all got a laugh out of that and he really had smoke, and became a regular. Next, I learned to curve a ball and got to be a fair country pitcher. Lefty wanted me to teach him how to make one break, so he became real good. If on, he could beat New York, but if not, he got pulled out by second inning. He pitched on a team we got going, and then, for Center High School. Lefty Warren is the guy I'm speaking of.

There were some men who played a little over on the Holt farm about three miles NW of here and some of us got to going over helping make enough for two teams to get in a little practicing. Also, at home, we had grown in number and size, so our cow pasture playground was too small, and we were ready to move up or out. I got the boys together and told them we had to have at least a half dozen gloves at least, so each of us tried to come up with one. What we lacked, we could maybe borrow from the other team. Several of us got one, and we got a bat and ball or two also.

We were allowed to put the baseball diamond in Lefty's dad's cow pasture. We matched a game with someone and had a turnout for the game. We passed the hat for a donation to buy balls and bats, and etc., but drew a blank. Of course, people did not have a lot. We returned to the game and did more weed and grass cleaning up on our diamond. If we hadn't, we might have had the same thing happen to us that happened to another cow pasture team. They failed to clean the weeds and grass much before matching game. So one of their visitors lined out into right center. The center field lost the ball in the grass. While he was looking, he saw a small rabbit sitting there and he grabbed it and threw it to the catcher, just in time for him to tag the runner homebound.

The umpire said, "You're out!"

The runner turned on the umpire and said, "He didn't tag me with the ball, he tagged me with a rabbit."

The ump looked down, saw the rabbit in the catcher's hand and said, "You're out by a hare. " Ha.

Well, after falling short on another donation try, I got the idea that we needed an elderly man as a manager, one who had played and knew the game, and mainly, one who could pull some help from these tightwads, and also do all else was needed. I thought I knew just the man, an uncle of two of our little leagues. He lived close by. I went to him. He didn't think he could help, but said he was willing to try. So I told the boys we had a new leader and that I wouldn't have anything to do with who got to play or who didn't. As we went, some more were added and some left out, but before long, another team split up and their best joined the best of us. Then there was a second team organized with another elderly man as manager. If we were not booked and they had a game, they would let me play with them. Also, the manager would let me line up where each played. One day, he asked me why we won when I lined them up and lost to the same team when he lined them up. I told him I thought it was because he let them play where they wanted to, while I put them where I felt they were best suited. You just can't go in there and play any position.

Well, good things don't come easy. The youngsters now have it nice. I had it nice in a country school for it was real close by, but we didn't have the money for me to go to high school. One Saturday, I went to town and the high school was in the building where the present elementary school is now located. So some of their boys were out on the ground court thawing out. I got off at the stop sign, went back and joined in the ring for lay-up shots and some from the outside.

Finally one of the guys said, "Hey fella, where do you play ball? Out here in the country?'

I said. "Yeah, anything wrong with that?"

He said, "Oh no, well, there's one thing. You very seldom, if ever, see a guy come out of the country that shoots a ball with class like you do, for most shoot whatever way they get the ball.

They ganged around me wanting me to come up there and play all types of ball with them. J.B. Taylor, one of our team boys, went and stayed with a farmer out on the edge of town and did chores to help pay his board. He retired just a few years back from the Center school as a math teacher. Willis Fults was another friend who played and helped Center Win District in football at least twice.

Kids now can ride a bus to school and many of the ones who desire to make the team have their own cars. Time changes everything. And now, where are all these tall boys coming from? Back 15 years ago only two guys in the NBA were over 6'5" and most were about 6'2" average. Boy, how we used to wish for a tall guy for center jumper. The ball went back to center after every goal, see, so getting the tip-off was as important as getting the rebound. One side could make eight or ten points before the other got the ball, if you got going kinda hot-handed. But of course, a time out was called to try to cool off the fire, and it would slow things down some. It really hurts to see kids nowadays toss expensive gloves and mitts around in the dirt as though they came out of Crackerjacks. It seems they don't realize how much they should appreciate having them.

Well, there's a lot more I could tell, but I thought someone might find interesting reading about our earlier sports. We had to use imagination and make do with a little of nothing and yet we all enjoyed our growing-up days. We had to invent ways of playing the ball we loved when it seemed impossible, but I guess this proves the old saying that "where there's a will, there's a way.

[This article was originally published in the local newspaper (*Champion?*) by Monroe Taylor…..PHA]

5

Lillie Mae Williamson

Days Gone By

By Joyce Wilson Bright

[The daughter of Lillie Mae Williamson]

Lillie Mae started her store in a very small little building and several years later she was able to build a larger store. For many years she went on Grocery Routes in a pick-up with a bed on it, full of groceries and feed, supplying people in the surrounding rural areas with groceries. Many years later, she was able to buy a large bread truck, which she had shelves built in for items so they couldn't fall off. She had a freezer she kept plugged in at the store, so when she left for her routes, she carried any item she sold at her store could be bought off of her grocery truck. There were many people that didn't have transportation and depended on her for their groceries. For many years she went 5 days a week, and later cut back to around 2 routes per week. Guy Lynch drove for her for several years.

When she got unable to take care of the store, my husband, Bill Weeks, and I stayed and kept the store open for a few years. She had many people who would go back to talk to her and tell her, when they were a little kid they bought candy off of her truck. That would really brighten her day. While we were there it was hard getting up at 5 o'clock and opening at 6. Some days we were open until after 9 o'clock. My sister, Velma Edge, lived at Lake Jackson. She and her husband, Jay Frank, would come up when they could and give us a break.

My son, Benny Bright, also helped at the store. She was so lucky to have such good help for several years. She had the store at Martinsville. Marie Mora worked for her, I believe 25 years. Mrs. Mills and Laverne Battles also worked for a few years. My mother also had Effie Mae Fenley who worked a long time. She was really a life saver when my Mother broke her leg and was down for around a year. Her help were dear friends and such devoted people. Later, Lea Crawford and Pam Crawford worked for her. My mother loved all of her workers and customers. It was such a hard thing to have to close the thing she loved so much.

On February 16, 1986, a record Black Bass, for the state, was caught in Pinkston Reservoir, weighing 16.90 lbs. It was weighed at Lillie Mae's store and held the record for a few years, being reported in one of the sports magazines for a few years. People stopped in the store from some towns several miles away, going there to fish. My Grandson, Camdon Bright, had been working around Chireno and drove there to fish every chance he got and had caught several large fish, one weighed over 10 lbs.

Joyce Bright: Pam, your grandmother was one of the sweetest ladies I've ever known. Mama thought so much of Pearline and Mr. Willie and all of the Hoopers.

Hoyt Hooper: The only ones that I can think of that didn't think the world of Willie and Pearline are maybe the devil and his crew.

Royce Lynn Johnson: Joyce, When I was plowing in the fields of Greertown, I would leave money on a fence post and Lillie Mae would leave me a soda water.

Jill Fountain Parker: Rhonda Chandler and I used to roller skate all around the game room. I honestly don't know how Mrs. Lillie Mae put up with us kids!

When I was young she stayed open late, like 9 or 10 pm, and always opened early. Not sure what time she opened, but she was always open early, like 4 or 5 am. There were times if some of us were sick, or our babies were sick, or sometimes just needed gas, or something important that we would call in the middle of night and she would get up and open the store just for what we needed. Not many sweet ladies would do that!

I remember when I went to the store in the middle of the day, there was a sign on the door; "Closed to run to the bank. Thanks, Joe." I was in shock, I had never seen the store closed in all my life! About 30 minutes later he was back and opened up for all.

Lillie Mae's original store Courtesy of Jill Fountain Parker

<u>Lea Osborne</u>: We lived next to White Rock Church on Lillie Mae's side, and we would walk to the store. Our daddy would give us .50 apiece. So my sister, Kara Osborne, and I would put our money together and we would play pool, Pac man, and pin ball and many others. Other kids in the community would meet there also: Jill Fountain Parker, Rhonda Chandler, Relissa Chandler Bailey, Tammy Whitton, Kelley Hancock, Janette Malecha, Ginger Russell, Reanna Glaze, and Jonica Glaze. Then we all meet up at Campbell's and we were all on mini bikes, mopeds, and whatever else we had, and we rode the dirt roads.

Lillie Mae Williamson

Janette M: I remember Angie Scates and my sister Debbie Jeans had a competition for the highest score on Asteroid. I also remember Mama and Daddy (Edsel & Janice Warr) would always run us by after a trip to Pinkston Lake. After swimming at the point and avoiding the drop off, and admiring Keith Brown diving off the tower, we would watch Ms. Lillie Mae make our slushes with much anticipation while Mr. Joe sat in the recliner watching TV. LOL! Good memories!

Jill Fountain Parker and Rhonda Chandler: The ice cream was amazing and the slushes were the best ever.

Mila Justice Smith: One of my favorite memories is the hand dipped ice cream cones. It was a great after-school-treat for me and my kids.

Alec C: I have so many good memories of that store and that lady. One bad memory of my daddy catching me riding my motorcycle down there, when I wasn't supposed to. He beat the daylights out of me! Totally had it coming! Then like two months later, he sent me down there in his old flat-bed to get diesel for the tractor! Like he didn't just beat the snot out of me!!!

Debbie S A: Jackie Berg and I walked to the store all the time from her house. We stayed down there a lot. We had some good times at that store!!!!

Sharon Fenley Prince: Just to add a note. I know Lillie Mae used to delivery groceries before she had the store. My dad, Gene Fenley, worked as her chauffeur when he was a kid.

Nina Jo Hudspeth Walker: Sharon, Mrs. Lillie Mae delivered groceries to my mom & dad (Mavy & Ed Hudspeth), when I was a small kid. "Wooo, I'm nearly 71, sooo that was a loooong time ago."

Ellen Luman Hearne: If I remember correctly, Mrs. Lillie Mae came through the Waterman community every Wednesday morning on her food truck route.

Jill Fountain Parker: Ellen, I do! We sometimes helped her load the truck on Tuesday night! The people she delivered to were mostly elderly people, that couldn't really go to the grocery store. They were probably grateful for her doing that!

Randy B: I played many a game of pool- actually learned how to play there- and once drank Beachnut Chew "spit" accidentally from Ricky Davis' Pepsi can... that'll teach ya to ask before just taking... lesson well learned!!

Karen Brown-Fallon: Sometimes Uncle Lowell or Granddaddy (Alvi Head) would stop by after a pea picking session & let us jump out of the back of the pick-up & get a treat! I loved how we kids would show up (foot/bicycle/horse/tractor/sometimes car) almost on a daily basis, get a cold soda pop,-candy, & a fresh dipped ice cream cone (always orange pineapple my choice) just to say, "CHARGE IT" to Momma's or Daddy's account-(Charles or Shirley Brown), & it was done! Mrs. Lillie Mae would usually take our word-then hand write a receipt,-put our items in a little brown bag, & send us on our way! No telling what that monthly bill ended up being with all 6 of us kids doing the same! Surely I wasn't the only one...good times/ simpler times!

Randy B: Karen, Larry and I rode our bikes down...couldn't count the times ... and yes... Orange Pineapple was amazing!! The most I remember the monthly bill for 6 of us back then during the summer... can't remember, but it was over $400.00. That's what I recall anyway.

Toni Berg Ford: Karen, orange pineapple was the best. Good times!

Katha Wyatt: Karen, I loved to ride my horse to Lillie Mae's.

Sharon Fenley Prince: Before I was 9 years old we lived in Houston. When we would come to Center for a weekend, our first stop was always at Lillie Mae's. My grandmother, Effie Mae Fenley Sharpston worked there at Lillie Mae's. We would stop and see her and get a slushy. James Wiggins built Lillie Mae's house and the hallway to the store.

Eldora Gilchrist: Rhonda, anytime we ever passed through Martinsville we always stopped at Lillie Mae's and got ice cream. It was the best in the country. She even made my little dog a little bitty ice cream cone. He would lick it just like we did, 'till it got down to the cone.

6
Mt. Herman

Days Gone By

By Jan Akridge

Billy's family goes way back, I'm a transplant! I was planted 50 years ago July 10, 1970. We lived in Mt. Herman by his grandmother, Fannie Mae Adkison. At that time there were 2 stores in Mt. Herman, Jess Warren's and Ura Lovell's. Mr. Jess' store was where the men meet and played dominoes. You could get a cold drink out of an old Coke box that had cold water running through it. You could also buy overalls there and shirts. Ura's was across the road. She helped me get my first job. She stopped me one day as I was walking to Barbara Scates house. She told me that Mrs. Gann at Center Floral needed help and for me to call her. Couldn't ask for a better neighbor. I can remember going to Ura's to get 2 potatoes for supper and her laughing that I only wanted 2, but that's all I needed. You could also get the best bacon there. She cut it off as you waited, then weighed it on the scales. After Tara was born when we stopped by she would put Tara on the scales to see how much she weighed that week. Wonder how many babies were weighed on those scales? I know Vivian and Earl did the same thing. At that time, Ura also had four washers and two dryers in a building behind the store. I used them every week. We were lucky to have some so close. Later on in years the other half of it was a beauty shop. Well that's my first story, more to come.

This is just a list of neighbors I remember when we lived by Mama Adkison (Fannie Mae). I'll start with her. She was still push mowing her yard in her late 70s. She had the prettiest flower gardens. She taught me so much, such as old wife's tales and saying that I still go by today! She made beautiful quilts and always had one hanging from her ceiling. She wanted me to learn to quilt so badly. I still have the one I started, (You notice I said started). It's about 2 ft. by 4 ft. That's as far as I got. Mama lived to be 102 years old. On down the road was the Fults family, Johnnie, Idell, Elze, and the older sister, I can't remember her name. Anytime you visited them you were sure to be laughing and having a good time. Mrs. Vada was next, she made the best popcorn balls for Halloween. My children wanted to go there first. She always had their bags all fixed up for them. Mr. Jess Luman was across the road. On down a ways was Preacher Lewis Johnson. He married us in 1970. In 1992 he married his last couple, who was my daughter Tara and Brandon Jordan. Wonder if he kept up with all the ones he married? Vaudine Williams Adams was on the old Pearl Lake Road, next to Charlie Fountain. Next was Auvey and Marie Adkison. Robert Warr lived down that way also. You knew a storm was coming when you saw his old black truck pass our house going to the Fults. They had a storm shelter. Donnie Warr lived down that way too. I remember Mae Choate lived on the highway. On this next one I think I'm right, if not let me know. My first name is Mavis. I never knew another person named that till I moved out here. And there was TWO, Mavis Taylor and Mavis Hudspeth. I couldn't believe it. The only Mavis I knew was the powder named Mavis. Mr. Carroll Russell and the Barbes lived on down past him. Across the way was the J.T. Holt family and the Elmo Rains family. I know I have missed some in Mt. Herman. But you can add to the story, and tell some from Aiken.

Nina Jo Hudspeth Walker: Jan, my mom's name was Mavy Hudspeth. Her name was pronounced (May-v). So, I guess you did only know one named Mavis, after all. LOL.

Jean R A: Ms. Fannie Mae was a fine Christian Lady. I went to church with her at Mt. Herman Church of Christ.

Tony Lovell owned the store first. Ura Lovell owned it next. Vivian (Ura's sister) and Earl Campbell bought it from her later. The store is closed at the time of this picture. Campbell's Grocery Store in Mt Herman 2022. Photograph by Pamila Hooper Adkison

Days Gone By

Taja Adkison Harvey: I didn't know Grandma Adkison was 102! I knew it was close though.

Royce Lynn Johnson: Older Fults sister was Elfe...married to Harem Tindol... only one of them to marry.

Jan Akridge: I knew she was the only one to marry, didn't know his name. Thanks Royce Lynn.

Royce Lynn Johnson: I took Johnnie to the emergency room when she was in her 90s. The nurse asked Idell who her family doctor was. Idel said she had never been to a doctor before!

Jan Akridge: I would believe it. When Elze died, Idell came running to our house for me to call for help. When I got her back up there he was already gone. I helped Johnny and Idel take him to his bed. They wanted to make sure he looked good when they got there. I was only about 17 or 18. I never batted an eye, just pitched right in there. People helped neighbors back then. Also, we knew our neighbors.

Janette M: Ms. Johnnie and Ms. Idell used to fly up and down our dirt road like bats outta hell.

Rhonda Chandler: I'll never forget Johnnie and Idell. Johnnie taught me the quickest way to get rid of a bull needle right there in the middle of the pea field.

Tammy D: Ronnie and I were married by him (Bro. Johnson) in their house in '82.

Jan Akridge: We were married in his house also!

Rex-Janie R: Jan, we were married by Bro. Lewis Johnson in March of 1967 at his house.

Debbie S A: Gene and I were married by Bro. Johnson in 1984 in his home!! He also married Gene's mom & dad! (Fate & Eva Dell Adams).

Pam Adkison: Bro. Johnson married us at Mama's and Daddy's.

Mila Justice Smith: Jan, I went with Jeanine to Tara's wedding. If I remember right, it was in J C and Venorah McSwain's yard. She was such a pretty bride!

Jill Fountain Parker: Bro Johnson married Steve and me in 1992, right there in his living room! He married Mama and Jeff in 1980 at Barbara's house!

Sharon Fenley Prince: He married my parents, Gene & Dorothy Fenley, Christmas Eve 1964 in his home. He also married Cole Hooper and me, March 9, 1991.

Tresa Danley Konderla: Jan, Yesss! Mrs. Vada did have the best popcorn balls ever. We made a stop by there coming from Salem going to Aiken and White Rock for Halloween.

Kerri L W: Another neighbor that lived right past Grandmother (Donnie

Warr) was Arlis and Beulah Tomlin. Also, Bo Scott lived down Pearl Lake Road and so did Don Lovell.

Jess Warren Memories

By Barbara J Scates

We lived in Mt Herman and in easy walking distance of Jess Warren's Store. The store was on Highway 7, but the Warren's owned a vast amount of land and their property spread down to the dirt road I lived on. The mail was delivered to our house about mid-morning and by the time the mailman made his way back around his route to deliver mail in the area of the store, it was midafternoon. So...and I am only guessing at this...the Warrens had a mailbox set up on the edge of their property on the dirt road beside our house so they could get their mail earlier in the morning. Sometimes they walked down to get their mail and sometimes they drove their car to the mailbox. They always got lots of mail, and although we never knew for sure, but I think they got a newspaper every day! That was almost unheard of back in the 1950s and '60s. Anyway they came every day to pick up their mail in that lonely mailbox that had no house in sight, except ours, and it was not our mailbox. If the mail was late, they waited...on foot or in their car. They had the 1950 or '51 black Ford that they won at the Shelby County Fair (at least that is what I always heard). Later Mrs. Warren had a sky blue 1958 (I think) Ford car. Both cars had a standard transmission with a clutch and Mrs. Warren had a hard time releasing the clutch for a smooth take off. I remember one morning (this was in the 1970s after I had married and was living on the corner by their mailbox) she got her mail and proceeded to back up and turn the car around. Well, I guess, she came out on the clutch too fast and ended up in the ditch. Jerry had to pull her out. Bless her heart, she was embarrassed.

Another quick story about the Jess Warren store...my mother sent my sister, Wanda, and me to the store to get a spool of thread. We walked in with our money and told Mr. Jess what color thread we wanted (I don't remember what color we needed, but I think it was red). Mr. Jess handed us a spool of thread and took our money. Wanda and I stood looking at each other, because he had given us the wrong color. Being the well-mannered children we were, we didn't tell him it was the wrong color. We walked back home knowing Momma could not use the color thread we were bringing home. Sure enough, Momma said we had to take it back and get the right color. She also told us that Mr. Warren was color blind. (I heard that from others when I got older). We worried all the way back to the store about how we were going to get the right color, if he couldn't see which color to hand us. All his thread was behind the counter and we could not go behind the counter to show him which color we wanted. Much to our relief, Mr. Warren set the tray of thread on the counter and let us pick the color. Whew...now we had the right color and we skipped all the way home!

The Warren store had a little bit of everything. Sewing supplies, overalls, nails, dishpans, garden tools, and candy, Cokes and lots more. I remember the big cookie jars sitting on top of the counter. I don't remember how much they cost, but you could point to the jar you wanted a cookie from and they would take the lid off, reach in and get it and hand it to you. It seemed like those cookies were as big as a saucer back then, but I am sure they weren't quite that big! I would love to go back just one more time and sit on that porch, dangling my feet and drink a Top Cola!!!

Pear Pie?

By Barbara J Scates

I saw that several were talking about picking peas...well, I also picked a few peas when I was young. I love to eat them, but to this day I hate picking them! I picked for Mr. Jess Luman. Mr. Jess and his wife, Mrs. Frances, were fine people. I don't remember how much he paid, because by the time we got finished picking the whole patch, I didn't care about the money. I just wanted to be finished and go home! I never liked hard work! Hahaha!

Many years later I owned a beauty shop in Mt Herman. Mrs. Frances was one of my patrons. She didn't drive, so Mr. Jess would bring her and sit in the beauty shop and wait for her. He always had a story to tell, so on this particular day, he proceeded to tell me the pear pie story. With a twinkle in his eye, he told how he had been out plowing and had stopped long enough to go in the house for dinner (that's what we called our mid-day meal). He went on to tell what all Mrs. Frances had cooked; a pot of peas, fried okra, some corn, a pone of cornbread, and for dessert she had taken some pears out of the freezer and made a pear pie. He said he could hardly wait to taste a slice of that pie! So, the time had come for him to get a big piece of that hot pear pie. He cut a big slice and put it on his plate. With his fork, he got himself a big bite. Much to his surprise, it was not pears at all! Mrs. Frances had mistakenly reached in the freezer and got a bag of turnips instead of pears!

Mt. Herman

"Turnip pie!" Mr. Jess said.

He was laughing so hard and Mrs. Frances was laughing too. They were such good folks, and I was pleased to have known this precious Mt Herman couple!

Mila Justice Smith: Barbara, What an awesome story!! I never got to meet the Lumans, and I know I missed a lot.

Kerri L W: So sweet! I loved Uncle Jess and Aunt Frances so much! Such fine folks! I enjoyed your story!

Phillip Holt: I remember Mr. Jess always had a story to tell!

Karen Bittick: Frances was a sister to my grandmother Ethel Warr McSwain. Aunt Frances and Uncle Jess were a good pair. Uncle Jess never met a stranger. Barbara, I loved your remembrance of them.

Eldora Gilchrist: Phillip, Jess Luman only had a milk cow. Just a wire fence separated the Luman property from our property. Each year the fence mysteriously got torn down and Mr. Jess always had a new calf come spring. Ha!

Katha Wyatt: They lived across from my grandmother. One day I climbed a big tree in her front yard and then couldn't get down!! Apparently, I was hollering so loudly that Mr. Luman couldn't go to bed, so he drove across the road and backed his truck up, got in the bed of it and coaxed me down!

Barbara J. Scates: Katha, I have seen some posts about your grandmother, Mrs. Vada Muckelroy, and the love and kindness she showed the kids in the community, but probably not many remember your grandfather, Mr. R. E. Muckelroy. I remember him from church at Mt Herman. Just a week or two before he passed away, I remember him talking to a group of us kids on the front steps at the church.

"I saw something last night that I will never get over," he said.

We were all excited to hear what he had seen.

With a twinkle in his eye and a smile on his face, he told us..."The moon."

He thought that was so funny that he had played that joke on us! I have always remembered that was the last time I saw him. I remember him always being a kind man!

Shirley Di Verdi: I seem to remember Mr. Jess' wife, Mrs. Ella, was very hard of hearing, if memory serves me correctly. She always revved up her car engine, you would think she was going to blow the engine up. She couldn't hear well enough to know she was doing it. That was always a joke, "better get out of Mrs. Ella's way." Didn't Mr. Jess sell overalls and boots? I picked a lot of peas with the Fults for Mr. Luman and Cletus Sharpton. Every summer if I wanted new school clothes, I knew I'd better pick those peas. We were picked up at daylight. The pickup bed would be full of people. The Fults sisters always picked peas in dresses. We picked until around noon every day, until it got hot. I remember it well, dragging those wet pea sacks around.

I think of it often, saying to myself, "It is no way girls or boys would work like we did."

Even our own kids would never do it. We would always stop at the store before he carried us home. Probably made a couple of dollars a day. I used to like putting peanuts in my Coke.

Mammaw Adkison was one of a kind. Her house was so hot. She was always working on a quilt.

When you would go to visit she would always ask, "What's yo news?"

She was a kind Christian lady that didn't mind telling you to go, when it got to be her bedtime, which was early. She would also start gathering your plate before you were finished eating. She was a gem. I have enjoyed the stories. They brought back some memories, I had forgotten.

<u>Royce Lynn Johnson</u>: Shirley, I'm 75 years old, and still picking peas! Pea picking then was 1 cent a lb. There were men who would pick 1000 lbs. a day, $10 a day. Today, it is 50 cents a pound. So one of those men could make $500 a day now picking peas.

<u>Phillip Holt</u>: Royce Lynn, I remember Daddy complaining about having to pay 5 cents a lb. to pick peas, when I was in high school. There's no telling how many 30 lb. sacks of peas I sacked...

Days Gone By

<u>Delores Harris Brown</u>: Loved your memory story of Jess & Frances. I remember them also. I picked peas, too, for my Uncle Kermit McSwain. I didn't like it, either. I think, I made 75 cents one day.

<u>Angela Johnson Lawson</u>: I love this story. Thanks for sharing it. Aunt Francis was my grandmother's (Ethel Warr McSwain) sister. I loved getting to go with her and my mother, Maxine, to visit Aunt Francis and Uncle Jess. Always lots of smiles and laughter.

<u>Shirley Di Verdi</u>: Laverne and D L Battles were our neighbors. Patricia was my friend. She would come over, and we would play for hours in the car cutting out models from the Sears and Roebuck catalogue. We would lick them and stick them all over the windows on the inside. That's what we called "playing dolls." Many a day we did this. I only remember playing this at my house, not hers.

<u>Eldora Gilchrist:</u> Pam, I also remember what beautiful quilts Miss Ella made. She quilted all the time. I went to Mount Herman School until I was in the fifth grade. After school I would go up to the store. Usually I had enough money to get a soda water and maybe a piece of candy. Sometimes Miss Ella would invite me up to her house. I would get to see it, all the beautiful quilts, and whichever one she was working on at the time. She made them for all her family. I wonder what happened to them all.

I had to walk on up to where the road was, pass the cemetery, and wait for the high school bus. My sisters would be on that bus. They and John Russell would get off, and we would walk home together.

We always walked to the store when the weather was good, and we always walked back. Mount Herman School had two rooms. Miss Woods and Miss Pate taught in one room, (at different times) one through third. Mr. Minton taught 4 thru 6th. The school closed down and I began the fifth grade at Excelsior and went through the 8th. Miss Lawson drove a pickup with a wooden shed over the bed with benches on each side. She would pick us up each morning and take us to school.

You know, women never played dominoes at Mr. Jess'. One day I went over there to get something for Mother, and they only had three players. They needed one more. They asked me to play 'till someone else came in, so I did. Mr. Jess and I played Uncle Lofton and Uncle Flex Lucas. We beat them on the second game. Grover Anthony came in and he took my place.

Another thing I remember about Mr. Jess. One day I went over there, and there was a beautiful woman sitting on the front porch sitting on a nail keg. Sure enough, it was the movie star Marilyn Maxwell, who was very popular about the same time as Marilyn Monroe. One of Mr. Jess' sons had married her out in California and brought her home to meet his parents. I never was so surprised and I have never forgotten it.

Living off the Grid

By Howell Adkison

Back in the '50s, my dad (Hollis Adkison) and most of his brothers went out west to the oilfields. They stayed a few years, and then, moved back to East Texas. Before he left, he had bought 20 acres off the southeast corner of Grandma Fannie Mae's (Adkison) place. He had started a house which was not finished on the inside before we left. There was not even an electric line to the property. You talk about living off the grid! We were! Over the next year or two, he completed most of the house. It became an ongoing process. About halfway down the road (CR 1205, today) to Grandma's house was a little dirt road turning to the right. The road crossed International Paper Co.'s land and came to an end at the corner of Dad's property where the house was. (My sister, Shirley Di Verdi, owns the place now). We were the only ones living down that road. Eventually, we got the county to grade the road, so the school bus would come pick us up.

When the road was graded, which wasn't very often, it would rain in the next three days. It never failed! Another sign of rain was when we could smell the paper mill way over in Lufkin, Texas. That's right, in three days it would rain.

Dad came in one evening and told us that he had seen a panther run across the road before daylight as he was going to work that day. A year later I was going out on my bike and saw it myself. Later years, we all heard it screaming at night. A very dreadful sound.

We hadn't been moved back very long, when Dad wanted to go over and visit Uncle Bill and Aunt Edna (Akridge). That's when I got to meet my first cousins, the Akridge boys. They had some fruit trees in their yard. Billy offered me one of what I was told was a "green apple." I take a big ole bite, and immediately, my jaws sucked in and my lips puckered out. They started laughing. I couldn't say anything for a while. Aunt Edna came out of the house and fussed at them a little bit. Uncle Bill had a little grin on his face. Okay, the joke is on me. It was a green persimmon. I was a little naive. I'm just glad that I didn't jump on them and beat them up. Anyway they became my best friends over the years. Jimbo, Gene sometimes, and I ran around together. Billy not so much, but he did get us out of a jam or two. Huh, Gene?

Gene and Jimbo was always daring me to do something, and getting me into trouble a lot. Hey, what are good friends for?

Billy remember the chinquapin tree on the Luman place? They were good.

<u>Jimmie Nell Adkison Lee</u>: Love these stories!! Do any of you remember chewing "Sweet Gum" from the sweet gum trees? I loved it and you had to know when to get it off the tree. When it was hard and somewhat crystallized, we would look for trees that had the bark knocked off and the sap was oozing on the tree. Well, one time our next neighbor had some grandkids come from Houston to visit. Prime targets for us country kids to introduce them to Sweet Gum, only that's not what I did....it was Pine Resin from a pine tree!!!!

I pretended I was putting it in my mouth and chewing. They followed suit. They chewed it. That mess stuck to their teeth...and gums. They could not spit it out. They ran home bawling, and their grandmother was fit to be tied. Not even a tooth brush would get it out! They had to chew on pieces of cloth to get it out of their mouth. Then their mouth was sore....I devoutly promised I had no idea this would happen. I got one heck of a switching!!! Their grandmother was raising all kind a cane, and finally Mama told her that at least none of them would need worming for a while!

Days Gone By

Mt. Herman School

<u>Royce Lynn Johnson</u>: Anyone remember the Mt Herman School? I went there in the first grade. I could have gone to Camp Worth also. Grades 1-6 were in one room and 7-12 were in the other room. Zettie Woods was my teacher. A Mr. Minter taught the other room. Cafeteria was mostly vegetables from local farmers.

<u>Jerry H</u>: I lived off Camp Worth Road. I walked to and from Mt. Herman School. I would pick blackberries and huckleberries on the way home. Sometimes after the road was graded, I would find railroad spikes.

<u>Phyllis Adams</u>: Jerry, we still find railroad spikes every once in a while!

<u>Royce Lynn Johnson</u>: You are right about the grades in Mt Herman School. I posted earlier that Mr. Minter taught grades 7-12, but I think now I was mistaken.

<u>Eldora Gilchrist</u>: It could have been that maybe, years ago it did go through the 12th. I don't know, but it was closed down when I started to the sixth grade, I believe, and that's why I went to Excelsior. Eventually my oldest brother James Gibson Barbe bought the school property. He and his wife lived in the teacher's house for a long time. Later he sold the old school building to the people that went to the Baptist Church up on the hill by the cemetery at Mount Herman. The Church of Christ kept the old church. The Baptist moved down the hill and made the old school their new church. Eventually, my brother built at my new house there where they lived until after he died, and his wife later moved to Nacogdoches.

Mt Herman School 1949

Notes from Linda Johnson Winder

In October of 1948 I was thrilled to start first grade at Mt. Herman, which was a two-room school house about five or six miles away from our house on Hwy 7. LaNell McSwain and I had both turned 5 in May, but at that time you had to be 6 to start school. The principal, Mr. Minton, apparently needed more students so he talked our mothers into letting us start school. He picked us up in the mornings in his car. School had already been in session for a month when we started. The first graders were writing numbers on the board the first day we arrived. We were sent to the board to write the number 8. The only way I knew to do it was to put one circle above another. LaNell and I learned quickly, however, and starting first grade so young never bothered us. Although we were always the youngest in our class, we did well in our studies.

Mt. Herman had one room for grades 1-4 and another room for grades 5-8. Mrs. Vivian Jernigan was our teacher. We always called her Miss Vivian. She was young, pretty, and nice. I thought she was wonderful. I loved school and wanted to become a teacher from then on.

Every day when I got home I would teach my brother, Royce Lynn, what I had learned. He was an eager pupil and I was somewhat successful. He said that when he started school, he already knew everything being taught in the first grade. I also got the great idea at the time that I would teach my cats how to read and set up a mock classroom in part of our old barn. Needless to say, I was not very successful and had to abandon that project.

During recess at school we were sometimes allowed to cross the highway and go to Jess Warren's store. The bathrooms were outside, one for the boys and one for the girls. A small lunchroom was in another building and hot lunches were provided. I cried one day, because all we had to eat were pinto beans and biscuits. Mama cooked dried lima beans, not pinto beans, and we ate cornbread.

I felt sorry for Mattie Parker. Her mother died having a baby, and the baby died also.

My friend Ella Rae Choate lived up the road from the school. There were maybe 10 kids in the family. One day she was sick, and the teacher had me walk her home. All of us girls wore dresses made from feed sacks. At the time farmers could buy feed for their animals in sacks. Some smart manufacturer decided to use cotton prints. Housewives would take the empty sacks and make them into clothes. Most kids wore the same clothes two days in a row. The dress was pretty wrinkled that second day, but that was what was done. Washing and ironing took a lot of time. Plus, children did not have that many clothes. Most of the boys wore jeans and overalls, which could be worn over and over. However, girls were not allowed to wear pants to school. Mama was a wonderful seamstress and did beautiful work, but I never appreciated it enough, because the material came from the old feed sacks.

Mt. Herman

Adults standing at the back are Merline Parker, Verna Mills and teacher Vivian Jernigan. Students, from the top, are Bob Wilson, Ella Rae Choate, Delano Warr (middle) Jerry H, LaNell McSwain, Peggy Taylor, Linda Johnson, Jeannette McSwain, Rachel Dennis (bottom row) Jimmy Hugh Lucas, _____, Edna Ray McSwain, Charlotte Parker, Mattie Katherine Parker, Cecil Ray Muckelroy, ____ and ____. Mt. Herman was a two-room school with grades 1-4 in one room and 5-8 in the other. There was also a separate building where lunches were cooked and served. The school was on the site of what is the old Campbell's Grocery Store in Mt. Herman.....Linda Johnson Winder

Mt Herman School Students and Teachers, Courtesy of Linda Johnson Winder

Phillip Holt: Yeah, Jerry, It's easy to recognize you with those big ears.

Jerry H: Phillip, they kept me very stable all these years.

Days Gone By

Karen Bittick: I always assumed you went to school in Center at the old grammar school. I noticed there are many that passed away long ago.

Adam J: Linda thanks for sharing. Vivian Jernigan is my grandmother.

Rodger McLane: Which one is Delano Warr? I've always heard stories about him.

Linda Winder: Delano Warr is the little boy in front of Miss Vivian.

Jerry H: J.B. was our bus driver, when I went to Center.

Sandra Wilson: Jerry, was this the last year you went to Mt. Herman?

Linda Winder: Do you know Ella Rae Choate who is in this photo? I remember her very well from school.

Russell Andrews: This is without doubt the best group I've ever been in, guess it's because I know of a lot of these families and the places.

Linda Winder: Eldora, I am not sure when this photo was taken or how many of the kids it includes. I don't think the fourth graders are even in this photo. I went to Mt. Herman in grades 1-3, and then, transferred to Center Elementary. I was very happy at Mt. Herman and did not like the big, crowded classes in Center. My brother, Royce Lynn Johnson, went to Mt. Herman the year I transferred to Center. His teacher was Miss Zettie Woods and she picked him up every morning.

Gwen Taylor Stewart; Linda, I think this may be a year or two later than 1949. Charlotte Parker was my first cousin and she was born in October, 1948—3 months after me. But it wasn't any later than 1951 or 1952 because that is when her mother-Marlene Parker- passed away.

Mt. Herman

Fred Borders: Gwen, I knew Bob Wilson and worked with him. I think he was about 6 years older than I, so he would have been born about 42. He looks about 8 in the picture so I'm guessing 1950. I must be misunderstanding you. How can Charlotte Parker be your age and be in a 1950 picture? You started 1st grade in 1954.

Gwen Taylor Stewart: We were both born in 1948. Started first grade in 1954.

Fred Borders: Gwen, I got that, so this picture must be at least 1954, or later. She looks older than 1st grade.

Gwen Taylor Stewart: Fred-I think the reason Charlotte was in that picture is because her Mom-Merlene Parker was there with her—maybe like a room mother or something. I don't think she taught.

Gwen Taylor Stewart: No-Charlotte is the smallest little girl on the front row. Her mother, Merlene, shown on the back row, died 05/21/1951 in childbirth.

Linda Winder: The photo could have been taken in 1949 or 1950, maybe even 1951. Charlotte Parker looks too young to be in school. I think, Gwen Taylor Stewart has it right that she was there because her mother was there as a room mother or something. I only went to Mt. Herman for grades 1-3. It was during this time period. I remember Mattie's mother dying in childbirth, so I may have been there in the spring of 1951.

Gwen Taylor Stewart: Merlene Parker was my dad's youngest sister. He was JB Taylor. Her death was a great tragedy for the family.

Linda Winder: J.B. Taylor who taught math in Center? He also boarded with my grandparents when he taught at Camp Worth.

Gwen Taylor Stewart: Yup! The one and only! Who were your grandparents?

Linda Winder: Lee and Ethel McSwain. At that time they lived at Salem. I just looked up some notes, however. J. B. Taylor boarded with the McSwain family when he taught at the Salem school, not Camp Worth. He was my math teacher at Center when I was in about the seventh grade. Math was not my thing, so I was a horrible math student.

Mt. Herman Tragedy

By Jan Akridge

This is a Mt. Herman Story about a group of friends. It was August 28 in the year of 1927. Two of those friends were James I. Akridge and George Wilkerson. It is said they were best friends, but that day they got into a fight and George left mad. When James started to leave the other men tried to get James to go the back way home, but he didn't. James married Mary Jane Hooper and they lived on the road that goes from Hwy 7 west to 711, about where the Old Jess Warren place would be now. George waited on him. As James reached the curve before his house, George shot James in view of his home and family. As James lay in the road, George would not let his wife, nor the older children, go to him. James died that day August 28, 1927. George Wilkerson was convicted of the murder and sentenced to 10 years in prison. My sister-in-law, Zandra, found the records for this case, years later when she worked at the court house. Just thought you might like the story. This would be the father of Luther (Bill), Slim, Corine Holmes, Virgil, RB, Macil and Mertie.

Cynda Jones: I've heard this story all of my life. Mary Jane Hooper was my grandpa's sister.

Jan Akridge: Billy's daddy was about 4 or 5 years old when this happened.

Jimmie Nell Adkison Lee: I remember Mrs. Holmes telling me that story. I couldn't believe it. Was awful.

Karen Bittick: Hard to believe he only got a 10 year sentence, especially since he would not let family go to him as he was dying.

Karren P: Wonder what the fight was about...

Jan Akridge: Karren, I was told they had been playing cards. I don't know if that was the cause of the fight. It was bad enough for the other friends to try and get him to go the back way home.

Karren P: Jan, wow. I enjoyed reading the story, but sure hate it happened.

Jan Akridge: I have a copy of the court records, but I couldn't find it last night. I might have to get another copy.

Karren P: Jan, I would love to see it.

Joy Tarver: My daddy shot a man with rat shot in the butt one time for stealing food out of our barn crib. Daddy couldn't figure out who it was. So, he laid in wait one night and got him. After he figured out who it was, he went to his house every day and gave that family part of whatever he had harvested for the day.

He told him, "Don't ever steal from me again, I will give you whatever I can."

He never told us who it was, and my parents took that info to their grave.

Mt. Herman Community

By Jan Akridge

I forgot to post this one last night. Mt. Herman Community was settled in the early 1830s. The dirt road from Center to Nacogdoches was paved and officially opened in 1937. Mt. Herman had a school and two churches. A Baptist and a Church of Christ. It also had a Post Office. It was named Word. To me that was a strange name to name a Post Office. It was located on the front porch of the Sam Brown home. His house was located on the old Nacogdoches Road at the top of the hill just before you got to Pearl Lake. The Post Office was opened April 29, 1892 and closed in 1912. (*Shelby County History Book II*)

Gwen Taylor Stewart: Our mom was friends with Dell Brown when we were growing up. Also, Mom and Dad purchased our home place on Nacogdoches Hwy from John and Annie Brown in 1949-50. It was about a mile towards Center from Jess Warren's store.

Jan Akridge: Gwen, I always thought your mom's and dad's house was so pretty. I hated when they tore it down.

Gwen Taylor Stewart: Jan, it burned down after Hurricane Rita. New owners tried to sonnet a generator to old and decrepit house wiring. Mom loved her flowers!

Eldora Gilchrist: Jan, check this out. The best I remember there was just one church when I was growing up and the Baptists met there. The Church of Christ didn't have a church or something. If they ever did, something must have happened to it. The Baptist agreed to let them have church one week, and we'd have church the next. I think that is how it went. I remember going to both at only one church, so you might check into that and see if that's what really happened. I do remember it being just one church. Then the Baptist let the Church of Christ have the original building, and they bought the old Mount Herman school building and built the Baptist Church down the hill. The Baptist bought the old school building from my older brother, James Gibson Barbe, who had bought the whole school property.

Royce Lynn Johnson: Eldora, yes, both had services in the same building, Baptist one week and Church of Christ the next. (Mostly same people at both services). When it was Church of Christ Sunday, they just put a quilt over the piano.

Mt Herman Church of Christ 2022, Photograph by Pamila Hooper Adkison

Karen Bittick: Royce Lynn, I remember us going to the Baptist church in Mt. Herman. I remember walking up the hill to the Church of Christ holding Ma Johnson's (Lena) hand and staying with her during their service.

Royce Lynn Johnson: The road from Center to Nacogdoches was CR 1168 crossing Pearl Lake. The new road was built and paved in 1937.

Jan Akridge: Royce Lynn that was the old Nacogdoches Road, right?

Royce Lynn Johnson: No...the old Nacogdoches Road went from Shelbyville to Nacogdoches, crossing at Bounds Hill, through Short, on to Jericho. The road is the same as now from Hwy 96 to Jericho, on to the January place where it went behind Pearl Lake to the top of the hill at the Word Post Office.

Reba James and I researched the old road. One of the first roads into Texas (map of 1829). It was traveled by early settlers, maybe by Davy Crockett on his way to the Alamo? Of course this was before Jericho and Mt. Herman...

Jan Akridge: I think the Pearl Lake Road was known as the old Nacogdoches Road in our time.

Royce Lynn Johnson: It was the road from Center to Nacogdoches at one time. The Shelbyville to Nacogdoches Road was much older. It was there before Center existed.

Jan Akridge: The one I was reading about was the one on Pearl Lake Road. Where the Post Office was at a Sam Brown's home on the hill before Pearl Lake road. They called it the old Center to Nacogdoches Road.

Royce Lynn Johnson: It was the only road to Nacogdoches, until they built Hwy 7 in the '30s.

Jan Akridge: Royce Lynn, where was the post office then? This is in the *Shelby County History Book #2*.

Royce Lynn Johnson: I thought it was at the corner in front of Donnie Warr's house. But you may be right about the Brown's house.

William Rudd: Royce Lynn, Do you or does the museum have a map showing the old Shelbyville to Nacogdoches Road? The Sam Brown home was located on which hillside from the lake, the one toward Center or the one toward Nacogdoches?

Royce Lynn Johnson: Nacogdoches.

Jan Akridge: William, Dowell Youngblood wrote this story and in his words he said that the Sam Brown home was located on the left of the old Nacogdoches Road at the top of the hill just before you get to Pearl Lake.

Sharon Fenley Prince: Is the old Nacogdoches Road the one where the old chip mill is on FM 711 and comes out on Hwy 7, near where Nig Tomlin lived?

Royce Lynn Johnson: Sharon, No... it's the one that runs through Short to Jericho, on through Mt Herman

Taja Adkison Harvey: Jan, where was the school?

Jan Akridge: Taja are you talking about the Mt. Herman School?

Jan Akridge: Royce Lynn, I just knew it was not behind the Mt. Pleasant Church. Mr. Youngblood in his story said it was next to the Campbell's store. That is a broiler farm now. Mr. Youngblood said he attended there from 1935-1938. A Mrs. Ruby Russell Strahan 1-3 was the teacher and J. B Taylor was the Principal. This is his story!

Jan Akridge: Billy said that the Barbes had chicken houses at one time beside the store.

Royce Lynn Johnson: Jan, James Gibson Barbe bought the property and the school building that was moved to become the Baptist church. Seems like he did build a chicken house there. I know it was close to the highway.

Royce Lynn Johnson: Mr. Minter was teacher and principal for older kids and Zettie Woods taught us.

Royce Lynn Johnson: I was referring to the Mt Pleasant School

Taja Adkison Harvey: Ok thanks. I was just wondering where it was.

Jan Akridge: Royce Lynn, I know, that's why I asked Taja if she was talking about the Mt. Herman School. I post stuff just to keep the group going. Stuff that will get people to comment on. I have family from out this way and your way. My grandmother was from your way. Family buried at Mt. Pleasant and Mt. Herman. I've only lived out this way 50 years. In fact my gggg grandfather is buried in the cemetery behind your dad's old place.

Royce Lynn Johnson: Jan, you are talking about the Lucas cemetery. Who was your gggg grandfather?

Taja Adkison Harvey: Yes ma'am I was talking about the Mt. Herman School.

Jan Akridge: Royce Lynn, I want to say Dick Lucas, but I think it is initials on the tomb stone. My aunt and uncle and I went by there. We are kin to Lillie Mae somehow. I have her records on it, will have to look it up. That was the first time I knew I had family out this way. Then found out I had it on my other side also. The Fults!

Royce Lynn Johnson: Jan, you can walk up to anyone in Shelby county and say "Hello 6th cousin". And most of the time you will be right!

Jan Akridge: Royce Lynn, I know, my uncle was married to some kin to Lillie Mae. When my aunt and uncle started looking up kin folks, they all got together and started going to cemeteries and looking up who was kin to who. That's how I found my roots out this way on the Adams side. Then later found out, my mother's family was from out your way, Fults on FM 711.

7

Employment

Days Gone By

Farming

<u>Eldora Gilchrist</u>: You asked about farming experiences. I have one. When I was probably about 9 or 10, we would be harvesting the crops. Since I was so small Daddy would set the gas to very slow on the tractor, and I would drive the tractor up and down the rows for them to gather the crops and load them in the trailer. When I go to turn at the end of a row, I was so small, I had to stand up and pull up as hard as I could on the steering wheel to have enough strength to mash the brake to make the tractor make the turn. Ernest Warr and the Fults sisters, Johnny and her sister, were all gathering. While I was standing up, Ernest threw a handful of grass burs in the tractor seat. Needless to say, I lost control with the tractor and ran into the fence, when I sat back down. Daddy got me off that tractor and whip my butt good, right there. Ernest apologized to me every time he saw me for the rest of his life, because he caused me to get a whooping.

Ernest Warr and his family lived in Mr. Jess' other rent house on the Johnson Road, and it had a dog trot down the middle.

<u>Delores Harris Brown</u>: Uncle Ernest Warr was a character. His wife Lid was my grandpa's baby sister. I remember that house and visiting them there. I was close to Mary's age and my sister was close to Shirley's & Betty's [ages]. We always had fun being around them.

<u>William Rudd</u>: If your Ernest Warr is Green Warr, I knew him well. In the late 1950s he and his wife lived in a home on my parent's place on FM 711. He also did some watermelon peddling for my dad. I recall that he was very mischievous, but very pleasant.

<u>April N Larry Scates</u>: Larry said he was known as Green Warr.

<u>Royce Lynn Johnson</u>: William, when Terry came from West Texas and moved to Jericho, he was mowing the lawn.

Ernest went over and told him, "We don't allow men to do women's work here. The women here will see you and expect us to do the same." Terry stopped the mower and went into the house!

Delores Harris Brown: Eldora, they came to our house often for 42 games. Uncle Ernest could make my grandma laugh, hysterically, with his stories and his picking. He could always cheer her up after my grandpa died. Aunt Lid was funny too, especially when they both got going.

Mila Justice Smith: Earnest and Lid Warr were two of my very favorite people. Lid was Velma Smith's, my mother-in-law's, aunt and they came by to visit her and Jack fairly often, when we were there too. Jack and Earnest had known each other since they were young and had lots of stories of their many adventures. We always had lots of laughs over their antics. I could have sat and listened to them for hours at a time. Lid was funny too, and I thought she was quite a character. She dipped snuff and always had her Planters peanut can to spit in! If I remember right, one of Shirley's sons recorded or wrote down a lot of Earnest's stories. It would be wonderful if some of them could be included in this book along with so many other memories of him and Lid.

Jerry H: I went overnight camping/fishing with Earnest and Lid. In the morning Lid was making breakfast. Someone tied a frog to her apron string. She grabbed a cast iron skillet and was going to hit me, if I didn't remove the frog. It wasn't funny at the time.

Rodger McLane: Jerry, they both seemed to be very tough people. Emphasis is on tough. My dad loved them though. He said he could remember Paw walking through the living room and raising his leg up to the light hanging from the ceiling on his 80th birthday and saying look what he could do.

Jerry H: They were good people. Always ready to help.

Delores Harris Brown: Rodger, they were tough people, to survive the losses they suffered, and still continue to raise their children and maintain their wonderful sense of humor. I loved both of them.

Royce Lynn Johnson: Jerry, my grandfather, Edward Johnson said that Ernest, Lid and the whole family lived in a tent at Tabernacle while he worked as a mule skinner in the 2000 acre virgin longleaf pine. This was in 1948.

Mitchell Anthony: Jan, how many ever had Mr. Buford plow up your garden? Lot of folks used to do that. I haven't seen anyone plow with a horse or mule in many a year... a bygone art form for sure.

Jan Akridge: In the early '80s Billy's dad plowed a garden here with a mule. The last time I saw someone do it.

Jimmy Nell Adkison Lee: Buford plowed our garden with his mule many times, and I can still see him in my mind riding by in a flatbed trailer of some sort being pulled by his mule. His sweet wife, Mary, was the sweetest lady and so pristine...her bonnet and dress always ironed perfectly. Isn't it funny at these little thing we noticed about the true gentlemen and ladies of our childhood? Their manners were silently being learned by all of us who were blessed to know them.

The Ride

By Howell Adkison

Back in the '60s, my Uncle Jessie and Aunt Jewel Adkison lived in a white house across the dirt road (CR 1210) on the left of Mrs. Danley's. I bet it wasn't 25 steps from door to door. Since then the house that is there now has been moved back. Anyway, my dad (Hollis Adkison) and Uncle Jessie logged together back then. They worked several areas around. They helped clear the land for Toledo Bend and Sam Rayburn Lakes. I remember the giant tree-crushing machines that was used to clear some of the land.

Mr. Velt Warr was also working for Dad as a mule skinner. No one was allowed to work his best team, but Mr. Velt. In the summer time Dad would take me with him to help out. I wasn't big enough to tote the stretcher rig behind the mules, but I could lay the chains out to roll the next log onto the load. Anyway, one evening Dad told me to take Mr. Velt's team to the corral, because they were going to scout another area for the next day.

"Stay off the mules," he had warned me.

Now, I had seen Mr. Velt ride these mules every day. So I get out of sight around a curve in the road and crawled upon one, thinking that riding is easier than walking. I thought I could get to the corral before they did, and Dad would never know that I had ridden the team. When I got to the corral they had made it back. BUSTED. Dad started chewing me out.

"Son, them mules ain't never let nobody ride them, except me!" Mr. Velt said, laughing.

Well, for a dumb kid that didn't know anything, it was my lucky day.

'Nuf said about that.

Now, Uncle Jessie had a pair of mules on the job that were big, black, and beautiful. He worked them hard. They were so black that when they got sweaty they would be blue in the sunlight. Hence the term blue mule. Ya think?

Velt and Joyce Warr on their wedding day. Courtesy of Helen Warr Windham

The Three Mile Bridge

By Howell Adkison

Back when Rayburn (Sam Rayburn Reservoir) was being built, Dad was logging down on Hwy 147 on the Zavalla side. The three-mile bridge had already been constructed from Zavalla to Broadus. Working that day were Uncle Jesse, who had Bob Wilson skinning for him, and Uncle Auvie. We had finished that block, so Uncle Jesse decided to haul the mules to the house. J.W. Adkison, Uncle Jesse's son, my cousin and best friend, was with us. Dad had to go somewhere else, so Uncle Jesse and Bob got the mules loaded. We were using a 1962, half-ton, stepside Ford pickup with a tongue-pull, tandem-axle, cattle trailer with an open top. Uncle Jesse tied the first mule to the front of the trailer to make sure it stayed ahead of the axle. Bob brought the second mule in behind it.

We took off down the highway with Uncle Auvie driving, Bob in the middle, and Uncle Jesse riding on the outside. J.W. and I were sitting in the pickup bed with our backs against the cab. The bridge was constructed in sections. When we started across it, the pickup starts rocking up and down. This scared the mules. The one tied to the front pulled loose and walked backwards. So now, both mules are at the back of the trailer. The shift in the weight caused the front of the trailer and the back of the pickup to rear up together. Uncle Auvie tried to brake, only to make the truck jackknife with J.W. and me in the back.

Now you have to understand there was no water under the bridge. It was built above the tree tops. As you drove over the bridge, all that you could see was the tops of the hardwood. They were between 80 and 100 feet tall.

"Soot! Stop this suckerbill!" I heard Uncle Jesse holler.

About that time the trailer got sideways and started turning over, pulling the trailer off the hitching ball. The mules spilled out on the pavement. The back end of the truck set back down on the highway. Then Uncle Auvie could stop. J.W. and I jumped out of the back, very thankful that we didn't go over the side. Amazingly, the mules got up. They were skinned up pretty good, but otherwise, they were okay. Bob got them together and we checked for damages. We turned the trailer back up and hooked it back on the pickup. No problems. We opened the gate to load them back up. Guess what? It's not happening. No way. Bob couldn't even get them close to the trailer. Now, it is starting to get late. The only thing to do was to walk the mules off the other two and one half miles of the bridge. So, Uncle Auvie drove us off the bridge and stopped past the last road banister to wait on Bob. Just about dark, we got them loaded. On the trip home we had no problems.

"Mule Skinners" living up to the name.

<u>Jimmie Nell Adkison Lee</u>: Howell, I love this story...Daddy never talked much, so I never knew this! I hope you know that there are very few men alive today that are as tough as you guys. Y'all were the hardest workers, and I know you and JW were very young. You are a great story teller! You seriously should consider writing a book on your life. When Uncle Hollis died, I remember you stepping up to the plate as a young boy and becoming a man fast. Our growing-up trials made us tough.

<u>Howell Adkison</u>: I have a couple of stories about Uncle A that I want to share, but you kids need to know how tough and hardworking he was. I have worked with a lot of men over the years, but three men stand out above all others in being tough and hardworking. Uncle Auvie is number one on that list. I do not give credit lightly.

Employment

Watermelons, Grit Newspaper, and Snake Root

By Howell Adkison

As a young lad, I didn't always work in the woods. One summer I decided to pick some peas and get out watermelons. Mr. J.T. Holt needed some help, so I went over to help out.

"I don't think you are big enough. These are big ole melons," he said, looking me over.

I stared up at him and said, "Don't let my size fool you."

"Hop on. Let's go," he said, kind of grinning to himself.

We got down to the field and hopped out. I knew, immediately, that I had bitten off more than I could chew. Do you know how big those ole Black Diamonds can get in these sand hills? About fifty pounds. I struggled a bit, but done my part. I only busted one…Okay two, but we needed a snack anyway.

That same summer, I decided to become a newspaper salesman/delivery boy. I had found an advertisement in a magazine for *Grit,* a newspaper. I'm not sure if it was monthly or weekly. My first customer was our neighbor, D.L. Battles. From there I headed out on my bike over to Mt. Herman and then to Aiken. Do you know how much knee grease it takes to peddle papers in an area like this? It wasn't near as many houses then, as there are now.

Okay, here's the kicker. The newspaper had an advertisement in it for buying snake root. I thought to myself that I needed to talk to Mr. Carter Hooper, whom happens to be a local root digger. The next week or so, I was going up the road between Uncle Jesse' and the Danley's store. I came upon Mr. Carter with a tote sack on his back. I stopped and started asking questions about snake root. He showed it to me and answered most of my questions. I'll make a long story short. When I got five or ten pounds, I sent it off for my money. Do you know how long it takes to gather five pounds of dried snake root? Too long! I am pretty sure Mr. Carter had a honey spot somewhere. My sparse diggings didn't cut it. I cut my losses (worn out bike and broken shovel). I went back to being unemployed.

Summer Produce, Photograph by William Rudd

<u>Jerry H</u>: We loaded two trucks with black diamonds.

Daddy said, "Put the small ones on one truck; big ones on the other one."

Small truck averaged 35 lbs. Other averaged 51 1/4 lbs. I don't remember what year or where it was. Too many years have gone past.

Howell Adkison: I think he weighed one that was 80 lbs.

Jerry H: We had some white seed Watson's that weighed over 100 lbs.

Phillip Holt: Howell, when were you helping my dad, J.T. Holt?

Howell Adkison: Don't recall the exact year, early to middle 60s.

Phillip Holt: Howell, I was born in '62, so if there was a little bratty boy hanging around that was me. I could see him saying exactly what you said above, and I could see that grin when he said it too.

Jerry H: I peddled in Shreveport many times.

Phyllis Adams: You had to be tough to work for Daddy, J.T. Holt!! He raised many a watermelon on those sand hills! If you were loading trucks at our house, you were fed lunch, cooked by Mama, Eldora Koonce Holt! I still don't know how she cooked a meal every day for all the hands. And with no air conditioning! Those sure were great days!

Jerry H: The meals were always good and plenty to eat; not fancy, just good and good for you.

Karen Bittick: One of the sweetest memories I have of your dad is him leading songs at Mt. Herman Baptist Church.

Howell Adkison: It is amazing how the mind triggers memories when other things are put down. Yes, Mr. Holt insisted that we go eat and I did. Now, when a man will feed you on top of paying you that is who I want to work for.

Phyllis Adams: Howell, yes, he wasn't going to let anyone go hungry! They fed everyone!

Jerry H: Phyllis, most of it was out of her garden.

Phyllis Adams: Jerry, oh yes! We helped pick and helped cook! Sandra Wilson and I helped in the garden and with the cooking! Mama did most of it! Still remember all the boys that worked for daddy eating her food! And she always had a dessert for them too.

J.T. and Eldora Koonce Holt

By Sandra Wilson

Several people have commented about Howell's post about my dad, J.T. Holt. He farmed most of his life. He never got rich, but he loved what he did. Growing up in his house, as soon as you got old enough you worked on the farm. There were good years and bad years, but of course we, kids, didn't know, because we always had enough to eat and clothes on our backs. Our mother, Eldora Holt, made most of our clothes and taught my sister, Phyllis Adams, and me how to sew and make our own clothes. There was never a question about whether or not to go to church, that was not an option.

Our younger brother, Phillip Holt, was several years younger than us, but daddy put him to work early. Daddy had a fruit stand on Hwy 96 South for several years and leased the land across the highway to grow watermelons. He would put Phillip on the tractor when he could barely see over the steering, and Phillip would plow for him. This almost caused several accidents, as people on the highway would see the tractor, but couldn't see anyone driving it. Daddy always had a good time telling this story.

Phillip Holt: Yeah, Daddy would sit under a shade tree and watch me. The back of the seat was higher than my head, so it looked like nobody was on (the tractor) when I was going away from the road! I don't know how old I was when he put me on there by myself, but I remember driving in the watermelon field pretty young.

Sandra Wilson: Phillip, you were just a baby! Maybe 6 or 7. I know he didn't set the tractor to go very fast with you on it.

Phillip Holt: Sandra, no, and I think I had to stand up to reach the clutch. I remember going up a little hill, and he was behind me in his pickup. I went to stop and pushed in the clutch (which was all you needed to do in the field), and it stopped, but started rolling back. Of course it stopped when it hit the front of his pickup. He wasn't too happy with me.

Alec C: I hauled melons with Phillip and Mr. Holt. Somedays I thought we would melt it was so hot, but then we would haul hay, and it really got hot! Those Holts are some fine folks.

Alec C: Jerry, yes sir, Mr. Holt favored those Black Diamonds. I preferred the Grays, but he didn't.

Jerry H: I remember, when he grew white seed Watsons. Some were over 100 lbs.

Alec C: Jerry, oh I am glad I never saw those. I must have worked for him from about 1980-1984. Phillip was my best friend.

Jerry H: It was a few years before that. It was sometime in the '70s.

Phillip Holt: Alec, I remember that field past San Augustine. One summer when you helped us, the brother of the guy we leased from thought we were gone for the day. He was in the field when we came back, and said he was getting some "hog feed". Daddy looked over in the back of his truck, and he had a bunch of 40# melons in there. That was one of just a few times I saw him really mad! We were all sitting in the shade watching the show!

Jerry H: Did he have his shotgun (never loaded) with him.

Phillip Holt: Jerry, pretty sure it was in the truck.

Jerry H: I am sure it was. Give me a call when you have time.

Alec C: Phillip, oh it was there! He was HOT! Do you remember when he talked about General Patton? I will never forget some of his stories. I thought he was a badass. I was right.

Jerry H: With a good heart.

Alec C: Jerry, the best of the best, sir. I learned more from what your Pa didn't say about folks, than I can easily express. He just didn't bother being petty or mean. I try to teach my daughter by the example set by men like him and my daddy.

Jerry H: Always even keel.

Fred Borders: Your dad and the Barbes farmed the Harris place next to our place about 1959 or '60 in watermelons. Farmers back then wouldn't put watermelons on the same ground consecutively. The next year they put it in corn. Levi Harris, one of the land owners, was a large cattleman and bought the corn. That was the first time I ever saw a corn picker. I think it belonged to Cletus Sharpston. The reason I think that is, because Mr. Sharpston picked some corn for me a few years later when I was about 15 years old.

Jerry H: Fred, I remember Levi would buy all the corn. Dad had a corn picker, I don't remember when, a lot of years ago.

Employment

Sandra Wilson: Jerry, I remember the corn picker. He also sold corn to Doc Watson.

Phyllis Adams: Yes! Daddy did the watermelons, and Mama helped him every day! We got to go to Jess Warren's store and pick out our feed sacks for new dresses! Mama was a very good seamstress! I thank them both for the good values they instilled in all of us kids!

Jerry H: I was 5 or 6. I would steer the tractor down the row. Daddy would be on the back of the tractor plowing around the plants. I remember, when Dad plowed with a team of horses. Then he had a Farmall tractor, then a John Deer (popping Johnny), then Ford and Massy Ferguson.

Delores Harris Brown: My grandpa, Bud Luman, was a watermelon farmer. He peddled the area south of Shreveport. I rode with him almost every day in the summer. One year he raised a melon that weighed 101 lbs. I'm almost positive it was a Black Diamond. He hung it from the rafters, cradled in a tow sack, until my uncle came up from Houston to see it. We did have a picture of him holding it, but we lost it thru the years. I remember him showing it off to many of his friends as they stopped by.

Jimmie Nell Adkison Lee: Do I ever remember those huge Black Diamond watermelons!! My step grandpa was a trucker. One day on one of his runs from New Orleans back to Houston where he lived, he stopped his truck at Ura Lovell's store and walked down the dirt road to our house to see us. He left a bag of chewing tobacco for Daddy (Auvie) in the mailbox. For our mailman, Mr. Spears, he left a sample of Banjo sweet snuff! Well on the morning we were to load an eighteen-wheeler of Black Diamonds, Daddy had scraped together all the help he could find. Edward, my brother, and I sneaked that snuff and tobacco to the watermelon field. He dared me to take a dip of that awful tasting snuff and chew tobacco at the SAME TIME! Oh my Lord, it was so hot! I took the dare!! Not long I was feeling sick and dizzy AND I had eaten a big bate of watermelon. To say I was sick and green is an understatement! I threw up watermelon and stuff I had eaten, I swear, that I didn't remember eating!! I rolled under that big truck and that's where I stayed...too sick and green to do anything. Had I not been so sick, Daddy would have torn me up. He knew I had learned a good lesson! Never did I dip or chew again!

Sharon Fenley Prince: I would peddle with my grandfather, Stokley Andrews, back around the time of 1975 – 1977. I can remember, if we still had melons around 3 in the afternoon, he would tell me to start yelling, "Watermelon, 2-bits".

Alec C: Jerry, I hauled melons for Mr. Holt. They were the best years of my life. Just me and him and Philip! Three melon tycoons. Well, at least Mr. Holt was!

Eldora Gilchrist: My parents, Roland and Christine Barbe, were farmers. Daddy was primarily a watermelon farmer. In fact in the '50s, he was the largest watermelon grower in the county. He also grew experimental crops for A & M. We had some of the weirdest cantaloupes and watermelons you've ever seen. Daddy would rotate his crops from Waterman to Jericho. We had different fields. Daddy always put terraces in his fields to help prevent erosion. We had two tractors. I drove one and my little brother drove one when we were gathering the crops. By this time I was a teenager, we had the community teenage boys picking up melons and loading. Daddy had gone to town to weigh out an 18-wheeler. Everybody got to agging me and my brother on to race to see who could get loaded and get back to the shade first. Of course we lost some of the melons racing over the terraces, and wouldn't you know my dad drove up about that time. He got me off of that tractor and whip my butt good, right there in front of all those teenage boys. I was so embarrassed.

In the winter Daddy would go up in Arkansas and buy a truckload of apples. While he was up there he became acquainted with other truckers, and so on. In the spring they would come down to our fields in their 18-wheelers, and we would sell them melons. That's how the 18-wheelers got to coming into the fields down here in Shelby County from Arkansas.

Cooking on a Wood Burning Heater

Jan Akridge: How many of you cooked on a wood burning heater? Not me, we didn't have one. Billy did at home and his Mama Adkison did also. One day when I walked in Mama's the whole house smelled of collards cooking. They smelled so good! She always said they were better after a frost fell on them. I know that day they sure made my mouth water. She always kept a can of water on the heater. You could smell the wood heater all the way up to our house. Sometimes now I will smell that smell and it brings back so many memories.

Royce Lynn Johnson: I did a few years ago when I started living alone.

Mila Justice Smith: I grew up with electricity and never had to cook meals on a wood stove. However, Gene Edward decided we needed a wood heater after a couple of winter storms that left us without power for a week or more. He could build a fire hot enough to fry bacon, then I'd put in a pot of pinto beans. I certainly didn't learn to fix very many things, but we didn't go hungry.

Royce Lynn Johnson: Mila, for some reason, pinto beans taste better cooked on a wood heater.

Mila Justice Smith: Royce Lynn, they really do! Maybe because you cook them longer. It seemed like I wasn't in as big a hurry to get them done. I remember making gravy to go with deer meat we'd cooked on the wood stove at the cabin many years ago.

Jan Akridge: All that sounds so good!

Eldora Gilchrist: I remember when I was little, mother was still cooking on a wood stove, and after school I'd have to bring in the stove wood for the next morning. Then mother got a butane stove which was a lot better, no more stove wood except for the fireplace.

Lonnie W: Mila, bacon and pinto beans, what more does a person need?

Mila Justice Smith: Lonnie, maybe a skillet of cornbread!!

Lonnie W: Mila, now you're making my mouth water.

Mila Justice Smith: Lonnie, we have a small fall garden and we ate collards and cornbread today. Sure was good!

Hay Bailing

Alec C: I'm nominating me and Phillip Holt as the best hay and watermelon haulin' team that ever was! We stacked hay in some places that was being held up by the hay! Best times I ever had! Phillip was a stackin' genius y'all! And me?? Well, I was just too d@#% stubborn to quit!!

Phillip Holt: Alec, those were the good old days! Except, the drawback to being a good hay stacker was, I always got stuck in those little barns with no air flow! No way could I do that now!

Alec C: Phillip, no way! It's hard to believe we could do that all day and then hit the square!

Rhonda Chandler: I don't know, my daddy and 4 brothers were pretty awesome back in the day. LOL.

Alec C: Rhonda, yep. I worked with a couple of them and they were tough men. Annnddd we partied welllll into the next morning. My brother Quirt had to pull the pulpwood truck over so I, and Ronald, could get rid of breakfast. Goooddd times y'all!

Rhonda Chandler: Alec, yes, they were good times.

Alec C: My daddy bought the majority of his land from Mr. Doyle Russell "on a handshake and my Daddy's word." They didn't sign papers till a couple years later.

Days Gone By

Army Years (1966-1968)

By: Joye Hodges

In February of 1966, my husband Johnny was drafted into the United States Army. He was first sent to the Fort Polk Base near Leesville, Louisiana for several weeks. During that time I wasn't able to be in touch with him. Then, he was sent to Fort Hood, Texas, in Killeen for his B.A.S.I.C. training which would be for six weeks. After that was finished, he would learn where he would be sent. When he went to Ford Hood, I learned that the husband of a friend and neighbor of ours was also there. By now, they were allowing, not only letters and calls, but also visits. However, sometimes the visits were only allowed in the parking lot out in front of the barracks. I managed to find a few people to go with me, so that I could make that long trip, because I didn't want to go alone. Johnny's brother and his wife went with me once. My parents went once. James and Sally Chandler went. I invited Barbara Scates, my friend and neighbor, to go if she wanted to, which she did, and a couple of other wives came along as well.

All in all, that was a fun trip. We had to take our husbands back to the base. I don't even know how the other couples got off and back on base. Maybe they called a cab. Their husbands were first cousins from Beckville. The wives rode back home with me and Barbara to my house where they'd left their car.

At the end of the six weeks, Johnny learned that he was being sent to Germany and he went over on an old ship that was making its last voyage. Johnny said it creaked and groaned like it was on its last leg and he said he heard that it sank on its way back to America where it was to go into dry-dock. Johnny was in Schweinfurt most of his time over there. They were pretty rough on them and he really hated it, but I was just thankful he didn't get sent to Vietnam. So the first time he went, he was there six months, came home for Christmas for a month, then flew back for 13 more months. I stayed here and worked at my job as a legal secretary with McDaniel, Hunt and Fairchild, Attorneys at Law.

That was the worst time of our lives being away from each other so long, but I wrote him two letters a day, about 15 to 20 pages long each, front and back. He saved them and brought them home in his foot locker. He said they would be out on long training sessions or bivouac and it might be days before the mail would catch up with them, but that he would always get a stack of letters. Yet, some of the soldiers never got any mail. He always felt bad for them, because there he sat with all those I'd written to him. He said he sure was glad I had, 'cause it helped him make it through. It was a way of helping me make it too. .I didn't mention that Barbara was expecting her first baby when we went up there. I was a few years older than she. I believe, she was 16 at the time. Johnny and I married in 1963 when I was 21, and now it was 1966 and I was 24. I am 8 years older than Barbara. We didn't have our first child, Tamara, until 1969 when I was 27, so Tam is 52 now. Mark is 47, with five years age difference due to my miscarriage between them. Having Barbara as a friend and making that long trip with me was most appreciated and I love her like one of my family. Going through that life experience, we definitely bonded.

Sand Hill Plant Farm

<u>Jill Fountain Parker</u>: Who remembers the Sand Hill Plant Farm? A bunch of us kids used to go up there in the summer and dump soil out of plant trays or flats as we called them. We got paid 25 cents (I think it was 25 cents) a tray to empty them out in a big pile of soil and restack the flats. We thought that was pretty good to get to play in the

dirt and get paid to do it. LOL. I remember my mother worked there with Shirley Berg, Earl McSwain, Ricky Davis, and a few more. That was a lot of fun!

Jill Fountain Parker: Pam, didn't your mom work up there too?

Pam Adkison: Yes, Mama worked there. She enjoyed working with the flowers, and the people.

Tammy D: Dana, see what Ricky has got to say on this.

Jill Fountain Parker: Tammy, when they relocated it, I think, Ricky was the only one that moved with them.

Tammy D: Jill, Ronnie said that a guy name Chester worked there, who moved with the plant farm, too.

Rhonda Ward: I lasted 6 weeks there! It was hot work! I found a banking job after that...LOL.

Joyce Bright: When I was a little girl Earl McSwain's parents had a store there.

Alec C: That's good money there. We didn't get but a quarter a bail for hay. And Daddy wouldn't put up a bail less than 85 pounds! Dang it!

Dana D: Ricky remembers working with Wanda Fountain, Shirley Berg, Roy Dale Fountain, Miss McSwain, and Chester Bammel, whom moved to Huntsville when Ricky did.

Yancy H: I worked there for a couple days. LOL.

Ginger Russell: I got dropped off at the end of the road after school, walked down and worked there almost every day.

Carrie Adkison Graves: My mom [Nelda Adkison] did!

Jana Ivy: I worked there during my freshman year of college at SFA while living at home, before I moved to Nacogdoches. Shirley Berg always made us laugh to pass the time!

Nina Jo Hudspeth Walker: My sister, Claudia McClelland, worked there.

Tina Lawson Brown: A while after Richard and I married, I was a planter, then I watered plants. Mostly I remember Maxine Johnson, my sister-in-law's mother.

Angela Johnson Lawson: Tina, yes, my mom, Maxine McSwain Johnson, who later married Bill Jernigan, worked there along with her brother, Earl McSwain. My best friend, Robin Holt, and I worked there for a while, too. I remember Mom training us how to transplant seedlings into larger containers and flower pots. We also moved plants from one green house to another. As teenagers we enjoyed getting to work with all the other ladies there. They made the hot, dirty work fun. My mom loved flowers and loved helping them grow. After Sand Hills Plant Farm left, my uncle, Earl McSwain, and his wife, Evila, started their own nursery near their home on Hwy 7 where the old McSwain Grocery had been. Linda, I'm sure you and Karen can add more info.

Linda Winder: I just vaguely remember going to see Mama at work at the Sand Hill Farm. I remember us talking about what a beautiful place to work with all the flowers and plants. Did Ferrell Russell own it?

Angela Johnson Lawson: Linda, Yes, I think he did. I remember him being there.

Karen Bittick: I think Rachel Brown Fountain, Melba Parrish McSwain, Barbara Williams Scates... just to name a few... worked there too. I thought it was a beautiful place to work.

Days Gone By

<u>Cathy A</u>: I worked there for a while.

<u>Cindy Scates Eubank</u>: Mother worked there with Wanda. She loved it.

The Sawmill

W H & B T Gilchrist Sawmill, Courtesy of Eldora Gilchrist

<u>Eldora Gilchrist</u>: Back in the thirties or early forties before Dickie Gilchrist, my husband, was born, his grandfather, W H Gilchrist, & his father, Dick Gilchrist, had a big sawmill in the area of where Lewis Johnson lived. We have a huge picture of the mill. It includes; several teams of oxen and their yolks that worked there before mules were

used, about 10 men & several kids & three boys on top of part of the mill's roof. We also have pictures of Dickies' father's first log trucks. He had three from the thirties and forties. Lewis Johnson and Carlis Gilchrist drove two of them and Dickie's dad drove the other one. Lewis Johnson married one of Dickie's father's sisters, Trudie.

Carlis Gilchrist, Lewis Johnson, Mr. Dick Gilchrist (Dickie's father), &W H Gilchrist (Gramps), Courtesy Eldora Gilchrist

<u>Pamila Adkison</u>: In the late 1970s, we bought a tie mill from Mike Edwards of Garrison and put it behind our house in Grigsby. We cut railroad ties from hardwood delivered by local loggers. We employed four or five men. Mr. Marvin Cherry was the mill wright. Yancy, Frank, and Henry Hudspeth rounded out the team. My brother, Cole Hooper, worked there some. Occasionally, Mr. Cherry would pick up an extra hand or two in Nacogdoches.

Mike introduced us to Mr. Cherry. He had retired from the Nacogdoches Lumber Company. It was located about a mile down a road on the right off of Main Street, before one got to the railroad tracks. That is if you're driving from Grigsby. Howell had delivered logs there many times. Our operation ran part-time, depending on when we could get the hardwood delivered. Mr. Cherry wasn't looking for a full time job, so Howell hired him.

I met him the first day he came to work. Mr. Cherry was seventy-five and none too tall. I'm five foot three. I could almost look him straight in the eyes. He wore a fedora-styled hat. It was stained around the hatband and a bit dusty. Over his work clothes, he wore leg braces on both legs. Each step he took was accompanied by a clickety-clank.

"I have my doubts that he can do the work," I told Howell, "but we'll let him set his own pace."

Operating the forklift, Yancy would unload the trucks, spread out the logs for scaling and keep the work area clean of debris. The bark on the slabs and the trimmings off the lumber would pile up. He would feed the logs onto the loading deck on the right side of Mr. Cherry.

Mr. Cherry faced the inside of the mill shed and was behind a partial cab. He would release the log onto the carriage that extended out about thirty feet, horizontally to the left of the cab. Pulled by cables the carriage would cross in front of the mill wright. The four foot, circular saw blade was connected by pulleys and shafts to an old inline Detroit. The logs moved back and forth as the slabs were cut off. The friction of the blade slicing through the logs would make it heat up. We had a hose spraying water on the blade to keep it cool. Mr. Cherry would flip the log after each cut, until he had a nice eight or six inch tie.

If any of the slabs would make lumber, Henry would take one and guide it through the trimmer. There were six or eight blades on the trimmer table set four and six inches apart. The slab went between rollers that had teeth on them which grabbed it and pulled it through. Sometimes those teeth would grab the gloves off the men's hands and choked the rollers down. Frank caught the lumber and stacked it for binding. He used metal straps, binding clips, and a binding tool for this purpose.

I scaled the logs. If we were shorthanded, I operated the fork lift.

Mr. Cherry knew how to run a sawmill. He built a storage shed, and another shed over the mill that was open on all sides, so we could work when it rained. He was patient with us. Howell and I knew little about running a mill. We were all green hands. And young. Because of labor laws, I had to get a signed document from one of the crew's parents. That's how young the crew was.

My doubts about Mr. Cherry were groundless, but he must have had his doubts about his new job. He never expressed them.

We closed the mill after about two or three years and sold it.

Hoyt Hooper: That saw mill work and cross-tie hacking must run in the family.

Nina Jo Hudspeth Walker: Yes kids started work when they were just babes back then!

Shane Williams: I remember that mill being there. I helped Uncle Clark put the tin on the roof of the shed over the mill. LOL. Howell thought it was hilarious when I would jump from the roof to the pile of sawdust to get down faster. My feet would get hot up there on that roof.

Pam Adkison: We didn't receive enough raw material to keep it open full time. I lost several good hands because of that.

West Shelby County Fire Department

Ben Burns: Fane Adams was chief and then his son Jerryl took over.

Alec C: My Daddy secured the first trucks from the Forestry Service. It was a 2.5 ton truck. They added a tank and pump. We fought several grass fires and a couple of house fires.

Tamara Tanner: My dad (Johnny Hodges) was fire chief for several years.

Alec C: Tamara, your dad and mine were great friends. They worked together on the first trucks! Excellent men serving their friends and neighbors.

Tamara Tanner: Alec, yes they were!

Alec C: Tamara, I can remember when my daddy would let me come along to your daddy's machine shop. I was in awe of all the stuff your daddy could make. They don't make men like that anymore. Good to talk to you.

Employment

Photograph by Pamila Hooper Adkison

[This is one of our fund-raising events for the VFD. We sold grilled-chicken plate lunches. We are in front of the old Walmart Store in Center, Texas. The only ones that I can identify are Mack Dillard (standing up with the apron on) and Earl Campbell (manning the meat slicer).... PHA]

8

Jericho, Camp Worth, and Mt Pleasant School

Donna Adkison: We used to walk the Jericho loop. It would take us all day. If we got thirsty we would drink out of the ditch. We would go in the store on 711. I don't remember the name of the store. We called the lady "Whistler", because she whistled all the time. Life seemed so simple then.

Delores Harris Brown: Was the lady Mrs. Buna?

Sharon R: Delores, yes it was. Mom worked for her part time when we lived in Jericho.

Delores Harris Brown: Sharon, a couple of days after my son was born, I drove to the store. We only lived a mile from there. She fussed at me about being out & about.

Karen Bittick: Wasn't Buna originally a Bradshaw? Also I think the store that is on the left of 711 across from the Rudd/Powdrill store was owned by John and Lou Cindy Bradshaw. (I don't know if it was a store or house). Y'all correct me if I am wrong.

Delores Harris Brown: Karen, the one on the left was the Powdrill's, Mr. Bob Powdrill, I don't know who had it before him, and then Uncle Lon & Aunt Della McSwain lived in it. I remember Mrs. Buna too. Seems like she was a Bradshaw. That's the same store Mr. Roy Rudd originally owned. William Rudd and I talked about that once.

Royce Lynn Johnson: Buna was Shade Bradshaw's daughter. Hershel's aunt...married Fate Buford later.

Mila Justice Smith: I always thought Mrs. Buna was a very kind lady. Gene Edward and I had just gotten married, and I needed to put gas in the pickup. I'd never had to pump my own gas, so I went in the store and told her what I needed. She came out and showed this "city girl" how to pump gas without making me feel dumb. I thought it was wonderful having a store so close and saved having to go into town for something in a hurry.

<u>William Rudd</u>: The store on the left going north on FM 711 was built in 1939 by my parents Roy and Elsie T Rudd. They sold it in 1947 to the Bob Powdrill family. Mr. Lon and Mrs. Della McSwain lived in it afterward. Currently the Ratcliff family owns the property.

<u>Delores Harris Brown</u>: William, so that's the store your parents owned. I remember Mr. Powdrill, but I was too young to remember your parents owing it. I do remember when Uncle Lon & Aunt Della moved in it. Prior to that, they lived in my great grandma McSwain's old house on down 711. It was a big old house with a separate kitchen off the back porch. Aunt Della cooked on a wood stove, she was a fantastic cook, and they didn't have running water. The well was beside the long back porch. Neither one of them ever drove a car. They would go to church and everywhere else on a mule drawn wagon. I know they were so proud to move into the store/house!

<u>Mack Borders</u>: William, I was born in 1947 so I don't remember your parents owning that store. I remember Mr. Bob Powdrill, who Fred and I called Uncle Bob. We would ride our donkey up there and buy a cold drink or a Popsicle. We spent many afternoons sitting on that front porch in a metal lawn chair talking to Uncle Bob. We would always buy our donkey a Popsicle as well. Funny the things you remember ... she didn't like lime popsicles.

<u>William Rudd</u>: Mack, I spent many hours sitting on that porch watching the world go by.

<u>Delores Harris Brown</u>: Mack, I remember his old drink boxes with the metal bars holding the glass bottles, with ice cold water running thru the box. I never liked pop / cola drinks, so Pa always got me a Dixie cup of ice cream! Mr. Bob used to say I was the strangest kid, didn't like drinks or candy!

Royce Lynn Johnson: William, yep, Jericho was our whole "world" back then.

Karen Bittick: I guess you and I are talking about two different stores. I am asking about the one across from Powdrill store on 711 that Mrs. Buna had for years. I was wondering if anyone remembered John and Lou Cindy Bradshaw. I think they are the ones that built that building.

William Rudd: The building was a store with house attached. I don't know anything about its history before the 1940s. In the 1940s, the building was occupied by the Blake Nail family for a period of time and by the Roscoe McSwain family for a while. Lou Cindy, the mother of Blake Nail's wife, Syble (sp?), lived there with the Nail family. I don't think the store was open during that period. I know the store was open when the McSwains lived there. I don't remember whether the Nails or the McSwains came first during the 1940s.

Royce Lynn Johnson: William, Lon and Della never ran the store...just lived there. One hot summer night Lon called me to check Della's fan in her bedroom. I fixed it and asked about his fan. He told me he had never used one!

Fred Borders: I don't think there was ever a store there again after the Powdrills closed it in the early '60s. They continued to live there for several years if memory serves.

Delores Harris Brown: Fred, I know they moved, I think Mr. Bob's health got bad. Janie had gotten married. So they moved around Center somewhere. That's when Uncle Lon & Aunt Della moved in, sometime in the late or mid '60s, I remember going to their house for a housewarming with the family.

Karen Bittick, William, John & Lou Cindy were the parents of Elton, Elzie, Morris, Elvie, & Syble. I have forgotten if there were more. I don't think there was a store there before Hubert and Alice Langford, but I could be wrong. Syble married Blake Nail and they had one daughter (Jerri, now deceased). Feel free to correct me if I have gotten something wrong.

William Rudd: Karen, there was a store there in the 1940s when my dad and mom had the store across the road. I think John built the building and opened the store but don't know how long they kept it open. I know one Christmas in the early 1940s my dad and a gang of young guys were shooting fireworks in front of our store. One of the chasers shot across the road into the gas pump of the other store and exploded, setting the pump on fire. They managed to put it out before anything was damaged. I know that store was operated in the 1940s for a period by the McSwains. It was closed while the Blake Nail family lived there. That was long before Hubert and Alice moved in. Now, I've forgotten if Buna operated the store before or after Hubert. I think she came after Hubert. I do know that she was there in 1965. I remember visiting with her then.

Fred Borders: William, I remember that store building being there in the '50s, but it was closed. After the Powdrills closed, there wasn't a store open in Jericho for perhaps a year or so. I think Herbert and Alice opened it about 1960. They were the first ones, I remember, to have a store there. Buna was there after the Langfords.

William Rudd: Royce Lynn, Roscoe and Eva Lee McSwain operated the store when I was a young lad. Mary Helen was over at our house a lot back then. It was in the early 1940s when I was 2 to 5 and perhaps early 6 years old. Eva Lee was the one that managed it most of the time. I assume Roscoe was farming and doing other things. I'm not sure exactly what year they moved.

Royce Lynn Johnson: That's why I didn't remember...I was born in 1945.

Linda Winder: When we were kids in the 1950s, we (Linda Johnson, Jeannette McSwain, Marsha McSwain, maybe Edna McSwain) would ride our bikes from where we lived around Hwy 7 down through the Big Woods to get a soda or ice cream at Powdrill's Grocery. I don't remember the store across from it until the Langfords had it in the 1960s. We would also go straight sometimes and take the back roads to the little grocery Tony Lovell was running at Mt. Herman. All on sandy dirt roads on regular old bikes. Gosh, we were all in good condition back then!

Angela Johnson Lawson: I remember Herbert and Alice Langford having the store in the sixties, and then Buna Buford having it around late sixties/early seventy. I was born in 1961, and I have fond memories of our bus (originally #2; later #5 in mid-seventies and still #5 today) letting us get off to shop for snacks while it went down both dirt roads to take kids home. Mr. Stokley Andrews was the first driver I remember. I was the first one on each morning, and Bus #2 was cold in the winter. He'd let me sit right behind him and put my feet where the heat was blowing out! Good memory! We all knew to be lined up to get back on the bus with our snacks when he came back through, or we might lose our store privileges. Also, he kept a five-gallon bucket at the front for us to put our trash into, and we did! Mr. Stokley was being nice letting us buy snacks, and we watched each other to make sure he did not have to pick up our trash! I remember my mom and dad discussing how important this was. Mr. Stokley was not expected to pick up after all us kids. This was supported by our parents as a way to help Mrs. Buna. Looking back they were modeling "shop local" when it was just what good folks did to help neighbors and one another. Also, the concept "it takes a village" — everyone helping raise our children, because everyone knew all of us and kept an eye on us!

Delores Harris Brown: Angela, Mr. Stokley was my bus driver too, I rode the bus with Karen & you too. Later on I think, '50s and '60s. He was good to all of us, but didn't put up with nonsense either. I miss the folks on 711, I grew up where Mary Scates lives now, on that farm with my Luman grandparents.

Royce Lynn Johnson: County Road 1273 that crosses 711 at Jericho was known as the Shelbyville to Nacogdoches Road. It is on a map Reba James and I found of 1829. It was one of 3 roads into Texas at the time. It followed a trail made by the Indians. Davey Crockett could have traveled it on his way to the Alamo. It went behind Pearl Lake, came out at the Loftin Warr place and through Mt Herman. You can still see the road cut behind Pearl Lake.

Delores Harris Brown: Royce Lynn, we use to go thru that way to come out on the Nacogdoches Hwy. Is it still in use? It used to be very sandy in places and you would get stuck!

Royce Lynn Johnson: Delores, all the roads were then. Blacktop now.

Delores Harris Brown: Royce Lynn, yes I remember my grandpa putting chains on his tires to go certain places.

Royce Lynn Johnson: Delores, no 4-wheel drive then.

Jan Cruse: I was asked how Peacock and Pearl Lake got their names.

Royce Lynn Johnson: Peacock from a family there, and Pearl Lake from Lonnie and Troy January, who won the name contest for the lake from the stockholders who built it.

Debbie B H: I never knew that!! Lonnie and Troy were my granddaddy's brothers!! My granddaddy was Elzie January.

Days Gone By

<u>Stel H J</u>: We used to swim and fish in Pearl Lake. My brothers and a lot of others were baptized there!

<u>Jan Akridge</u>: Has anyone else driven down Camp Worth Road and come to Whisky Springs and felt the temperature go down? Most of my and Billy's dates were down the dirt roads or at Barbara and Jerry Scates' house. We took our children to swim in the Iron Ore Creek.

<u>Barbara J. Scates</u>: I remember when we were young enough to go four-wheeler riding on Saturday night, how I couldn't wait to get to Whiskey Springs to feel that cold air!!!

<u>Rhonda Chandler</u>: Lonnie W and his family are carrying on the tradition of still swimming in Iron Ore.

Jan, last time I was there I was with my kids and Cord Fountain. A black panther came to close for our comfort. I haven't been back there since.

<u>Jimmie Nell Adkison Lee</u>: How many of y'all played at Big Ditch and walked through Gunnels Cave. As a kid they looked huge!!

<u>Jerry H</u>: Jimmie Nell, many times.

<u>Karen Bittick</u>: Do any of y'all remember having baptisms in Big Iron Ore Creek?

<u>Jill Fountain Parker</u>: Karen, they also baptized in the [Lowell] Russell pond right there in Aiken.

Delores Harris Brown: Mt Pleasant used to have baptisms at Pinkston Lake. It was just down the hill from the church. There used to be a lodge house there a long time ago. I think when Mr. Pinkston still owned the newspaper.

William Rudd: It was known as Peacock Lake, before Pinkston bought it. I have been to baptisms there.

Sharon Fenley Prince: I remember a house, or maybe the lodge, there by Peacock Lake. It had a dog run.

Delores Harris Brown: Yes, it did & a fireplace. The best I remember, it was built with logs, or maybe part of it was.

Mila Justice Smith: Delores, Gene Edward's folks lived in that little house on Peacock Lake. He was born there. The house was still there when we married, but nobody lived in it and apparently hadn't in years. It burned down a few years after we married. I don't remember exactly the cause, but I'm thinking somebody was there partying and it caught fire. Gene Edward's sister and brother-in-law bought the place and built a house on it. That house was struck by lightning and burned to the ground. They rebuilt then several years later, and sold it to the Goodwins who still live there.

Delores Harris Brown: Mila, it's a beautiful place! I have admired it for years. I had no idea it was one of Gene Edward's sisters. Which one? The last time I was there in October I thought I saw a for sale sign.

Mila Justice Smith: Delores, Betty Sue and Aubrey bought the place and lived there for a number of years. They sold it to the Goodwins, and they still live there. It's a really pretty place. They tried for a while to sell it. I don't know why they didn't, but they're good neighbors, and I'm glad they stayed.

William Rudd: Karen, my mom and dad, Roy and Elsie Tee Rudd, built and operated the W.R. Rudd Grocery store and Station at the Northwest corner of the Jericho crossroads. Today's FM 711 and CRs 1005, 1272 and 1273, from 1939 to 1947. They sold the store to the Bob Powdrill family. The McSwains also operated a store on the Northeast corner of the crossroads in the 1940s.

Delores Harris Brown: William, which McSwain family? I remember my grandma saying something about it, but I don't remember who she said had the store.

William Rudd: Roscoe and Eva Lee McSwain owned the store, I recall perhaps wrongly, because I was very young. She was the one that managed the store. I assume, he spent most of his time on farming and other business activities. I think, that was in the 1950s and perhaps the 1960s.

William Rudd: Delores, yes, I knew all of them and yes, Mr. Lon could be stubborn. After Mr. Lon and Mrs. Della died the property was sold to Michael and Sharon Ratcliff.

Delores Harris Brown: Karen, isn't she the one that played the piano at Salem? She could make that piano jump!

Delores Harris Brown: William, he was a good man, Ma's next-to-the-eldest brother. He sure loved to sing in Church.

Jericho, Camp Worth, and Mt Pleasant School

<u>Joyce Bright</u>: Now they have a nice paved FM 711 to travel, but when I was a little girl we had to turn off at McSwain's store that was located on Hwy 7. Then we had to go thru a big sand area. We really had to get a running start to not get stuck. That was before you got to Jericho. In Jericho, the Powdrills had a store. We lived a few miles down, off of that road. It was really in the Sandhills. We had so much fun back then. Foy Bradshaw lived on the road that we lived on. He raised a lot of peas and I remember picking peas for him. Mrs. Bradshaw would cook big dinners for the workers and it was so good. Their son or grandson, Charles Bradshaw, became a famous football player and later became a Lawyer. It's hard to believe the school bus came all the way to our house to pick up Velma and me for school in Center.

Sometime around 1946, there were a lot of animals, including foxes, with rabies. Velma's good friend's (Laura Jean McSwain) little dog got the rabies. All the kids that had played with the dog had to take shots. Velma had to take them, I think it was around 14. It was a real scary time.

We used to go swimming in Iron Ore Creek. I don't know how we all kept from getting snake bit. We also went to Big Ditch and Gunnels Cave. I think those were the good ole days. The younger generation just doesn't understand how much fun we used to have. We were very poor, but I guess we didn't know it. For a long time we didn't have electricity or running water. Before we finally got a box to hold block ice, we would have to put our milk in a syrup bucket and put it down in the well to keep it cold. We had to take baths in a tub after it had set in the sun and warmed. Gosh, I hope we went to school clean!

Sometime around 1946 or 1947 a tornado came thru the area, which would now be FM 711, not too far from Jericho. It did a lot of damage and completely demolished a house, killing a lady and baby. The house beside it was not touched. That happened when we lived on my Uncle Edward Johnson's property, which was probably 3 miles from there. I'm sure it did a lot more damage, but it stuck in my mind about the woman and baby being killed.

Royce Lynn Johnson: Louise, Evelyn, and Larry, the baby....only killed the mother..... Larry was badly hurt. Must have been around 1950.... Louise was born in 1945, and she was 5 or 6 then.

Delores Harris Brown: Royce Lynn, I remember Larry, Louise, & Evelyn when they lived with Mr. John & Mrs. Minnie behind our house. They walked up to catch the bus with me & Helen. Larry always called me his girlfriend. I was only 6 or 7 years old. He had a hard time with his legs. He was always so sweet to me. They also went to church with us. They are all in the Sunday School picture I have from 1955.

Beth B A: Pete Andrews' mother's name was Mavis Bernice. They lived in Crowderville.

Jan Akridge: Beth, Amanda's and J.C's baby is named after her and me!

Beth B A: Jan, yeah I knew that. I just forgot.

Eldora Gilchrist: Someone else you can learn a lot from would be Owen Warr. He lives up here in town, and he remembers when they lived at Camp Worth. When he was a kid, Bonnie and Clyde would come down there and hide out at the Muckelroy's, who (they were kinfolks) were teaching school at Camp Worth at that time.

Owen said when his mother saw Bonnie and Clyde come flying down

Jericho, Camp Worth, and Mt Pleasant School

the road, she would yell at Oren and his brothers, "Get out of the road here comes Bonnie and Clyde."

He said he [Clyde] drove like lightning.

I think one time, Wayne Hopkins told me that they lived at Camp Worth, and his [Clyde's] daddy was the school bus driver to pick up the kids and drop them off.

Rodger McLane: After Oren Warr's funeral last week, I got online and bought some signed pictures of the Four Mints. I also found this book by Gene Warr. Do y'all know if this is the same Gene Warr from Shelby County? (I know Oren wasn't in the group, but his visitation brought the group up in conversation.)

Jan Akridge: We did an estate sale for James Paul Wilson about a year ago. He was one of the Mints. He had 8 by 10 glossy picture of the man that played on Laramie. I still have an album and some 45s of the Four Mints. When I had Making Memories at the old Hughes house on Hwy.7 West, we had KDET (James Paul Wilson) to come out and do an on air interview with him signing records. It was so much fun!

Sharon R: My dad, Gilbert Rains, said. "This is Oren's brother."

Tonya McSwain Andrews: I grew up on Farm Road 711 close to the Shelby/San Augustine County line. I remember going down to Woodland Acres Lake and swimming with my brothers and sister (Roscoe McSwain, Stacey McSwain, and Cecilia McSwain Boles) and any other kids that were around. Momma (Venorah McSwain) would

Days Gone By

let us ride on the tailgate and go fast to give us a thrill. I often thank God for protecting us. We enjoyed swimming and picnicking there. We went to Old Salem Church. It didn't have a baptistery, so I was water baptized in the Woodland Acres Lake as well.

Tresa Danley Konderla: Tonya, I still use the term "dig out" like when we would ride in the turtle hull of Aunt Nora's car going down those sand roads!!

Tonya McSwain Andrews: She would get arrested today for the things we did back then. LOL!

Tresa Danley Konderla: Oh, my gosh, YES!! And we loved it and lived to tell the stories.

Tammy Fenley: What? Your mom, Venorah McSwain, let you ride on a tailgate? Y'all HEATHENS! LOL! CPS definitely needs to hear about this! ... I'm dying from laughter.

Cherry Martin Murphree: I remember those days, as a child going to the Sandhills to pick muscadines to make jelly. We would actually go out San Augustine Highway to get to the Sandhills. This was actually one of the childhood events that made a lasting impression.

Jarry Co, Jerico, Jericho

Fred Borders: What do y'all think about the spelling of Jericho community? There are many of the older people of the area that say there is no "h" in it, and the proper spelling is "Jerico." I have an old Champion article where it's spelled without the "h." The article is not dated but it was about 1949-50.

William Rudd: I've read both versions and don't know which one is the original. It may have been Jerico, if the name evolved from Jarry Co, an adaptation of the Jarry family name as I have suggested in an earlier post. My mom, Elsie Tee Rudd, preferred the Jerico spelling. I know they are not an authority on the subject, but Google Earth satellite and street level photos use Jericho. Unfortunately, there is probably no final authority on which spelling should be used, but I am willing to go with either option. ... I vividly remember the Sunday morning tornado discussed in the article. The Fults family lived about a mile from our house. We had a private phone line and provided local communication access to medical and law enforcement assistance during the event.

Mack Borders: Fred, February 12, 1950, was the date of the tornado. I was only three years old, but I have some vague memories of the aftermath of the storm.

Mack Borders: Fred, is this storm the same one that got Pa Andrews' barns?

Linda Winder: Fred, do you have the entire article on the storm?

Royce Lynn Johnson: Fred, Jericho got its name from W.A.F. Jarry, a prominent early family that settled in Jericho. It was originally Jarry Co.

Mack Borders: Royce Lynn, right. William Alvie Fitts Jarry. From what I found it seems he came to Shelby County from Arkansas after serving in the Civil War. I also read that he died in 1923 and is buried in the Mount Pleasant Cemetery.

Mack Borders: William, I googled W.A.F. Jarry and this came up under *findagrave.com*. Also, it seems there was a book written entitled, *William Alvie Fitts and His Descendants of Shelby County, Texas*. It is, of course, out of print and I don't know the name of author, the publisher, nor date.

Mack Borders: Fred, that's what I thought. I remember you and me walking around, and there were a lot of people cleaning up the damage. They built back one big barn to replace all the smaller ones.

Fred Borders: William, if Miss Elsie Tee preferred Jerico, its Jerico.

Fred Borders: Linda, no, I screen shot this from Facebook. I think it was one of William's posts.

Mack, I remember Pa's head got cut in the storm, probably from a broken window in his bedroom.

William Rudd: Fred, I think I'll do some more research on the name and perhaps if it should be Jerico, then we may need to launch a campaign to make it so.

Mt Pleasant School

Sandra Wilson: I have a picture of the old Mt. Pleasant school house that was behind the cemetery. It has 3 or 4 rows of children sitting or standing on the steps. On the bottom step is my daddy, JT Holt and Marcus's daddy, Travis Wilson, sitting side by side. One of the January ladies gave it to us and she wrote all the names of the children on it.

Row 1: Travis Wilson, J.T. Holt, Norris Andrews, Earl White
Row 2: Patty Wilson, Lester Rudd, Pearl Williams Galvis Andrews
Row 3: Lester Adkison, Donise Peacock, Wanda January
Row 4: Marie Peacock, Jessie Adkison, Eula Mae Bush, Sylvia Bradshaw, Mozell Williams, Vergie Dale Hailey
Row 5: Loren Williams, Vaudine January, Buna Bradshaw, Audrey Adkison, Louise Hailey
Courtesy of Sandra Holt Wilson

Schoolmates abt 1944

Mt. Pleasant School
1930's~1940's

School Site Today

Courtesy of William Rudd

1930-1945 Mt Pleasant School

By William Rudd

The Mt Pleasant School behind the Mt Pleasant Church was a two-room white building, front facing west, with a kitchen for preparing student lunches. The "big" room was for grades 8 through 12, I think, and the other room was for grades 1 through 7. The building was located on a knoll just north of the Mt. Pleasant Cemetery. The land for the school was donated by Frank Rudd, my grandfather. After the school, along with most other rural schools, was consolidated with the Center school system in 1945, the land reverted back to my grandfather. Many years later Royce Lynn Johnson bought the Frank Rudd place, including the school grounds. I have photos taken in recent years of some of Shelby Johnson's vegetables growing where the schoolhouse stood.

As a young lad, I often visited the school and spent the day there with my sisters, Glenda and Bobbie, until I was almost six years old, the year of the consolidation. My best memory of the visits was the delicious hot chocolate that the lady who cooked, Ms. May, made for me. Normally, students who lived nearby walked to and from school. After school on one of my visits, Ms. Twyla Campbell, a teacher, loaded her car with students, including me, and took us home. It was 1943 or 1944, in the midst of WW II. During the drive, Ms. Twyla led the group, mostly girls, in singing the Army, Navy, Air Force, and Marine theme songs along with the *Star Spangled Banner*, very inspirational for a lad of 5.

I was invited to visit the school once for a special bible-based presentation (A world apart from today's modern, advanced society of hate, destruction, and beatings, and no bible-based discussions in school). After the school bell rang, they announced that Mr. and Ms. Oley (sp?) would be "putting us on a show" (jargon of the day) at the end of the class day using flannel board images. I was 4, maybe 5. Now, I'm thinking, how are they going to do that, "put us on a show?" Are they going to mash us flat so that we will fit on the board? I panicked, was inconsolable and fell asleep crying. I was awakened at the end of the show and on the walk home found a copy of the little red book of John in my overall bib pocket that the Oleys always gave to the children following their presentations.

The previous, unpainted, Mt. Pleasant, one-room schoolhouse became the Mt. Pleasant church building and was remodeled in the 1940s. The school room had a stage at the far end from the front doors and wall boards at waist-to-head height were painted black to be used for chalk writing.

<u>Sandra Wilson</u>: When my daddy, J.T. Holt, finished school at Mt. Pleasant, he went to Camp Worth and graduated from there as valedictorian. He had to stay out of school for a couple of years to work on the farm. Even in his older years he could add a column of figures faster than I could on a calculator.

Mt. Pleasant School, 1920's/1930's

Mt. Pleasant Building Today
(After Renovation in 1940's)

Courtesy of William Rudd

<u>Royce Lynn Johnson</u>: The school was in a forest of virgin, longleaf pines. No underbrush. It looked like a giant park. It was not cut until 1948. What if they would have left a few acres? Shelby County would be famous!

Jericho, Camp Worth, and Mt Pleasant School

<u>Sharon Fenley Prince</u>: My grandfather, S.H. (Stokley) Andrews, went to school here, along with his brothers and sisters.

<u>William Rudd</u>: Sharon, my dad and mom had a very close friendship with Stokley and Adele. They played 42 together on Friday nights for many years, and they hunted together. Doug and I were the same age and were in school together all the way through Texas A & M. Doug was best man in my wedding, and I dated your Mom some.

<u>Sharon Fenley Prince</u>: William, I would love to hear some stories sometime, especially on Doug. My favorite one on Doug is him getting my grandmother, Adele Andrews, to sign a paper stating he was born a different year than he actually was, just to win a bet.

<u>Delores Harris Brown</u>: Sharon, I loved Mr. Stokley. He was my bus driver.

<u>William Rudd</u>: One of the nicest persons I have ever met.

<u>Delores Harris Brown</u>: William, yes he was, and he made some of those wilder boys on the bus toe the line. They soon learned he meant business. He would sometimes stop at a store and let kids get a drink or something special at the end of the school year. He caught me skipping classes one time when I got on the bus at a stop sign. He let me know that it should be my last time doing that, or he would tell my grandma. I didn't attempt that again!

<u>Jan Cruse</u>: Sharon, Mr. Stokley was the best bus driver I ever had. The bus did not move until we were all in our seats and fairly quiet. Also, we went to church with him and family. Good memories!

Days Gone By

<u>Mike Mills</u>: Y'all were talking about Camp Worth. My mother, Dorothy Mills, started her teaching career there in the early '40s. She left there and was hired by Martinsville about '48 or so.

<u>Shane Williams</u>: I was in her classes at Martinsville.

<u>Russell Andrews</u>: My daddy went there [Mt. Pleasant School] in the late '20s. His name was Talvis Andrews. His brothers were Norris and Ferris and had sisters, Donna, Hattie, Brooksie D, and Laverna Andrews. Hope I didn't forget anyone. My grandparents were Talmadge and Della Andrews.

<u>William Rudd:</u> I knew everyone on your list. We lived less than a mile from Talmadge and Della Andrews. Norris built my dad's and Mom's house on FM 711 in 1973. I moved to Dallas in 1962. I remember your family when they lived on the old Nacogdoches Road not far off FM 711, but I don't remember you. Are you a younger child?

<u>Russell Andrews</u>: William, I was the baby of the family. I remember your folks. Miss Elsie T was a tough woman and a worker, taking care of the cattle and mowing fields. You name it she could do it.

Jerico-Mt Pleasant History

<u>Jan Akridge</u>: Ok, Royce Lynn Johnson, keep me in check! This history of Jericho-Mt. Pleasant came from Reba January James. The beginning of the twentieth century this was a thriving community.

There was a school, three churches, and stores. They also had their own doctor, Doctor Bailey. Dr. Bailey took care of his community. He was known to race his buggy at full speed to get to the sick. In 1930 C.B. January and his wife Maude built a canning house. They sold to surrounding towns. Prominent families at that time were; Andrews, Bradshaw, Jarry, Hailey, Anthony, Johnson, Fults, Lucas, January, and Peacock.

Royce Lynn Johnson: I don't know what happened to all of the books and research that Reba had.

Jan Akridge: This was from the *Shelby County History Book # 2*. There was a bunch of us that submitted stories to make this book up 20 years ago. When I was looking up to make sure of the dates about the murder of Billy's grandpa, that I had put in there, I began reading other stories. I thought some might like to see them.

Royce Lynn Johnson: Jan, I would...I read the 1st one, but not the 2nd. I got lots of the history of the area from Idell Fults and Lewis Johnson.

Jan Akridge: Royce Lynn, she might have left her research to the museum. You need to write some post on here, so we can see what stories you know!

Royce Lynn Johnson: Jan, her daughter had a garage sale before I knew. I hope not! I will write one on Pearl Lake sometimes.... built in 1922.... soon 100 years old. It has an amazing history!

Alec C: Royce Lynn, my momma's Uncle Buddy Mason and his wife, Blanch, lived up the hill from Pearl Lake when I was a boy in the early '70s. We would drive up from Houston on the weekends so my daddy, Russel Cline, could help them farm. He would let me run trotlines with him at night. It was a little spooky on that lake at night! I was also baptized in those dark, sweet waters by Brother Warr by the loving mercy of our Lord. Sometimes, I can still recall just how the nights on that lake sounded and felt. Feels just like Home, if only for a second.

Linda Winder: Royce Lynn, when the weather gets too cold for you to be out farming, you need to write down all the stories you know. You have a fantastic memory, and all that history that you know needs to be recorded. I have said I was not going to do any more books, but I will definitely volunteer to put together one that you would write.

Angela Johnson Lawson: Linda, I was just thinking you need to help Royce Lynn get some of his stories written. He knows so much. He doesn't even realize how much he knows...no one does.

Linda Winder: We have talked about it several times. Probably need to get a tape recorder and get him talking! He has a fantastic memory and is a good writer so we need to keep pushing him. He heard so many stories years ago, and I am sure he remembers them all. I may need to start copying all this stuff he is putting on Facebook.

Sharon Fenley Prince: I did not know the history of Jericho/Mt Pleasant. I know my aunts, Rene and Ethel Andrews, and Honnie Andrews Borders, would tell us stories when we were kids, but I do not remember any of their stories. So please, Royce Lynn, I would love to read a book of stories about the community.

Jan Akridge: We sold the hard back books for $200.00 at the antique shop. They are hard to find. They did a remake to make money for the museum. I think they sold them at one of the festivals for $80.00.

Delores Harris Brown: Debbie Bryant Hutchins might know. Her mother was a January, I believe Maude was her grandmother. I'm not sure if she's a member, but I will send her a message.

Karen Bittick: Delores, there is nothing wrong with your memory either!

Delores Harris Brown: Karen, it gets cross-sided sometimes.

Shane Fenley: Wish I had asked my grandma more about the Andrews side of our family. I don't even remember my Papaw Stokley. What I do remember of Mammaw Adele, she wasn't talking anymore after having her strokes.

Mitchell Anthony: Shane, Mr. Stokley was a good man!

Shane Fenley: If the name didn't give it away, I'm the grandson of Dorothy Andrews Fenley and Gene Fenley. The one they raised. And of course, as a kid, I never asked questions, because I wasn't concerned. Now when I want to ask, it's only the grandkids and great grandkids of Stokley and Adele alive.

Karen Bittick: Shane, you can be very proud of your grandpa Stokley. I rode his bus all through high school. He would give us all little red New Testaments on the last day of school. I had to ride in the seat behind him several times for misbehaving. Your uncle, Doug Andrews, would drive for him sometimes. Doug was the one who taught me how to make change.

Fred Borders: Karen. Making change is a lost art. The change now is whatever the cash register says.

Sharon Fenley Prince: Fred. I have been at a cash register and my husband gave the girl a twenty. Then he proceeded to give her change, but she had already hit cash tender for $20. Blew her mind when he handed her a quarter. All we needed was the bills and a nickel in return. She had to go get her manager for him to tell her how much change we needed.

I worked for George and Geneva Burns at their store Handy Andy on Hurst St. If you did not know how to give the correct change without the register telling you, you would not be working long for Geneva Burns.

Dr. Bailey

<u>Fred Borders</u>: Dr. Bailey had two children that I know about, Bryan and Lyle. I've heard my mother, Honnie Andrews Borders, talk about walking to Mt Pleasant School with Lyle Bailey and Jewell Stephens Sanford. Dr. Bailey also had the first car in the community, and my mother, as well as the other kids in the community, learned to drive with it.

<u>William Rudd</u>: Dr. Bailey's home was on the hillside at the southeast corner of the Jericho crossroads. My dad and mom, Roy and Elsie T Rudd, owned that property for more than 40 years. The chimney and foundation bricks and rocks of Dr. Bailey's home were still on the place then.

<u>Fred Borders</u>: William, I never thought to ask where Dr. Bailey lived. I always assumed it was down the road past Stokley's. So his house was on the right of the road that goes east from Jericho? Was it there where that old black walnut tree hung over the road?

<u>William Rudd</u>: Fred, the doctor's house was up on the hillside about 100 to 200 yards from the road going east from Jericho and probably 200 to 300 yards from FM 711. I assumed it was facing the road going east (not sure) because of the foundation brick and rock arrangements.

The bricks and rocks are probably still there unless David Wheeler removed them. I sold our place to him in 2013 after my mom died. I remember the black walnut tree hanging over the road, but I don't remember exactly where it was. I've never seen a photo of the Doctor's place. There are no trees in the immediate vicinity of the house site.

Dr. Sidney Lafayette (Fate) Bailey

By Cherry Martin Murphree

My great-grandfather, John W. Bailey, was from Coffee County, Alabama, in the New Hope Community near the Pea River. He served in the Civil War with Company H, 61st Alabama Infantry, CSA. John evidently got married in Coffee County in 1871. I feel sure that John and Berry Bailey came with their mother, Clarissa Harlow Bailey to Panola County in 1872. Shortly after arriving in the Buncombe Community, they went into Shelby County and settled.

John Bailey farmed and operated a watermill and gristmill near the Short Community. This watermill operated from what was called the Bailey's Lake near Center. There were two water levels...that ran into the mill that caused the mill to operate the gristmill to grind their corn meal, and it would also split house shingles, etc.

John and Berry Bailey had 12 children. One of their children was my grandmother, Inez Bailey Martin, who was Dr. Sidney Lafayette (Fate) Bailey's sister. Inez was a twin. Inez Bailey Martin and her husband, John Benson Martin, Jr. had ten children. One of their children was my father, Woodrow (Dutch) Martin. John Benson Martin, Jr. and Inez

Bailey Martin are buried at the Old Salem Cemetery. They raised their family in the Harmony/Brady area near the Short Community.

A Younger Generation's Perspective
By Shane Fenley

I've seen a lot of post in this group about our area well before my time. I definitely love the history lessons, but I haven't really seen much of a younger generation's perspective. So I figured why not, I'll share mine.

I am the grandson of Gene and Dorothy Fenley and the son of Sharon Fenley Prince. The last generation of actually remembering our roads as dirt, the store was Mr. Johnny's before it became McSwain Grocery. The last to spend our days out riding bicycles, and the first generation of kids everyone typically got mad at for riding our four-wheelers up and down the dirt roads, usually at a high rate of speed.

We would ride the 8-mile block (I've checked it in a truck!) out of my grandparent's driveway to turn right at the "T" by what was my great aunt's and uncle's (CB and Maudie Gilchrist) to the Short area, swim in the creek along the way, then turn right again to go to the 4-way at Burton Egg Farm, and then right again back to the house. As everyone knows, with how the chicken trucks made the dirt up and down the roads, just how much of a task this was in the summer. We would ride to McSwain Grocery to go get drinks and hang out during the summer. We played baseball in the pastures, shot at things we probably didn't need to be shooting at, and just went about being kids.

Back when there used to still be two really high embankments along the road before you go closer to my grandparents' house, my brother, Dameon, and I built a clubhouse right along the edge of it to where we could see the road. Even tried to make a zip line from one side of the embankment to the other. It broke on the 2nd try. Thankfully, it broke with him and not me. We dug holes up the embankment to be able to climb from the road up to the clubhouse.

Once my grandparents got a 4-wheeler. When they weren't using it, I rode it to meet up with friends to go to the Sandhills. That is a spot just past the 4-way at Burton Egg Farm, if you go straight toward 96. Lots of sand had built up just right to ride around climbing hills and just goofing off.

We also used to go behind my great grandparents' house, Stokely and Adele Andrews, to go fishing in the pond back there and go camping. We used to catch some good-sized fish in there. I just haven't been back there since my teenage years.

I say all that to say this. It was nice to grow up in Jericho and be the kid I got to be [and to grow up] before video games, cell phones, and tablets took over kids' brains. We were the last of the outside kids that knew about the time it started to be getting dark, we needed to be getting home. The last of the kids who knew not to go in asking for a drink 'cuz we would be told there was a perfectly, good, water hose outside, and we knew to wait a couple minutes for the cold water.

As a kid, you always can't wait to grow up. But as an adult, it's nice to look back at memories made as a kid. I'll always have fond memories

Joy Tarver: Shane, my family always went to hear your granddaddy and dad play and sing. They were so good. Everyone loved your family and the get-togethers. They inspired me to learn guitar and piano, but I was never up to their standard.

Shane Fenley: Joy, his way of teaching me guitar was; "just watch my fingers and listen." I think I learned one song he always played that way, and I can still play it. The guitar I have of his I have to get fixed at the top of the neck. My oldest son Connor is wanting to learn guitar, so I gave him one of his old ones over the weekend. Although he was my grandpa, he was also my dad, because mine hasn't been around. He always talked about passing down his old things to my own kids, and that was the first I got to do so. He died a month after Connor had turned one. My youngest, Dawson Eugene, is named after him.

Shane Fenley: Yes! Walked those roads with Ma and Kathleen a lot picking berries and buckeyes! Don't see either anymore on that road. Berries are here and there, but not like it used to be. How everything was covered from the store to what was y'all's house doesn't really grow anymore.

9

Jericho and World War II

Days Gone By

World War II Louisiana and East Texas Maneuvers – 1941

By William Rudd

One of the largest peacetime training maneuvers ever conducted by the U.S. Army took place in 1941 in Louisiana and East Texas. The Great Louisiana Maneuvers were the first of a series of exercises held in 1941, 1942, and 1943 that eventually involved more than 400,000 troops and more than 3400 square miles of sparsely populated rural areas in north and west central Louisiana, as well as a large section of East Texas. Most events consisted of a series of exercises that were executed and evaluated before moving on to the next. Umpires observed the fighting and ruled on who and how many were killed or damaged. The 1942 and 1943 maneuvers were smaller than the first one, and planned exercises in 1944 were cancelled so that soldiers could be part of the D-Day invasion in Europe.

For the 1941 maneuvers, the top military commanders, including George Marshall, Dwight Eisenhower, George Patton, Joseph Stilwell, and Omar Bradley, among many others, came to central Louisiana to either command troops or observe the exercises.

There were two phases to the maneuvers' war games. In Phase 1, "The Battle of the Red River," both sides were given offensive missions. The Red 2nd Army would cross the Red River from the east side on September 15 and invade the Blue homeland. The Blue 3rd Army would move north to intercept the invaders and drive the Red force back across the river. All Phase 1 action was halted on September 19 when the outcome was no longer in question, as the Red east flank continued to crumble. East Texas was minimally involved.

In Phase 2, "The Battle for Shreveport," the Blue Army's mission, from its assigned territory southwest of the city between the Sabine River and Red River, was to advance upon and seize Shreveport, Louisiana. The Red force was much smaller and tasked largely with positional defense for a 100-mile zone west and south of the city. On September 28, the war games were halted by General Headquarters, "not by the tactical situation, but by the calendar."

Tactically the Blue forces were struggling to close in on the southwest side of the city. But a wide two-pronged envelopment of the Red west flank was underway by the Blue Army's 1st Cavalry Division. One column, led by General Patton, made a wide circuit through Nacogdoches and Henderson in Texas, attacking Shreveport from the northwest. An inner envelopment column crossed the Sabine in the vicinity of Logansport after passing through San Augustine and the important crossroads town of Center. General Patton led his 1st Armored Corps north around Caddo Lake, behind Shreveport's defenses and was on the outskirts of the city when the maneuvers were terminated. (Gabel, 1992)

World War II Louisiana and East Texas Maneuvers –1943

(William Rudd's first-hand account of the World War II Louisiana and East Texas Maneuvers)

I was only 22 months old during the first military maneuvers of 1941. So, the maneuvers that I have personal memories of must have taken place in 1942 or 1943. I was almost 4 years old in the summer of 1943.

During the War Years my parents, Roy and Elsie Tee Rudd, owned

Days Gone By

and operated the W. R. Rudd Grocery Store and Station at the Jericho crossroads, today's FM 711 and CRs 1005, 1272, and 1273. Jericho is about 8 miles southwest of Center, Texas.

About mid-afternoon on a summer day, there were loud roaring and clanging noises coming from over the hill to the East in front of our store on today's CR 1005. Soon what seemed to be an almost endless convoy of jeeps, tanks, motorcycles, artillery, troop carriers, and supply trucks began streaming over the ridge. The whole column turned north onto today's FM 711, leaving a huge arc of ruts 1 to 2 feet deep since none of the roads were paved or graveled then. Many of the practicing warriors were delighted to find a store at the crossroads and stopped for food and supplies. By the time the whole convoy had passed, they bought almost everything in the store.

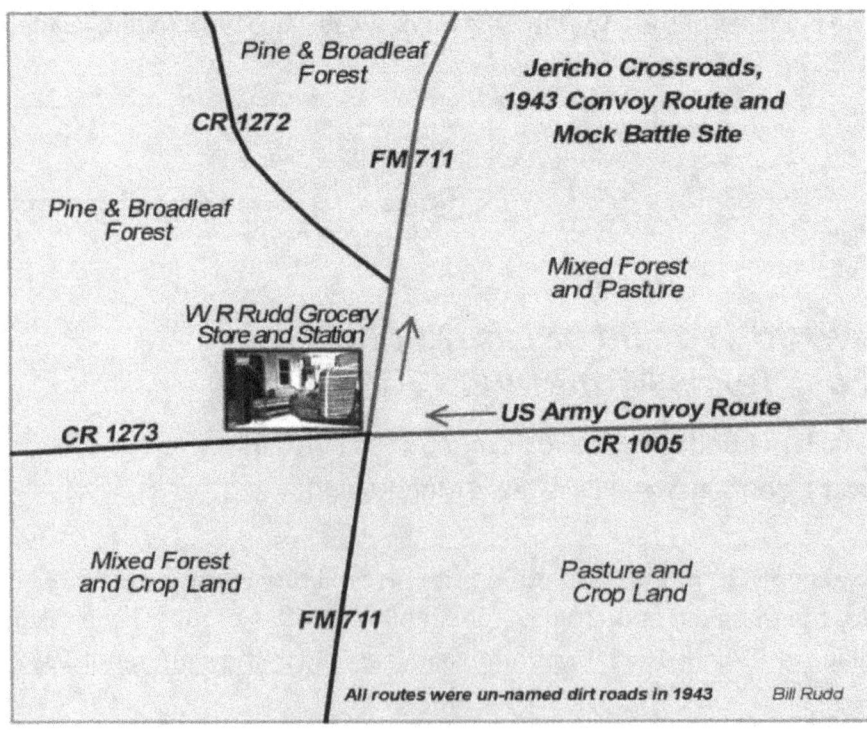

Courtesy of William Rudd

I watched from the front porch of the store as a tank came roaring across and lurched to a stop in front of the gas pumps where our truck is parked in the store-front photograph. Two young combatants popped the hatch on the tank, crawled out, went in the store, and returned with candy and Cokes. They opened a small compartment on the deck of the tank, put the Cokes in and crawled back inside, battened the hatch, and roared off to the north with the rest of the convoy.

There was an active battle in progress in the area, and I watched as soldiers of one team captured two enemy combatants under a small bridge that crossed the road in front of our store.

Many of the young soldiers replenished their canteens from our water well which was readily available on the south side of the store. Drawing water from the well was a new experience for some of the northern, city kids. They had a hilarious time pulling on the rope and stepping on it in order to make the next pull. It was an awesome day for a young 4 year old.

Howell Adkison: That had to have been an awesome day!

Jan Cruse: Wow! William, never knew so much excitement in our neighborhood.

Linda Winder: Very interesting story! I have never heard any of this. Thank you for sharing, and for having a great memory, and a great talent for research.

Karen Bittick: Linda, I guess the military maneuvers were before I was born. This is the first time I have ever heard of this. Thank you, William Rudd, for the photos and your memories of our Jerico Community.

10
W.R. Rudd Grocery Store

Jan Akridge: William, there is a story about your parents in the history book also. It has a picture of the store and a little boy and girl in front of the store. That was going to be the next post I put in here. You might want to tell the story.

William Rudd: Jan, thanks for thinking about me. I had considered submitting that write-up, but was concerned that it may be too long. Glenda Spradley, one of my sisters is the bigger one standing in front of the truck in the store photo. My other sister, Bobbie Smiley, is the smaller person in front of the truck. I was a recently born baby at the time.

Courtesy of William Rudd

W. R. Rudd Grocery Store and Service Station – Jericho, Texas

By William Rudd

On October 1, 1939, William Roy and Elsie Tee Youngblood Rudd and their children, Glenda Mixia, and Bobbie Evelyn moved from their home near the Mt. Pleasant Church of Christ into their newly built home, country grocery store and service station at the crossroads in the Jericho community. On October 30, 1939, just twenty-nine days after they moved, William Edward was born, making the family complete.

The store was located about five miles west of Center on Hwy. 7 and then three miles south on a crooked country road with deep sand beds in dry seasons and muddy hills in the wet seasons. The store was open seven days a week from 6:00 a.m. until 9:00 p.m. or later except for scheduled worship times at the Mt. Pleasant Church of Christ where the Rudds were faithful members. With time, this family store and its owners became the "Hub" and an important part of the bustling farming, logging, and ranching community.

A large long warehouse with a very smooth wooden floor was added to house feed and fertilizer for the customers, but it served two purposes. As Roy and Elsie Tee sold the feed in the winter and the fertilizer in the spring, room became available for roller-skating. With this in mind, Glenda and Bobbie received roller skates for Christmas. Then, much to the delight of the neighborhood children, there was a skating rink in Jericho. Later, an outside basketball court was added near the warehouse. Elsie Tee, having been a basketball star in school, spent many Saturday and Sunday afternoons teaching her children along with others. Teams developed and entire families joined in the fun.

Roy and Elsie Tee even provided a building for voting in the elections, and this was a source of community pride. On voting day, Jericho at the crossroads was the place for locals to gather, share family news, and discuss politics. Roy's father, Frank Rudd, being well informed because he was a keen reader, enjoyed spending hours with his friends talking politics and sharing his views in support of "his" president, Franklin Roosevelt.

Roy often said that Elsie Tee could have been a doctor. With snakebites, severe burns, illnesses, accidents, and expectant mothers giving birth to babies, she was called upon often by the community to administer first aid and give nursing care. Roy furnished ambulance service with his car.

Roy used his pickup and truck to deliver groceries, or feed and fertilizer to families without vehicles in the community. Elsie Tee took the orders and then minded the store while he was delivering and visiting. This helped to keep them abreast of the news, activities, and needs of their neighbors.

Following the bombing of Pearl Harbor, as many as eighteen young men from the community were called or volunteered for a branch of the service. Also, some families moved to the Gulf coast to work in the shipyards. But, those remaining tightened their belts with patriotic fervor and dealt not only with the loss of their young men and families but with food stamps and the rationing of shoes, sugar, toothpaste, automobiles, tires, and gasoline.

The community's surprise visit by uniformed soldiers on maneuvers from Louisiana, said to be General Patton's army, created excitement and a local awareness of the seriousness of World War II. Noisy tanks, jeeps, motorcycles, and foot soldiers were seen and heard as they arrived in the early afternoon. Their mock battles were fought around the store, skating rink, barns, culverts, and up and down the crossroads before they rallied around the water well. Locals still remember some of the soldiers trying to draw water from the well by pulling the rope down and holding it with a foot while pulling the rope again as opposed to pulling it up in the typical hand-over-hand fashion. Then, they converged on the store and bought literally all of the candy, cookies, soda pop, and other snack foods. Because of rationing, there was a waiting period before the items could be restocked. As the maneuvers moved on the next morning, all felt this was an experience of a lifetime even though the three-foot deep ruts from the motorcycle trips around the store had to be filled before customers could approach the gas pumps.

Party line telephones were available, but it became apparent that the business and the community needed a private line. Roy made a deal with the telephone company, hired help, purchased telephone wire, poles, transformers, etc., and built and paid for a private line to Center for the service. The phone buzzed day and night with war news and family messages. The death messages, and especially the loss of sons in the service, were the hardest to deliver.

Much activity was generated by Ollie Lovelady's decision to locate his sawmill within walking distance of the Rudd's store. Log haulers created even more traffic and there was much more business for the store. Most days the mill hands could be seen eating lunch and visiting with customers on the front porch of the store. Vienna sausage, potted meat, sardines, cheese, peanut butter, Cracker Jack popcorn, moon pie, and RC Cola soon became grocery staples. Often, one could smell dust from passing log trucks, freshly sawed lumber, and smoke from the burning slab pile, but no one seemed to mind.

Along with the grocery store, Roy, always pursuing a way to make a dollar and working hard to get it, hauled produce, cottonseed, logs, lumber, and apples. He even moved people. He and Elsie Tee grew large gardens, as well as peas, melons, and cantaloupes for the market, and they raised cattle, mules, hogs, and chickens. They always employed others to help. For some, part of the pay was room and board. It's hard to believe they managed all of this without electric lights, butane gas, running water, or bathrooms.

Truly, being the "Hub" of the Jericho community created a better place for living for the Rudds and for all of the families living there.

W. R. Rudd Grocery
Texaco Sky Chief & Fire Chief

Courtesy of William Rudd

Royce Lynn Johnson: Amazing....a part of the history of Jericho I didn't know. I guess it was sold later to Bob Powdrill, whom I remember.

William Rudd: Royce Lynn, my parents sold the store to the Powdrills in 1947.

Royce Lynn Johnson: William, where did they live before building the store?

William Rudd: Royce Lynn, they lived in the house across the road from the Mt. Pleasant church building.

Royce Lynn Johnson: William, the house was later owned by Lester Rudd?

William Rudd: Royce Lynn, yes Lester and Florence lived there for a few years. Then Lester built a new house next door toward Jericho. They subsequently built a new house near the Center city limit sign on HWY 7.

Royce Lynn Johnson: William, so the house they lived in was the Elton Fenley house, directly across from the church.

William Rudd: Royce Lynn, yes.

Delores Harris Brown: I remember when Lester & Florence & Carl lived across from the church. Then moved to Center. I think, Carl is in the 1955 Mt Pleasant Sunday School picture I posted awhile back.

Jan Akridge: Love this! See it was better you doing this than me hitting the high spots, LOL.

Debbie B H: WOW!! As many times as I went to that store as a child, I never knew that your parents originally owned it. Thanks so much for taking the time to write all of that down. Who are the two little girls in the picture? Glenda and Bobby?

William Rudd: Debbie, Yes. Thanks for the comments. They are probably 4 or 5 and 8 or 9 years old. An interesting item in the photo. The gas sign: 17 cents a gallon. Another unrelated note. I don't know if you know that Dianna and I were married in the Hurst Street Church building, and your Dad conducted the ceremony.

Debbie B H: Awwww, I did not know that, but I know that my mom and dad thought the world of your mom and dad.

Shelby Johnson: While standing at the crossroads a highway patrol asked me if I owned the road.

I told him, "Yes, I do. Two miles in both directions." Jerico blessed.

Jan Akridge: You go Shelby!

Rhonda Mc: Shelby, is this the Ratcliff house now, or the Old McSwain Grocery?

William Rudd: Rhonda, this property is currently owned by the Ratcliffs. The old McSwain Grocery was across the road (FM 711) from this property. That building is still there, but it is not occupied.

Shane Fenley: Mr. William, it actually is occupied. While the store isn't open, one of Ronnie and Donna McSwain's daughters lives inside the house part of the store. After Donna's mother passed, who lived inside the store for years, it has had a few of her kids living in it as well. At least the building I'm referring to is the old McSwain Grocery.

Karen Bittick: I really enjoyed this article. The photo of the store in Jericho brings everything into perspective since I was born in 1947. It is hard to believe that I never knew any history prior to Mr. Bob Powdrill. I knew Mr. Roy and Mrs. Elsie Tee mostly as farmers.

Delores Harris Brown: William, your dad's & mom's store was the exact location as the Powdrill Store? I would love to see a picture of your mother & dad. She was my Sunday School teacher for several years. I thought a lot of your parents.

William Rudd: Thanks Delores, My mom taught bible classes for almost 60 years. They sold the store to the Powdrills in the fall of 1947.

Delores Harris Brown: William, I know your mom is the one that found Uncle Burt McSwain when he went missing. She found him in the woods. I think she was squirrel hunting.

William Rudd: Delores, yes, she and her sister, Duetta, hunted squirrels together. They were hunting on my Mom's old home place on the old Nacogdoches Road not far from Mt. Herman. My Mom noticed what she thought was a pile of clothes someone had thrown away near the creek. When they were ready to go home she walked over to check them out and found that it was Burt. She said he was lying on his back, and he was holding his wallet and his hat. I don't know if they came to any conclusion about why he died.

Delores Harris Brown: William, it was strange to my grandma. She had cooked a big dinner for Thanksgiving. Uncle Burt didn't feel like coming to the house for dinner, so my uncle took him a plate of food that afternoon. He wasn't seen after that. They searched for him for about 3 weeks. There were a lot of rumors floating around, but the final investigation said he suffered a heart attack and died probably the same day.

Royce Lynn Johnson: Delores, He was a long way from home. It was snowing. He became disoriented and lost. Probably died of exposure.

Delores Harris Brown: Royce Lynn, was it true he had gone hunting with his little dogs?

Days Gone By

<u>Royce Lynn Johnson</u>: Yes...they never found it.

<u>Fred Borders</u>: I remember the Powdrills well. I was aware that the Rudds had established the store. We lived about 1.5 miles southeast from the store. My brother Mack and I walked, bicycled, or rode our donkey there many times for a Coke and candy bar or 22 shorts for our single shot rifles.

The Jericho Community – A Vital Contributor to Shelby County's Economy

By William Rudd

The Jericho Community is a key contributor to the Shelby County, Texas economy. Community residents participate in several county economic drivers, with poultry production being a major one. My family, one of the earliest participants in the county's poultry business, built our first chicken house in 1948. Back then it took 10 to 12 weeks, or more, to produce market-size birds. Today there are about 70 chicken houses in the immediate community with each one housing 10,000 to 50,000 (average 20,000) chickens. From day-old baby chicks, growth to market-size birds takes about 7 weeks, permitting growers to cycle up to 150,000 chickens a year through each house. That's a lot of chickens, more than 10,000,000 per year. So, if you are grilling chicken, you may be grilling Jericho chicken.

Photographs by William Rudd

In addition to enhancing the local economy, this industry promotes county and area-wide development of hatcheries, feed mills, processing plants, building and supply businesses, trucking, and other commerce. It also produces an abundance of chicken manure fertilizer to improve pastures and hay meadows, creating a symbiotic relationship that has enhanced cattle production. Lesser, but important, businesses include timber production, oil and gas production, and vegetable farming. Pine forests, growing crops, green pastures, grazing cattle, and chicken houses dominate the community's landscape. Numerous community residents are owners and operators of major wholesale, retail, and service-oriented businesses in Center and other locales across East Texas and Western Louisiana.

Photographs by William Rudd

Photograph by William Rudd

Delores Harris Brown: Loved growing up there! I do remember how bad the flies were in the summer though. I spent many summer days with a fly swatter in my hand.

Angela Johnson Lawson: Delores, We still keep a few fly swatters around, because they are needed at certain times of the year!

Linda Winder: Those early chicken houses were so primitive compared to today's houses. I saw a feed scoop at an estate sale years ago, and the people running it said they had no idea what it was.

Delores Harris Brown: Linda, one of the first jobs I had was debeaking chickens in some older houses. My best friend & her family lived on an egg farm. I would help them when I was there. I'm sure it's totally different now. There are a good many chicken farms here in South Georgia too.

11

Tabernacle School

Days Gone By

Joyce Bright: Has anyone given you any information on the Tabernacle School, which would have been near where you turn to go to the Church and Cemetery off 711. Mama [Lillie Mae Williamson] and my Aunt Vircle McSwain went to school there. I think it's great you're taking your time to do all of this.

I know the school there would have been probably sometime around 1930. They also had a syrup mill in that area and I can remember it when I was a little girl. I think Shine Hooper had it. Becky could probably find out from Vivian. I wish I had a better memory. The book will certainly be interesting.

Russell Andrews: Tabernacle was right below were Justin Lee and Anna Boles Lee lives. My dad went to school there for a while, walked from Jericho every day to Tabernacle School.

Barbara J. Scates: I remember my mother, Vaudine Luman, talking about living at Tabernacle. Momma was born in 1926. I am not sure if she went to school there. I do know she went to school at Camp Worth. Her parents were Selmer and Eunice Luman. All their children were named with a V; Velma, Vaudine, Vernice, Vastine, and Verlon. A generation gone, but not forgotten.

Delores Harris Brown: My mother, Merline Luman, went to school there also. She went to Camp Worth and Tabernacle too. I have some school pictures from there. Mama was born in 1924.

Karen Bittick: Delores, My mother and daddy both went to Tabernacle & Camp Worth Schools. They were both born in 1925. There was also a small store across the road from James Lee and Mildred McSwain. Uncle Roscoe McSwain had it back in the fifties & sixties. The little store sat on the right on 711. It was probably a mile from old Salem Church. It didn't have gas pumps. I think it was something to keep Uncle Roscoe occupied. I remember him always having a cigar in his mouth. LOL.

Russell Andrews: Delores, my sister, Janie Graves, used to help Murline on a newspapers route. A very nice woman.

Delores Harris Brown: Russell, I remember Janie. I was probably in the car too! I usually sat on the newspapers, rolling them. Thank you for the compliment on my mama.

Tabernacle I

Interview with Billie Oice Johnson

Born July 12, 1927

Daughter of Edward Johnson and Lena Anthony Johnson

By Linda Johnson Winder

I began my education at 6 at the Tabernacle school, a one-room school. My older brother Royce and I walked about a mile to school each day, usually, going down a trail through the woods from our house. My mother, Lena Anthony Johnson, had gone to Tabernacle when she was a child in the early 1900s. She attended several grades before she had to leave school to stay home and help her mother, who was sick.

I don't know if I went to the same building as she did, or whether it was a new one. I did hear the story that horse races had been held at that site before it became a school.

When I attended in the 1930s, the school building had no indoor plumbing, no running water, and no electricity. The boys would go to the spring behind the school and get a bucket of water for us to drink. We all drank out of dippers.

A wood heater supplied the only heat. We would be so cold after walking to school on winter mornings that we would have to be careful and not get too close to the heater too fast.

I can remember children from several families attending the school – the Andersons, Scotts, Mancils, Lumans, Uncle Leo McSwain's kids and Uncle Lon McSwain's kids, James Lee McSwain, the Holts. Joe and Jackie McSwain came later. Usually about 20-40. By the time I was in the fourth grade, there were two teachers and a partition was put down the center of the room. The school was well-built with a stage and double front doors.

Daddy was one of the trustees as was Mr. Anderson. Foy Bradshaw may also have been on the board.

We had both a morning and an afternoon recess. The favorite games at recess were jump rope, London Bridge, Ring a Round the Rosie, Pop the Whip, and softball. The boys would play Mumbley Peg with knives.

There was a Flying Jenny at Tabernacle. It was built using a split log, and boards were on each end to hold onto it. The big boys would have to turn it and spin it. It would really go fast, but I don't remember anyone ever getting hurt on it.

Every Friday there was a spelling bee. The older students competed against one another, and the younger students competed against one another.

I considered myself a good speller, and I did well in the competitions.

We mainly studied the basic stuff, spelling and arithmetic. My favorite subject was geography, because it was more interesting.

We had books and took them home to study. Mama made me a little book satchel. We didn't have electricity at home, so I studied by lamplight.

All the students brought their lunches from home, many using syrup buckets. These lunches usually had a biscuit with ham or sausage leftover from breakfast. Some brought baked potatoes or sweet potatoes. If there was dessert, it was homemade teacakes. It was rare to have fruit.

Every December the students would put on a Christmas program, with all students having speaking parts. They always had a tree in the school decorated with homemade ornaments including strung popcorn and construction paper chains. I remember Norman Anderson putting soot on his face to do a blackface part.

Miss Ursela Jarry was my first grade teacher. Her sister, Norma, also taught there, as did several girls in the Jarry family. Royce's first teacher was Miss Hulon Biggers. We didn't have any screens on the windows or doors at school, and one time a dog wandered in. She threw a book at the dog. At some time Miss Swanzy taught 1st through 4th, and Mr. J.B. Taylor had 5th through 8th. Mr. Duff Warren taught after Miss Swanzy and Mr. Taylor left. Zettie Wood taught there at one time.

Miss Octavia McSwain taught one year. She got her daddy's truck and put a tarp over the back of it and drove a bunch of us students to Timpson to see the movie *Snow White and the Seven Dwarfs*. It was my first movie, and the greatest thing I had ever seen. I almost didn't get to go because I had the croup, and it was a cold night. I was getting hoarse, so they let me ride in front in the cab on the way home.

We only had school for seven months. That was all the trustees could afford to pay a teacher.

After I finished seventh grade at Tabernacle, I went to Camp Worth for the eighth and ninth grades. I remember Miss Wilma Watkins teaching at Tabernacle while I was attending Camp Worth, because she boarded at our house. It was 1941. The trustees had several places she could stay, but we had a new house, and she wanted to live with us. We didn't have electricity or running water, but we had a butane stove and refrigerator and butane heaters. She and I had to share a room, but she was a very sweet lady, and I did not mind.

Mr. Jim Anderson, who was one of the trustees, did not want Tabernacle to consolidate with Camp Worth. He insisted that the school consolidate with Center.

TABERNACLE SCHOOL ABOUT 1905. Ledora Warr, who was born in 1892, is labeled at the top right. Her sister Ethel Warr, who was born in 1899, is believed to be the little girl on the front row with her hands close to her face. Warr siblings Noah and William Tom are probably also in the photo. Ethel Warr attended classes for all eight grades offered at the Tabernacle School.

1905 Tabernacle School, Courtesy of Linda Johnson Winder

Tabernacle II

Interview with Maxine McSwain Jernigan

Born February 5, 1925

Daughter of Lee McSwain and Ethel Warr McSwain

By Linda Johnson Winder

[This is an interview with my mother (Maxine McSwain) on Tabernacle School. I found it very interesting that my grandmother (Ethel Warr) went there and that my grandfather (Lee McSwain) went when he was grown. LJW]

I started school at Salem or the Ironosa School in San Augustine County, which was down the road from our house in Shelby County. Teacher J.B. Taylor boarded at our house. He would walk with us to school, but we always had to walk behind him, never in front of him.

I went to Tabernacle in the third grade. My sisters, Janie and Christine, and I all walked several miles to school each day.

My mother had gone to school there in the early 1900s, probably from 1906-1914. She went to school until she was in the eighth grade and would have liked to have gone more, but the only school with more grades was in town, in Center, and she had no way to travel there. Walter Williams, who was later her mail carrier, was one of her teachers at Tabernacle. Another teacher was _____Warren, Jess Warren's sister.

My father, Lee McSwain, also attended school some at Tabernacle about 1916 after he married. He had broken up all the land he was going to cultivate so, while he was waiting for time to plant the crops, he went back to school for a while. He was already about 25 then, but he wanted to get more schooling.

The Tabernacle school had double desks. I shared one with Odessa McSwain.

Herschel Anderson was one of the students. He was crippled, so his older sister, Thelma, would take him to school. She would then sit outside until recess was over, making sure none of the kids picked on him.

I went back to school at Salem for the fourth grade. Miss Hulon Biggars, who later married Carlton Dance, was one of the teachers. She lived in Brady and would ride her horse seven or eight miles through the woods back and forth to school every day. The horse was named Easter. My sister, Janie, spent the night with her one night and got to ride behind her on the horse. The Salem school was in a big two-story building with two large rooms on the bottom for the school. The Masons had the top of the building.

When I was in the fifth grade Salem consolidated with Camp Worth, and I went on to finish high school there.

We were able to ride a school bus to Camp Worth. My uncle, Hooker Warr, drove the bus some, as did Pa (Edward) Johnson. Royce Johnson, who was a student at Camp Worth, started driving the bus when he was 16. There were no paved roads anywhere and he, absolutely, delighted in driving up rainy, slick hills. He would get a running start and gun the bus up the hill, going from the ditch on one side of the road to the other with all of us screaming and trying to hold on. We never got stuck. He was a good driver.

Linda Winder: I liked her description of Daddy driving the school bus. I remember how he loved to drive up muddy hills with everyone screaming and trying to hold on while he went from one side to the other.

I found my original notes from this interview. Mama also mentioned that Bill (Daddy's sister) sometimes drove the bus to Camp Worth. One day the bus was running hot and caught on fire under the hood and Bill jumped out and beat out the fire with a book. She was probably about 14 or 15. Things were very different back then!

Tabernacle III

By Linda Johnson Winder

In the late 1960s, somebody was rummaging around on the Foy Bradshaw property and said a bunch of old desks were stored up on the top story of the barn across from his house.

Foy Bradshaw had died, and no one was living in the Bradshaw house then, which was at the beginning of the dirt road that went from FM 711 to our house.

Mama said the desks were from the old Tabernacle School, which had been close by. It was a school from the late 1800s to the 1930s. Lots of family members had attended - Ma Swain and her siblings, Mama and her siblings, Ma Johnson and her siblings, Daddy and Bill, etc. Pa Johnson, and Foy Bradshaw had both been school trustees.

Mama wanted one of the desks, so one day we stopped her little Falcon in the middle of the road. I don't remember if she climbed into the barn, or just watched the kids and did a lookout for somebody passing by, but my sister-in-law, Louise, and I got into the barn and got some desks. Most were in bad condition, but I know we got 4-5. I have no idea how we got them home in that little Falcon.

Pa Johnson said we really weren't stealing, that he had as much an interest in stuff from that school as Foy Bradshaw did.

Mama still has her old desk near her back door, holding magazines and papers and dog leashes.

I used mine as a side table for years, but took it up to the History Center a few years ago to use in a display for school stuff from the early 1900s.

Tabernacle School

The school was in a forest of virgin longleaf pines. No underbrush. It looked like a giant park. It was not cut until 1948.

Royce Lynn Johnson: What if they would have left a few acres? Shelby County would be famous!

Lena Anthony

Grandmother of Royce Lynn, Linda, Angela, Karen

Lena Mae Anthony is listed on the school census records for Tabernacle School on May 28, 1915, as being a 12-year-old white female. Her brother, Eddie, age 15 is also enrolled. Familiar surnames on the records include; Fountain, Holt, Hatton, Jernigan, Lucas, McSwain, Peacock, Warr, Wheeler, and Wilson. The census taker lists 51 names of children, all aged 7 to 15. The Anthony land was close to the school, and she and her siblings walked through the woods to the building.

History of Tabernacle School

By Mattie Dillinger

"The Tabernacle School was establish in 1893 when the trustees were W.B. Metcalf, T. Faulk, A.G. Cook, and R K Gibbs.

The next year the trustees were J.J. Walker, W.A. Pounds, W.H. Franks, and N.B. Wheeler.

Miss Eula Griffin and Willie Dear were teachers in 1895. Other early teachers were W.C. Cartwright and Elbert Lane (1910); Jeff Bridges (1911); J.B. Shofner (1912 when there were 48 pupils}; J.W. Williams (1916); Dura Wheeler and Josie Glynn (1919); Linnie Holt (1920); Sam Monk (1921); Jessie Beck and Nora Anderson (1922); Mrs. Vessie Morse (1923); Miss Twila Biggars (1924); Mrs. Viola Rudd (1925); Sam Monk (1926); Miss Fleta Thomas (1928-31); Miss Norma Jarry (1931-33); Mrs. Ford Walker (1933-35); J.B. Taylor and Mrs. Vera Swanzy (1936); M.D. Warren and Mrs. Zettie Wood (1937); Miss Octavius McSwain (1938); T.A. Cook (1939-42), when there were 22 pupils.

In 1949 the school was annexed to Center in July.

June 4, 1938, Tabernacle No. 50 was divided into two parts. The south joined the Camp Worth No. 14 and north Tabernacle joined Center No. 901. (Dillinger, n.d.)."

12

Old Salem School

Linda Winder: 1930s Salem School? I found this photo in my files, but am not sure if this is Salem School. I think it is because my mother, Maxine McSwain is pictured, and she mentioned that Clarence McSwain went to Salem with her. She also said J.B. Taylor taught school there and boarded with her family. She went to both Salem and Tabernacle before going to Camp Worth. The names are on the photo. She was born in 1925 so this would have been in the early 1930s.

Back row: Vivian Sharpton, Velma Luman, Valeria Sharpton, J. B. Taylor, Addie Mae Golden
Middle row: G. W. Golden, Clarence McSwain, Vaudine Luman, Maxine McSwain, Paul Whitton
1st row: Verniece Luman, Fannie Golden, Brown Golden, R. C. McSwain, Willie McSwain, Mamie McSwain

1930? Salem School group picture, Courtesy of Linda Winder

Jan Akridge: Barbara, your mom looks like a little Wanda! I love these old pictures!

Gwen Taylor Stewart: Thanks so much for sharing. I had never seen this picture before. This was before Dad and Mom were married, and all of those Lumans and Goldens and McSwains were our mother's cousins.

Gaye T L: Our dad talked about going to college a while, and then taking time off to teach, until he finally graduated.

Royce Lynn Johnson: This is Salem School. Not many know of it. It was just below the county line in San Augustine County. Mama said J.B. Taylor boarded with them and walked to school with them while he taught there. Years later he taught me at Center.

Russell Andrews: Royce Lynn, Mr. J.B. taught me in the 7th grade. That would have been somewhere around 1975. His wife, I believe, was secretary for the high school principal.

Gwen Taylor Stewart: Russell, our Mom was the Business Manager for the school district. I think Mildred Ashby was secretary back then.

Russell Andrews: Gwen, I knew she had something to do with the school. Also, how many years did your dad teach all together?

Gwen Taylor Stewart: Russell, My brother and sister say 38 in Center. Not sure how many more before that.

Karen Bittick: J.B. Taylor taught me in eighth grade. That would have been in 1961. I remember him getting all of us signed up with Social Security.

William Rudd: J.B. Taylor taught me in 1951 at the Center Elementary School. One of my favorite teachers. He and my Mom, Elsie T Youngblood Rudd were neighbors during their early years.

Adam J: Vivian Sharpton was my Grandmother.

Russell Andrews: All the Lumans' names started with a V.

Mila Justice Smith: Russell, 3 of the Luman girls are pictured. Vastine and Verlon, the only boy, were the youngest and I guess they hadn't started school yet.

Pam Adkison: Mr. J.B. Taylor taught me in the seventh and eighth grades. I remember him walking around campus with his math books tucked high under his arm. Good man.

Jerry H: J.B. Taylor also was a bus driver.

Joy Tarver: If you brought him cashews, he let you chew gum in class.

Russell Andrews: Joy, he loved chinquapins too. If he caught you eating in class, he would say, "You got enough to go around?"

I would say, "No sir."

He would say, "Get on down to the office. I'll be there in a minute" and you would get a paddling.

Pamela Johnson Sanford: I loved Mr. Taylor!! He was an awesome teacher, and it was fun to be in his class!

Old Salem School

J.B. Taylor, Courtesy of Gwen Taylor Stewart

Cemetery

<u>Linda Winder</u>: Cecilia McSwain Boles spearheaded a project to get a historical marker for Old Salem [Cemetery]. The dedication was held in 2013. Jean Anderson and I held silent auctions at McSwain Reunions to help pay for the marker, and Cecilia got other donations.

Linda Winder: The plaque on the front of the marker notes the contributions of the McSwain families to Old Salem.

Rodger McLane: I find Old Salem to be so peaceful and beautiful. I don't know much about my family that way, but I think they settled in one of the prettiest areas of Shelby County. Once a year I try to ride the road from Old Salem to Mount Olive and Old Sardis to check on everyone's headstones. It's beautiful country.

Mila Justice Smith: I grew up in Corpus Christi, and the cemetery where my mother's family is buried is very large, and there are always people around. So the first time I went to the Old Salem cemetery I thought it was such a lonely place. But I quickly came to realize the beauty and peace that's there is what is most important. There are people that I love very much that are there now, and now it feels like home.

Delores Harris Brown: Mila, I understand that peaceful feeling. I feel that at Old Sardis when I go there. I usually stay for a good while and sometimes take lunch and just sit.

Funeral Wakes and 24-Hour Vigils

Jan Akridge: I don't know why I was thinking about this today, just wondering if any of the older ones remember when friends or loved ones were laid out at their homes after they died. They had people that sat up with them all night. I myself never knew anyone. After I married, Billy and Jerry Scates were asked several times to sit up with friends and family at night at Magnum's. They don't do this now!

Helen Windham: The Warrs continued to stay all night at the funeral home until fairly recently. My brother, Jimmy, stayed when my dad was at Magnum's, and I stayed with my mom at Watson's.

Brandi McLane Kelley: Helen, I remember Dad, and I'm sure some others, staying at Mangum's when Ma Warr died. I remember Lacie and I spent the night at Mamaw Ruby's.

Helen Windham: Brandi, Yes, I think my daddy stayed also. Daddy and some of his sisters stayed when Grandpa died. I don't remember who all it was.

Erma Bush Parrish: When my daddy, Travis Bush, died in 1968, he was brought to our home, and a couple of men would sit up all night. He always told my mom, that he wanted to spend his last night at home.

Mila Justice Smith: After we married, Gene Edward was asked to sit up at the funeral home several times. I remember he and several other men stayed all night in shifts.

Jan Akridge: That's right Mila. They did sit up in shifts.

Helen Windham: I have pictures of my uncles, EC and LC, in their coffins at our grandparents' house at Aiken in 1957. My great grandmother Warr was in a bedroom of her daughter's house in town. Aunt Essie and Ernest Stanfield lived on Appleby Sand Road.

Delores Harris Brown: I stayed all night at Magnum's the first night when my 2 year old son died. Everyone tried to make me leave, but I wouldn't. A few people had already said they were staying also.

Jan Akridge: Delores, I'm so sorry, I would have done the same thing also.

Days Gone By

<u>Delores Harris Brown</u>: I know my Grandpa Luman went several times also to sit up at the funeral home and people's houses. We all went when Mr. Adam Bradshaw passed away, his body was at their home. I was pretty young, and every time I walked into that house for years after, I could still see his coffin sitting there.

<u>Angela Johnson Lawson</u>: My dad, Royce Edward Johnson, often stayed at night at area funeral homes when a relative or friend passed away. As a little girl in the '60s, I can remember being curious as he'd be preparing to leave to go to the funeral home to stay for the night or for a shift.

As a child, I wondered how these men who were asked were brave enough to stay at the funeral home at night. Apparently, fear was not a problem for these men like it was in this little girl's vivid imagination! LOL!

Also, I knew how my daddy was normally in bed by 8:30 pm, because he was tired and had to get up early for a new day's work. I knew most of the men had to do the same. Dad tried to explain how he and others stayed, because it was an honor to be asked.

<u>Rex-Janie R</u>: Angela, it was also out of respect for the person that had passed away.

<u>Linda Winder</u>: Daddy was constantly on call to "sit up" at funeral homes and/or be a pallbearer. Was this tradition still in effect when he died? I don't remember. I do remember that someone was at the hospital ICU waiting room day and night the 10 days he lived after the tractor accident.

<u>Angela Johnson Lawson</u>: Linda, Yes, someone stayed around the clock while he was in ICU for 10 days, and they did at the funeral home, too.

Jill Fountain Parker: I remember my granddaddy (Jack Fountain) spending many nights at the funeral home with different family and friends. It used to be a custom, but time has changed so much. I think, you can still request it at some funeral homes. The last one I remember someone staying all night was in 1995. I think, that same family has lost more family since and stayed all night with them. Some being pretty recent! They were firm believers in that!

I also remember the funeral home calling Mamaw (Rachel Fountain) 2 or 3 times a week to come and sing at funerals. Sometimes she knew them and sometimes she didn't. She would take off work and go sing at them. I went with her a good bit and we would go in the back door and be in a little room, that nobody could see you, with music instruments (piano, organ ...) and microphones. They would have live music, not recorded like they do now. She sang at a many funerals!

Angela Johnson Lawson: Jill yes, she did! I remember Mrs. Rachel singing at many funerals.

Shane Fenley: I've done it once in my lifetime as a kid. When my grandpa, Billy Wayne Hooper, passed. I remember staying the night up there with Cole and Dameon. As a kid, I slept pretty good on the couch. As an adult, idk [I don't know] if I could sleep on that couch again!

Jill Fountain Parker: Shane, I remember staying one night with my granddaddy too. It was a little strange, but I guess I slept pretty good too, 'cause I don't remember much of the night!

Shane Fenley: Jill, now I can't tell you how many times I remember your grandma and my grandpa singing at funerals!

Jill Fountain Parker: Shane, no telling how many they sang at!

Shane Fenley: There's honestly not. Then growing up, at least for me,

Wayne Hopkins always hitting them up to sing specials at church. Which they were all already in the choir!

Joy Tarver: Ms. Rachel could sing like a bird. I loved to go to church when she was there.

Shane Williams: The last time I remember anyone doing this was at Carla Davis McSwain's funeral. My dad was asked to stay a shift. That was the first time I had ever heard of it happening.

Elaine Belanger: The last one I knew of in our family that actually was laid up in home for viewing was my Uncle Charley Williams -Tammy D's dad. Grandparents (George and Venorah Williams) lived there in Aiken on the first dirt road passed Excelsior School on route, going toward Nacogdoches, and just this last couple of years we have had no family standing by to sit up with family at FH.

Karen Bittick: Wakes, or keeping 24-hour vigils, are another lost tradition. As far as I know they are no longer popular.

Delores Harris Brown: Karen, sad too, that it's gone. Neighbors, family, and friends always gathered around to show their support and offer comfort. Grieving families didn't have to worry about food or cooking. I think about that Ray Stevens song "Sitting up with the Dead" he nailed it. (He was born here in Albany, Ga where I live).

Brandi McLane Kelley: I mentioned this to my Mom, and she said 20 yrs. ago when my grandpa died that they wanted to do this, but the funeral home wouldn't let them.

Helen Windham: Brandi, really? Do you know the reason they would not?

Brandi McLane Kelley: Helen, no, Mom said she remembers asking about staying, but can't remember the reason the funeral home gave for not letting them.

Pam Adkison: Howell's maternal grandmother, Grandma Turner, told a story of when she was twelve. Her mother sent her with another lady to a family whose mother had passed. Her task was to help prepare the mother for burial. They laid her out on a door, and prepped her for viewing by the community. Those were definitely hard times.

Sharon Fenley Prince: My Grandfather Fenley was the only one that I ever remember being brought back out to his home. His name was Ira Fenley, or most knew him by his nickname, Big Bud.

Gaye T L: I was only 2 when my Grandma Taylor died, but I remember vividly my dad picking me up so I could see her. We were at the old Taylor home in Mt. Herman that later burned. I remember Daddy sitting up with people at the funeral home. The story behind that tradition was before embalming, somebody had to be responsible for keeping the body iced down.

Delores Harris Brown: Gaye, I have a similar memory of my Great Grandma McSwain, Mama holding me up to touch her face in her coffin. This was at Mt Pleasant Church, 1953.

Jan Akridge: I remember reading it was to keep cats and other animals away.

Joyce Bright: I remember when they used to bring the deceased bodies to the homes for Visitation. Mr. Willie and Ms. Pearline had a beautiful baby girl who died. She probably was around 2 years old. They lived in the little white house, past Aiken, going around the curve on the hill before you get to Shirley Gilliland's, right on Hwy 7. It's grown up around there now, but I never pass by there that I don't remember that precious baby. I wasn't very old, but it was so sad.

Days Gone By

Lost Near Ole Salem

By Pamila Hooper Adkison

A few years back Mother and I were going to the graveside services at Salem for a family member. I had never been there, but got directions from Tonya Andrews, who was working at Sardis Church, and Venorah McSwain (via cell phone). We took the road past Venorah's, like they told us. When we got to a certain tree, where five roads met, we took the right. We kept going and going and going. Somehow we came back to that tree. Therefore we reasoned, it was the left one to take. We kept going again. We traveled until the road, which the oil companies had topped with white limestone, turned back into gravel. I think, we would have come out at Grigsby on Highway 7. Before we got to 7, we met the funeral procession at a narrow, low place in the road where a creek crossed. As soon as the cars had passed, we looked for a place to turn around. When we finally found a big enough area to turn around, we headed back. We increased our speed and tried to catch up, but all that was left to follow was the dust that the others had stirred. Then someone in a big hurry passed us. We kept on going. In a few minutes he comes barreling back toward us. He gets even with us and stops. I don't know this crazy-driving person. We're in the piney woods of East Texas. Only God knows we're here. Besides I wasn't going to lower my window, until the dust cloud he choked us with had blown over. I inched my window down.

He yelled, "You going to Salem?"

We nodded, "Yes."

"Follow me," he said.

He turns around, and takes off. What did we do? We followed, until he turns onto a road between some trees. From the well-maintained road we could see the edge of a house. We looked at each other. Should we follow? No, we kept going. We stopped at a house that had a Texas DOT pick-up in front and got directions back to Camp Worth Road.

We made it out of there. We never found Ole Salem. One day we may try to find it again.

There are two things that I surmised that day: 1) The other driver is probably my kinfolk. There are a lot of Hoopers in this area. Some of us do lean toward the quirky side. 2) Always have a full tank of gas.

Mila Justice Smith: That's too funny!! My Dad would have said you were so far back in the woods they'd have to pipe daylight to you!

Jan Akridge: You can get lost on those roads!

Pam Adkison: Jan, We have that habit of getting lost, but we always find where we want to go. Not that day!

Jill Fountain Parker: Jan, and in the woods! Randy and I got lost walking in the woods down by Camp Worth. We parked in an area right behind Momma's car. She was already in the woods walking the old railroad tram. She was looking for arrowheads. Randy was a little kid the last time he had been back in the woods there. I had only been one time, but went in a different way. I was convinced I could find it, if I stayed by the creek. Well, we didn't find it, nor Momma, and got lost in those big woods. For 9 hours we walked. We came out past Woodland Acres down by the big metal bridge right past Fountain town. We had to borrow someone's phone and call Granddaddy to come get us and take us back to where we parked. If we would have left the creek like Randy wanted to, we would probably still be lost today. But we did get to see some beautiful hills and valleys, beautiful woods! Most all my kin are at Old Salem on my mother's and daddy's side.

13

Grigsby and Martinsville

Days Gone By

At the Foot of Grigsby Hill
By Venorah McSwain

Clark Paul Williams, Sr., my dad, was a generous, loving man and a very good neighbor. He was a produce farmer and sold produce in Timpson, Nacogdoches, and Shreveport. Emma Fancher Williams, my mom was a hard worker. She helped Dad in the fields, and so did the children; Shirley Berg, Edwena Higginbotham (Edwena didn't help much in the fields. She stayed in and cleaned house.), Venorah McSwain, Thomas Williams, Clark Paul Williams, Jr., and Carolyn Caldwell. On Saturday nights Daddy would reward us by taking us to the drive-in theater. All that could fill the bed of his pickup went.

The neighbor kids were not left out either. Dad loved kids. He gathered up all that wanted to go, especially the Danley kids. After farming for years, Daddy built a grocery store at the foot of Grigsby Hill. He would let everyone charge, whether they could pay it back or not. That was the kind of man he was. He was going broke, so he started selling bibles door to door. He gave praise to the Lord for this turn of events.

There was a Church of Christ on the Yarbrough land next to the railroad track across from the grocery store where the old post office was and the depot. Dad's sister, Vida Williams Wakefield, was the postmaster. She eventually moved to Oklahoma City. Daddy's sisters Eva Russell and Marie Widmer moved to Maryland and worked for the Internal Revenue Service. Aunt Beurl contacted a fever at age fourteen. The fever went so high that she had brain damage. I remember us all loading up and going to San Antonio to see her. Dad even brought her home one time, and let her stay for a few days! Such a big hearted man. Many years later Aunt Eva brought her to Oklahoma City, where she and Marie retired, and put her in a nursing home to be close to them. She passed away there; happy.

Daddy's father, Thomas Ubanks Williams, was the country doctor in the Grigsby-Aiken community. T. U.'s brother, Dr. Thomas Williams, resided in Beaumont, and his brother, Walter Williams, was a rural mail carrier in Shelby County.

Mother made us kids stay out of the candy case. Daddy came in the store; hot and tired and hungry. He got a piece of candy, ate it and wanted another. Being an adult, he got another piece of candy. I was a little child watching him, knowing that I couldn't have a second piece.

I said, "No way! You can't have another one Daddy!"

He blew up and using his size twelve shoe, kicked my butt out the front screen door onto the dirt outside. As the story goes, the building was a lean-to, and I hit my head on the ceiling as I came down! The moral of the story is; "Don't poke the hungry bear."

The Monk Smith family lived just across the dirt road, and he passed away leaving a wife, Della and four kids (Minnie Mae Luman, James, Carl Jr. and Geraldine). Geraldine never married; she worked at the Tenaha School for Doc Watson. Della cooked lunch for Daddy and all of us kids. They lived in the old depot. I remember Della running around the table and stirring all the bowls of food, so we could see steam rising, when she would see Daddy coming. He was their only meal ticket!

She would say, "Dr. Bill is coming!"

Daddy rode to house calls with his father, and one day a man followed him to the buggy and said; "Are you teaching Dr. Bill how to be a doctor"? I can't pay you today, will a dozen eggs be ok? Keep letting that boy go with you."

That's how my dad got his nickname, and "Dr. Bill" stuck with him all his life. I sure wish his grandson could have known him. Doc. Dr. Bill Caldwell.

How I Learned to Make Biscuits

Mother had what we called a bin in her cabinet, and a large wooden bowl that had flour in it. Hull out a hole in your flour, put baking powder, a ball of grease, a teaspoon of salt, and two cups of buttermilk. Mix thoroughly. Grease an iron skillet and pinch off a ball of dough and put it in your hand and then turn it in grease and put it in the pan. Will make about 8 large biscuits. Then, put the bowl of flour back in the bin for the next time. O yeah, I had to stand in a chair to reach the bowl and put it back! Mother would rather go to the field to work, than to cook.

The first batch that I made, she and Uncle Lovis were planting tomatoes in hotbeds. They gladly ate the biscuits.

Old man Yarbrough would come in the store and get him a bottle Coke and take four good swigs, all at one time and finish it off. All of us kids marveled at it!

Tommie O T: Great stories! My Mama Oliver and Mother made biscuits that very same way.

CarlenEmma W: The simplicity of this lifestyle brought tears to my eyes. We plan to make biscuits just like this says.

Cecilia Boles: Yes, I remember; tomato fields, also the smokehouse behind Mamaw's house, and the old chicken house with the old cars, where we would play and drive those old cars!! (No telling how many snakes and tarantulas we shared those pretend rides with each time). I remember going pole fishing and digging worms with Mamaw behind her house at that lake. She always told us there were alligators in the swampy side behind the dam.

Memories of Grigsby

By Edwena Williams Higginbotham

As told to Tonya McSwain Andrews

My parents were Clark Paul Williams, Sr. and Emma Fancher Williams. They were very generous, and friends and neighbors were always welcome. One of my fondest memories is playing volleyball. On Saturday and Sunday afternoons, neighborhood kids could come to our house. We would play volleyball for hours. Momma would make a pot of chili, or whatever she had to cook. Everyone was welcome, and no parents were worried about where the kids were. Later, we would go to the drive-in movies. Momma and Daddy would take anyone that wanted to go. Sometimes we would go to Center, and other times we would go to Nacogdoches. They charged by the vehicle, so it wouldn't matter how many went. Daddy would get popcorn and drinks, and we would all have to share. We would sit on the top of the truck, in the back, on the hood, or even the ground. When we came back, Daddy would drive all the kids to their houses.

The Game of Chicken

Vehicles were scarce, but Lamar Martin and Larry Hargis each had a pickup. They would go around the community and pick up some of us kids. Then we all would gather at the Attoyac River. This was my first exposure to the Game of Chicken. We would stand in the back of the truck. Lamar and Larry would drive toward the river. The one that stopped first was the loser. Lamar Martin would win every time, because he was a daredevil. No one ever drove into the river, but they came scary close on many occasions. One night, L D. Byers had a new pair of shoes. He was being so careful to keep his shoes clean. I pushed him into the water. He almost cried, because I got his shoes dirty. Once I saw how upset he was, I felt bad and apologized over and over.

Barfield Store/Martinsville

We would walk to the store at lunch from the school. Daddy had a charge account. One day, he went to pay his bill and it was $30. Remember that things were much cheaper back then. Come to find out, the bill was high because I had signed the bill for all the school kids to get a snack. After that, I learned that the charge account was only for my family.

Dr. Thomas U. Williams was my granddaddy. He got the first vehicle in our community. He didn't drive, but he had a driver. One day they were driving down a country road to treat someone. The driver got to going too fast and lost control of the car. They ran off the road into a creek.

So Dr. T.U., being used to a horse and buggy, said, "Drink you SOB, drink."

My daddy, Clark Paul Williams Sr., rode around with his dad, T.U., doing house calls. Someone called him Dr. Bill one day and that was what he was called for the rest of his life.

My parents had Williams Grocery Store or Grigsby Store. I'm not sure what it was called. Everyone had a small book with a piece of carbon paper. Each time someone charged, we would write it down. Then when the crops came in, customers would come in and settle their account. People would sit in front of the store and talk about everything. It was a local hangout, and you could catch up on what everyone in the community was doing. Momma and Daddy worked the store, except when they were working their own crops.

Shirley Berg was one of the best volleyball players in Shelby and Nacogdoches Counties.

Lowell Russell's dad called Dr. Williams to his house one night. Lowell had an earache. He told him to go get a Bessie bug, break its head off, get that white juice out of its neck and put it in his ear. So they did it, and he never had another earache.

["Bessie bug" or "Betsy Bug" is harmless and feeds on rotting wood.] (Old Farmer's Almanac, 2020).

Dr. Bill sold bibles. Mother took us to the Church of Christ at the Yarbrough place. Bro. Barron was preaching and Edwena was too short for her feet to touch the floor.

When the preacher said, "Praise the Lord," Edwena said, "Praise the Lord."

Often, Dr. Bill would take us to a non-denominational church

14
Waterman

Eldora Gilchrist: Waterman sawmill paid their hands with sawmill tokens, and the general store was owned by the lumber company, where they were considered same as cash. The Waterman tokens are highly collectable & rare.

The Waterman Train Wreck

By Pamila Hooper Adkison

Waterman, a sawmill town, was established on the banks of the Attoyac River in Shelby County. It was a settlement for company housing for the mill hands and woodsmen. Waterman was known as the front, because the railroad tracks ended there. Narrow gaged tracks networked into the surrounding woods from the Santa Fe spur in Waterman. Other businesses built up around the mill to provide services for the families. The community had a hotel, school, churches, and a commissary. It had the largest payroll in Shelby County at one time. The payroll consisted of native residents and migrant workers which followed the timber baron. The lumber company issued its own tokens on payday to its employees that they could redeem at the commissary

The development of the railroads across the nation pushed the growth of the country inward. Raw materials were easily transported between inner sources and markets. Because the population of the interior of the country was sparse, laborers followed the lines to new jobs and new lives created by commerce. The commercial lumbering industry benefited from this expansion. Before the railroads, the logs were rafted down rivers to the mills. The difficult phase of the operation was getting the timber from the inlands to the rivers. The railroad lines became the perfect solution. The tracks were built web-like throughout the forest, and the railroad cars increased the capacity per load. The railroads provided a means to harvest the timber economically and efficiently.

Even so, in mountainous regions or rolling hills the commercial harvesting was on a small scale. The locomotives could not pull a very steep grade. Therefore, the tracks had to be built fairly level, requiring fill-in dirt or built-up trellises to traverse the terrain (Burns, Logging Railroads: History and Operations, n.d.).

Edmond Shay began developing a locomotive that operated on gears in 1872. It was slower, but could negotiate the steeper grades of topography and could wade creeks and streams. With the reliable Shay Engine (Burns, "Shay" Steam Locomotive, n.d.), the logging industry expanded into the old growth timber by building tracks, quickly and efficiently, whenever needed. The ultimate goal was production. The closer the mill was to the source of timber, the less expensive the operation. When the area had cut out, a company could just as quickly pull up the tracks and move to another location. The railroads transported the finished product (lumber) from isolated places (Waterman) to the construction markets throughout the nation.

In 1905 William M. Waterman began his lumber company. The longleaf pines along the river bottom in West Shelby County became part of the large scale commercial enterprises of the lumber industry. The trees grew a hundred feet tall and four or five foot in diameter. With no undergrowth to clear out beneath the canopy, it was easygoing to build railroad spurs through the old-growth forest from Waterman. There were around seven lines that extended further from the town. The engines carried the flat log car into the woods to the work site and returned back to the mill loaded with the logs in the evening. The flatheads, loader operator, and skidder men hitched a ride on the empty cars each morning. At the end of the day, they rode back to the mill on top of the logs.

In 1913 Mr. Waterman shut down the operation and moved to Deadwood, Texas, of Panola County. This new location was called Waterman Front. This sudden move led to the controversial discussion by some concerning the reason for the shutdown. Was it due to the area being cut out, or the beginning of World War I? William Waterman was a German by nationality and had gone back to his native country.

The harvesting procedure of the time was to clear cut and move out. The logs were dragged to the trackside by the loader, which was mounted on the cars. Steel cables wound around a power drum, then up to the crane and boom. After the flatheads laid the trees on the ground, a skidder man drew out the cables and attached them to the logs. On signal the operator began drawing the logs to the tracks. He, subsequently, loaded the logs onto the cars. When that section was clear cut, the tracks were extended deeper into the Big Woods.

In the 1820s, Moses Austin and Stephen F. Austin brought Anglo-Irish descendants from the United States into Texas which was claimed by Spain (Mexican municipality of Tenehaw). Family men with their wives brought an aspect of civility to the area. (Wikipedia, 2022).

Shelby County was part of the "Neutral Ground," a strip of territory along the west bank of the Sabine River. In order to preclude a border dispute between the United States, after the Louisiana Purchase in 1803, and Spain, these countries declared the area neutral. Without any law enforcement, predictably, this no-man's-land attracted bandits and renegades fleeing from justice of both nations. This area of Texas was notorious for its lawlessness and violence. The "Regulator and Moderator War" (1838-1844) was centralized in Shelby County. President Sam Houston of the new Republic of Texas sent in a militia to quince the uprising in 1844.

Prior to the expansion of the railroads in the early 1900s, the subsistent farming and arduous, daily life made the Shelby County residents self-reliant and independent. Cooperation among the neighbors enabled them to make a decent living for their families.

Accidents in the lumber industry were endemic. Eye witnesses at the Waterman Mill recounted frequent accidents of fatalities and debilitating injuries. The mill had inadequate safety standards, and in the woods, operations were worse.

At the woods site, anything or anyone (unaware of the signal) was crushed as the log was reeled in. The cables could entangle unsuspecting workers dragging them to their death. If the cable snapped, it whipped through the woods and critically injured or decapitated workers.

There are no official records giving an account of the Waterman train wreck. The Texas Workmen's Compensation Board was not established until 1913. Even after regulations were implemented, the lumber industry was grossly underreported. Companies of that time did not have adequate, safety guidelines and were reluctant to admit the poor working conditions. A photograph of the wreck taken by a local photographer, Preacher Loving Sabel, is the principal document of the tragedy. Any article written in the Shelby County newspaper, *Champion*, was lost in a fire in the 1970s. Orally, eye witnesses have passed down the train wreck narrative to the next generation.

There are variations on the cause of the accident. One is that the brakes failed on the locomotive as it came down Shoat Hill. Another is the cars became uncoupled and left the narrow gaged rails. (Burns, n.d.). Still, another is the train came over one hill, down into a valley, and up another hill before approaching the mill. Four cars uncoupled from the engine at the top of the last hill and rolled back down through the valley and back up the first hill. Just as the pendulum returns, the cars retraced their path to the top of the hill where they had uncoupled. The momentum created by this action was enough to carry the cars over the rise and down into Waterman. When the cars reappeared over the knoll, the engineer realized he had a run-away and sounded the distress signal (Minton, 1991, pp. 180,196).

Judge V.V. (Verbon Vester) Pate gave this account in an interview for John Minton, of the train wreck (Minton, 1991, pp. 180-182).

> "And Mr. Eli Sanford lived down there right close to where it happened and he told me that he heard the whistle as it began to scream, because the train was running away....Eli Sanford told me that he was a-plowing....Mr. Sanford said it was a curious, most blood-curdling sound that you ever heard in your life and said just a few minutes he heard the thump and the bump and the logs and things a-falling....those logs was driven into the ground twenty, twenty-five feet deep."

In an interview for John Minton, Buren McNease gave this account by None (No-nee) Scoggins. She lived nearby and was accustomed to hearing the different whistles (Minton, 1991, p. 196).

> "But anyhow, when they heared this she said it was one of the lonesomest whistles she thought she'd ever heard, but they knew there's something wrong....but in a few minutes they knew what it was."

Life was difficult for the folks of Shelby County. They were used to a brutal existence and settled matters on their own, but the Waterman train wreck affected many families, and the sorrow of the survivors affected the next generation. Decades later the wreck was discussed among the residents. Those who knew the words would sing the "Waterman Train Wreck" song.

Along with the picture of Mr. Sabel, a ballad of the accident has survived. The writer was said to be a drummer (a traveling salesman of clothes, or shoes, etc.). He was staying at the hotel that day and composed the ballad as he observed the activities and heard the accounts of the accident. The neighboring residents adapted and added their own verses to the song. Several version developed from the original. Family and friends sang the ballad while working their farms and doing their daily chores around the house. An accomplished musician on the guitar and the piano, Tommie Sabel, son of Loving Sabel was instrumental in preserving the ballad. Tommie, a farmer, who picked up odd jobs to make ends meet, became associated with the ballad as an entertainer. He wrote the verses down from memory for Buren McNease, a relative, in 1960.

"tommie

Rote By tommie Sabel 19-60

it was on one friday morning the train

was some lonesom tune it went out into

the log woods it was on it daley rome

and on it way returning this sad accident

ocurred the train did wreck and did kill to men

later to more did die it was own one Sunday

night at Eleavon tharty o clock we heared the

cryes of mercy that cause me to start

I stept into the Watermon Hotel and gaze

up on the Bed and it concurring this reck

Mr asbery adam was dead. it was in

Days Gone By

> *sept 1911 the day the reck occured the train*
> *did Reck and did kill to men and later to more*
> *did die the sun was sloly sinking the*
> *Bird had gone to rest all thro the day*
> *is lonely we all shall meet again there*
> *Be no Wreck up younder cause By the*
> *Watermon Wreck the Engion near says*
> *to the farmer we must shead down the train*
> *the train has lost it manel guide to*
> *Wreck this train its Bound"*
> *(Minton, 1991, pp. 196-197) "*

Several men were critically injured in the train wreck. These are the ones who rode that train to their death;

Mr. Asbery Adams, Mr. Mansfield, and Mr. Haynes, and Mr. Ernest Wise.

[Tommie Sabel was a member of White Rock Baptist Church when I went there. Since my sons were preschoolers, we would sit near the back row, so we wouldn't disturb others. Tommie would come in after Sunday School and would sit on the end of the same pew. That must have been mid-to-late 1970s.

There are other versions of the song in the journal about *The Waterman Train Wreck: Tracking a Folksong in Deep East Texas by*. John Minton.... PHA]

15

Other Topics

Days Gone By

Road Runners in Southwest Shelby County

By William Rudd

In the early 1950s, some roadrunner families lived in the back pasture of our farm and ranch in the Jericho community of southwest Shelby County Texas. They nested in a deep ravine that provided a natural habitat of tall weeds, dense underbrush and low level trees. We would see them often racing down a cow trail when we visited the area. Unfortunately, pasture improvements to grow grass for cattle grazing in the mid to late 1950s destroyed their habitat and they disappeared.

Road runners are slender, black, brown and white streaked, fast running ground cuckoos. They have head crest, long legs, strong feet, and a dark bill. Typically, mature birds are 22 to 24 inches long and weigh 8 to 15 ounces. They make a dove-like cooing sound. Normally, they prefer running instead of flying. Their deceptive track mark is an 'X' making it difficult to tell which way the bird is running. They can fly at speeds up to about 25 miles per hour when necessary to escape predators or capture prey.

Roadrunner diet normally includes insects, small reptiles, rodents and other small mammals, small birds, eggs, fruit and seeds. They usually race after prey and may leap to catch insects. They have been observed banging some prey against the ground to overpower it. Because of their quickness, they also prey upon rattlesnakes.

Roadrunners inhabit the southwestern United States, eastward to parts of Missouri, Arkansas, and Louisiana, as well as Mexico and Central America. They live in arid lowland, mountainous shrubland and woodland and stay in their breeding area year-round. Breeding pairs are monogamous and mate for life. During spring and early summer courtship displays, the male bows, alternately lifting and dropping his wings and spreading his tail. He parades in front of the female with his head high and his tail and wings drooped and may bring an offering of food.

Roadrunner nests are often composed of sticks, and may sometimes contain leaves, feathers, snakeskins, or dung. They are commonly placed 3 to 10 feet above ground level in a low tree, bush, or cactus. Roadrunners generally lay 2 to 6 white eggs per clutch. Both sexes incubate the nest and feed the hatchlings. For the first one to two weeks after the young hatch, one parent remains at the nest. The young leave the nest at two to three weeks old, foraging with parents for a few days, then they strike out on their own. (Wikipedia Creative Commons Attribution-Share alike License 3.0., 2022).

Royce Lynn Johnson: William, you will still see them on the Big Woods Road above Jericho.

Mila Justice Smith: There are still roadrunners in Jericho. We live at the top of the hill and see them fairly often, especially during the summer. There is still a good bit of brush, tall grass and trees around for them to hunt and nest. They seem to think our blueberry bushes make a pretty good habitat too.

Royce Lynn Johnson: I watched one kill a snake once. When the snake would strike and miss, (They always do because the bird is faster than the snake.) he would peck it on top of its head. He would do it again and again, always in the same spot until the snake is dead.

Phyllis Adams: Lots of them in Mt. Herman also!!

Angela Johnson Lawson: Definitely still have a few in Jericho. I've seen a few this summer.

Tammie L: I see them in the curve before my house.

Little 'Gator

By Clinton Howell Adkison

My brother, Heath, and I were around 10 years old, give or take. Nobody believed we had an alligator in our pond, until we started bringing people over to see. We took pictures of it with a 110 camera, but back then in the mid to early '80s you had to send the film to Walmart to be developed. It may be a week or two to even get the pictures back. There was no such thing as an IPhone nor digital cameras.

For Heath and me, the alligator didn't run us off from the pond, but made it more exciting to go down there. At first the little 'gator would keep an eye on us, and we would be watching for it. We had a makeshift raft out of 55 gallon drums and old boards. We would fish and swim off of it. He was always around just watching, and after a while he got used to us being there, disrupting his peace and quiet.

One day we were fishing for catfish and had a red and white bobber on the line. The 'gator got curious, so he swam up to the bobber and bit into it and it shattered. So we, being boys (mischievous boys is what Momma might say) looked around in the tackle box and found a Hula Popper, which is a top water bait that was painted like a frog, and had 2 treble hooks on it, and would make a popping noise when you jerked it across the water. We tied it on and cast it out. The 'gator didn't notice it at first, until we started popping it. Here he come, made a B-line straight for it, and bit down just as calm as can be. We started reeling it in, because that is what you are supposed to do when you catch something. He very calmly let us reel him in, no fighting at all. The whole time this was happening we had no idea what we were going to do when we got him in, much less, how we were going to handle him, or even get the hook out of his mouth. No gun with us, so I couldn't holler "chooot em," like they do on TV. The closer we reeled him to the bank, the more nervous I got. When he finally got to the bank, he was a little bigger up close than what we remembered, because he was always in the water. Now he was on dry land. Once he was on the bank, he planted all four feet and went thrashing about. I guess we didn't have much common sense, we reacted just as if we had a big fish and went to yanking back on the line. I don't know what pound test we had on that old Zebco 33, but the line was not breaking and the gears were stripping. Finally that Hula Popper came flying out of his mouth, and shot past us, landing on the bank behind us. The 'gator left out of there in a mad hurry. I don't know who was more relieved when he got loose, us or him.

Who's Been Eating My Fish

By Pamila Hooper Adkison

When we lived at Grigsby, Howell built a stock pond on the back of our property. He also made a road from the house to the pond for our two sons to ride their 3-wheelers, and later, their motorcycles. The road wasn't too long, but it had a couple of rolling hills. With a few dirt mounds built into the road, it became a respectable, obstacle track. They would ride down the road, across the dam, and back to the house.

We stocked the pond with catfish fingerlings, hybrid blues. We fed them for about a year. That summer, when they got about pan-size, the boys planned a big fishing day. They had lots of fun catching them on a little rod n reel. They had about seven or eight on a stringer by nightfall. Each fish weighed about two or three pounds, nice size with white bellies. The boys couldn't wait for their dad to get home to show him. For some reason, Howell didn't get home until well after dark that day. It was too late to go to the pond. Since we had left the fish on the stringer in the water when we walked home, we thought they would still be alive the next day.

The next morning the boys rode their 3-wheelers down to the pond to bring the catch back to clean. I expected them to be back soon, but had not paid any attention to the time. I did think that it was taking them a while, but didn't worry any. After about an hour one of them did come in.

"Where are the fish? I asked.

"They're gone. Something ate them." he said, "An alligator ate them!"

Alligator! The pond was only a couple years old. It wasn't mucky and over grown. It couldn't be a suitable habitat for an alligator.

It was there, though. It had eaten four or five of the fish, not the whole animal. The upper half of each was still on the stringer. The remaining fish had died during the night.

The boys had been throwing rocks at it every time it came to the surface. It would submerge when a rock came close to it and resurface in another place. Most of the time only his eyes and snout were visible. It remained still in the water, watching. When it swam, it moved slowly, even lazily. We could tell it was moving when the water swirled about a foot behind its eyes. After a few days, I had a chance to see it out of the water. It was about 2 1/2 feet to 3 feet long. It had bands in yellow and dark green around its body and tail. Its eyes were yellow. On the bank, it scurried high on its legs and was fast. Maybe, it was retreating to the safety of the water, whenever we showed up.

Elections

Jan Akridge: Since it is the night before the election, I was just wondering if some of the older ones remember, if they showed the results of the presidential election on the big board on the square like they did local races years ago.

Mack Borders: I remember that when I was very young. Daddy went every election night and let Fred and me come along. We would run all over the square and play with other kids while the adults watched the changing election results. It was great fun for us kids.

Karen Bittick: Wayne and I were just talking about that. The first time I voted, Daddy carried me and showed me what to do. We marked our ballots underneath one of the big oak trees in front of the courthouse across from John C. Rogers Drug Store.

Eldora Gilchrist: We loved it, it was so much fun watching the returns come in.

Jan Akridge: The only one I remember going to was after I married, and we went to the square to see the results.

Days Gone By

Pamela Johnson Sanford: Darrell and I were talking about that the other day, too!

Elaine Belanger: How did they post results or returns?

Royce Lynn Johnson: Elaine, on a chalkboard....as the results came in by cars delivering them.

Jan Akridge: It was a BIG chalk board.

Karen Bittick: Jan, on the back of a large flatbed truck.

William Rudd: Remember very clearly election nights with the big board on the East side of the Square, being continually updated with eraser and chalk as the votes were being reported. The 1948 election of Harry Truman is most vivid in my memory. My dad and I were there most of the evening, the weather was a little warm and there was a big crowd. I don't remember if we stayed until it was announced that Truman won.

Jan Akridge: William, WOW what a great memory!

Karren P: Great fun. Last one was 1990, I believe.

Elaine Belanger: Wow! 1990.

Mila Justice Smith: I don't think anyone expected to get the final results of the presidential election that night because of it being a national election. Everybody was more interested in Texas offices, but especially the county offices. Who won the race for sheriff and for the commissioners had all the local interest that night.

Delores Harris Brown: I remember the board. It was very interesting. I wish someone had pictures of it.

Other Topics

John Woods Park

Jan Akridge: Who was John Woods? He has a park named after him on Hwy.7 West, right before Mt. Herman. It's been there for as long as I can remember. The first time I met all of Billy's family, they were having a get-together there. Children were running everywhere. Does anyone know when they made the park? People still use it, mostly to rest or use their phone. I used to go there to get tree moss for the wreaths I made.

Eldora Gilchrist: When I was little, the church (I think) had an Easter egg-hunt for us at the park each year.

Delores Harris Brown: Eldora, I have a picture of our Sunday School Class from Mt Pleasant at the Park, dated 1955 I think. We had an Easter Egg Hunt & Picnic.

Nina Jo Hudspeth Walker: I remember Excelsior School used to have wiener roast there & took us kids by bus. I'm not sure of the occasion, maybe end of school term looong time ago!

Royce Lynn Johnson: The WPA built it in the 30s when HW 7 was built.

[Works Progress Administration is an organization started by President Franklin D. Roosevelt in the 1930s to relieve the 25% unemployment rate caused by the Great Depression. Eligible individuals were employed through the WPA and Civilian Conservative Corp (CCC) to build the infrastructure of the nation. The CCC enhanced our natural resources, developed the highway system, and built public buildings while providing financial relief to a distressed nation……PHA] (Wikipedia, WPA, August 2023)

Days Gone By

McSwain Hill

<u>Rhonda Chandler</u>: Does anyone know how McSwain Hill got its name? I've been curious for years.

<u>Linda Winder</u>: McSwain Hill on Hwy 7? Leon and Alma McSwain and their children lived on top of the hill, and Lee and Ethel McSwain and their children lived on the bottom going towards Center. I think the McSwain teenagers named it McSwain Hill.

<u>Delores Harris Brown</u>: Kermit McSwain lived right in that area also and Joe McSwain.

<u>Linda Winder</u>: I just remember them living on Hwy 7 past John Woods Park.

<u>Delores Harris Brown</u>: Linda, yes and Joe still lives there. I saw him the last time I was home. I'm not sure how far that is from McSwain Hill, I remember asking about that when I was a kid. Something about the roads being muddy, and trucks & cars sliding down, having to get a team of mules to pull people up the hill. I assume from the McSwains.

<u>Royce Lynn Johnson</u>: All the McSwains who lived there...Leon, Elton, Warren Gee, Lee McSwains. And all the kids, a bunch of them!

<u>Linda Winder</u>: Yes, on the side of the hill on the dirt road is were Elton and Melba Rene and their kids, and Warren G and Lillian and their kids lived. Come to think of it, at one time there would have been about 15 McSwain cousins on that hill – Bobby, Earl, Jacqueline, Aubie Jean, Betty Jo, LaNell, Judy, Marsha, Terri Lynn, Bradley, Gene, Jeannette, Edna Rae, Travis...I forgot Kerry Grant.

<u>Karen Bittick</u>: Are you talking about where the big water tank is? When I was growing up, there were all MCSWAINs living in this area

and the community is listed in the county archives as Covington or Crowderville. Over the years many of the MCSWAINs have died, and their properties have been sold to outsiders. But it is still referred by many as MCSWAIN Hill.

Royce Lynn Johnson: Karen, the name Covington came from Alonzo Covington who farmed and was the original owner of the land. The father of Vera Covington who taught us in school at Center. Crowderville was named by Bobby and Earl because of the crowder peas grown there.

Karen Bittick: Royce Lynn, I knew about MCSWAIN Hill, Covington, and Crowderville, but I didn't know the history. LOL

Angela Johnson Lawson: Karen, and Royce Lynn, I remembered Daddy telling me Crowderville was from crowder peas being grown there, but I didn't know Bobby and Earl McSwain gave it the name! LOL Probably tired of planting, growing, and shelling so many. I think that's when I was told the story as a young teenager who was complaining a little bit! LOL!

Karen Bittick: Yes, Daddy said it was from growing Crowder Peas. One thing I remembered on that hill was plenty of grass burrs and red ants.

Royce Lynn Johnson: Linda, so are we double second cousins or double third? I forget how to figure that.

Linda Winder: We are double second cousins. First cousins share the same grandparents. Second cousins share the same great grandparents. In this case, we share the same great grandparents on the Johnson side. (Ed Johnson and Nannie Koonce) and the McSwain side (Daniel McSwain and Mary Jane Murdock). Don't ask me about third and fourth cousins - too complicated. I like your comment on how most people in Shelby County are probably sixth cousins!

Delores Harris Brown: Linda, the same with Allen P. McSwain & Margaret Savannah Murdock McSwain, Allen & Daniel were brothers (right?) and Mary Jane & Margaret were sisters. So their kids would be double first cousins. My grandma being one of Allen's daughters. There are so many McSwains, but it seems they are all related somehow.

Royce Lynn Johnson: Delores, they are definitely all related....all came from the four brothers.

Delores Harris Brown: Royce, didn't two of the brothers return to Alabama?

Royce Lynn Johnson: Delores, I think so....so we all came from two brothers....Linda can help us out.....

Delores Harris Brown: Royce Lynn, I'm thinking so, I have a copy of the McSwain Book, but haven't pulled it out lately. I know I brought my grandma here to Georgia to visit me back in the '80s, and we went to Ozark, Ala., & Abbeville. She met some of the McSwain relatives there. It's just across the state line from me.

Royce Lynn Johnson: Delores, I visited there once. The same names in the cemetery there as are here. The McSwains were not the only ones from there coming to Texas.

Delores Harris Brown: Royce Lynn, you're right! I think several families came together. The funny, strange thing is my Georgia-born husband's father's people are from Abbeville & Ozark. We both have ancestors buried in the same cemetery over there!

Linda Winder: Delores and Royce Lynn, Daniel McSwain III came to Texas with his brothers Allen Patterson and Sanford Bunk. Daniel returned to Alabama, but his brothers stayed and sent for their families. Later four of Daniel McSwain III's sons moved to Texas - Sanford Bunk (same name as uncle), James Roscoe, Euell Lee, and Colon D - and stayed and raised families in Shelby County. That is why there are so many McSwains in the area - lots of descendants.

Delores Harris Brown: Linda, is it true that of the original McSwain brothers came to work on the Courthouse? I had heard that story from my grandmother, I believe, or one of my great aunts.

Linda Winder: Delores, Not sure if all worked on the courthouse, but this is from the McSwain book I did on my grandparents ..."Daniel is believed to have returned to Texas in 1885 and worked for J.J.E. Gibson, building the Shelby County Courthouse, which was built in the style of an Irish castle. Daniel was a highly skilled bricklayer. Once again, he made enough money to return to Alabama. While living in Alabama, he would buy land, sell the timber, clear the stumps, then sell it at a good profit and do the same thing again."

Gwen Taylor Stewart: Sulane, my goodness! I remember looking forward to sitting by you on the bus! (Don't remember whose bus-sometimes I rode Mr. Arthur D's, sometimes my dad's, sometimes Mr. Luman's-my grandfather). I always thought you were so sweet and so pretty!

Linda Winder: There are two different McSwain books. My aunt, Christine McSwain Mahan, did the first one, which covers all the family tree and all its branches. I did a second one a few years ago, including a lot of her research on the family but focusing more on stories of my grandparents, Lee and Ethel McSwain. Hers lists all the family members with dates of birth and death and children, etc. but mine is just pictures and stories. What is your family line?

Delores Harris Brown: Linda, I'm the great granddaughter of Allen Patterson McSwain. He & Margaret Savannah had 11 children. My grandmother was Nonie McSwain that married Bud Luman. Merline Luman was my mother.

Days Gone By

Chris M: Linda, Daniel McSwain did work on the Shelby County Court House. Mary Danley and I placed a picture of him there. It was still there the last time I visited.

Shelby County Courthouse 2022, Photograph by Pamila Hooper Adkison

Nicknames

Barbara J Scates: Many people had nicknames.

Rhonda Chandler: Dicey Jane!

Debbie S A: Robbie's was Cob!

Shane Fenley: There was Big Bud and Little Bud Fenley. I was always called Bud.

Brenda H: Francis.

Eldora Gilchrist: There was Big Eldora (Holt) and me, Little Eldora (Barbe) Gilchrist.

Cindy Scates Eubank: My mother was Vader Tater.

Sharon Fenley Prince: Sharon Jean.

Catherine L: Some called me Kit Kat. Should have been peanut butter cup. Daddy called me Cat.

Tresa Danley Konderla: Both my brothers had nicknames (Dink and Rowdy) and the only person who kind of called me a nickname on occasion was Daddy. He would call me Sissy. Several friends from high school still call me TD that started back when CB radios were popular. My handle was Tiny Dynamite.

Three Counties Junction at Attoyac River

Joyce Bright: Pam, I thought about something else you might want to check on. Not too many places have 3 Counties in one location, but at the river there's Shelby, San Augustine, and Nacogdoches. Mama told me that years ago there was a night club at the river, I think, in San Augustine County.

Eldora Gilchrist: About 44 years ago Ruddy Mitchell drove Dickie & me all down where his house & land were down there close to the river. He showed us where the old road was that crossed his property. Wagons went through there. If you looked back, then you could still see the ruts where that road was. He also said as they followed that road on the place to cross the Attoyac River, instead of going by Highway 21. The road that was on his property went across Attoyac at a higher crossing place going toward the settlement of Nacogdoches instead of the lower road. Do you remember where the dipping vat was on his place? That road was close to that. It's just off the main road that goes through there now. I have permission to go on his property, if I choose to, but I don't go during hunting season. I haven't been in many years, because they do have the hunting rights leased.

Royce Lynn Johnson: The crossing above HW 21 was called "Packs Bridge". This was before HW 7. It was built about 1900. The two roads converged on this side of the Attoyac with one coming from Mt Herman and the other from Ironosa, crossing Tupergum [Tupelo Gum] Slough. Jess Luman told me it was there.

Eldora Gilchrist: Royce Lynn, that must have been the crossing Ruddy was telling us about.

Sharon Fenley Prince: Royce Lynn, growing up, when we would ask Daddy (Gene Fenley), "Where are we going?" One day we were driving through the backroads to Spring Ridge Homecoming, and he pointed out Tupergum Slough.

I looked at him and replied, "It's for real?"

Delores Harris Brown: Tupergum Slough was the favorite camping & fishing spot of the Lumans. We went almost every weekend when my grandpa was alive. He & Fate Luman built a boat from the hoods of two old Dodge trucks. It was so heavy! I was privileged to go with them in the boat a few times, running trot lines.

Early Trails and Roads Across Shelby County Texas

By William Rudd

Many of our nation's highways and byways closely follow the routes of ancient Indian foot trails. As far back as seven or eight millennia ago Native Americans were creating some of those trails. During historic times East Texas Caddo Indians, an agricultural people with a highly developed culture used well established trails to conduct commerce, facilitate inter-tribal social gatherings, access hunting grounds and enhance mobility in warfare. By the mid1800s, many of the paths were being used as wagon trails with some subsequently becoming modern roadways.

An 1856 map shows the locations of three wagon trails thought to be adaptations of earlier Caddo Indian foot trails, along with ferries, and villages in Shelby County at that period of East Texas history. In the map below, I have reconstructed the 1856 trail routes using landmarks and site locations published in recent US Government Survey maps. From an 1841 map I also added the village of Tinaha (Tenaha) with a north going trail extension from there.

Days Gone By

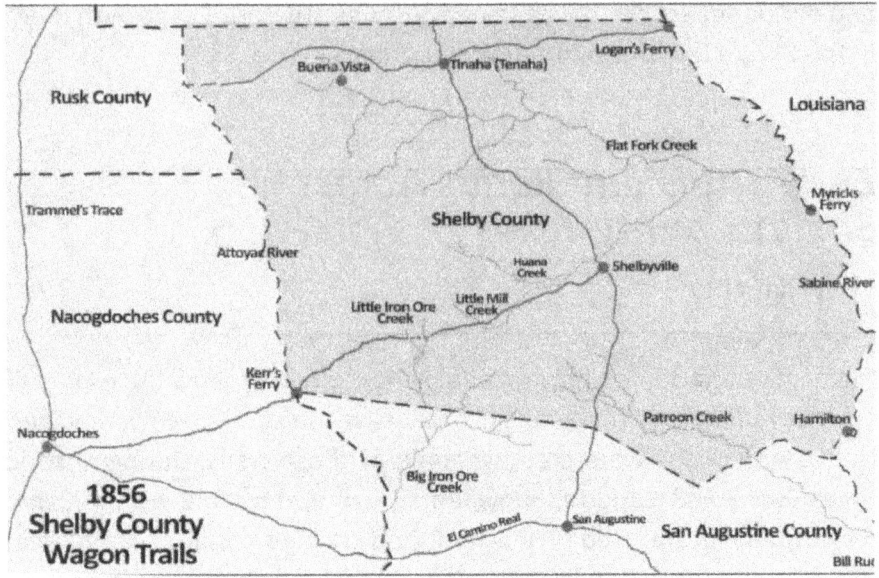

1856 Shelby County Wagon Trails Map by Bill Rudd

Before the 1800s two east-west trails across the county most likely supported Caddo travel between East Texas, North Texas, Louisiana, Arkansas and Oklahoma villages. In the mid-1800s, the routes became wagon trails between northern and eastern parts of the country and El Camino Real at Nacogdoches, "The Gateway to Texas."

One of the wagon trails crossed the northern part of the county, coming from the north and from Shreve's Landing on the Red River. It ran west from Logan's Landing, passing through Tinaha (Tenaha) and crossed the Attoyac River. An 1845 map shows it joining Trammel's Trace going south from the Mt. Enterprise area to Nacogdoches.

The second (southern) east-west wagon trail entered Shelby County from the west at the Attoyac River crossing on Kerr's Ferry where Shelby, San Augustine and Nacogdoches counties meet. It linked Nacogdoches directly to Shelbyville and likely served as an alternate route from the north to El Camino Real. Although the map shows the trail terminating at Shelbyville, wagon trail crossings at Myrick's Ferry would have made it a logical destination for extending the east-west route from Shelbyville to the Sabine River.

In addition to the two east-west trails, there was one north-south trail through the middle of the county. From the north, it crossed the east-west trail from Logan's Landing at Tinaha (Tenaha). Going south from there it crossed the Flat Fork Creek and then curved southeastward to Shelbyville. From there it ran generally south to El Camino Real at San Augustine, crossing Patroon Bayou before leaving the county.

Modern Road Segments Sharing Wagon Trail Routes

Many segments of the wagon trail routes are still in use today. In the following maps, modern roads are plotted in red where they closely track wagon trail routes. Where the routes differ significantly, they are plotted in black.

Northern East-West and North-South Trail Routes

US Highway 84 crosses the northern region of the county, closely tracking the east-west trail there except for a sector in the vicinity of Buena Vista. US 96 runs along the north south trail from the northern county line through Tenaha and across Flat Fork Creek where the trail turns eastward on its way to Shelbyville, as US 96 continues southward to Center.

Days Gone By

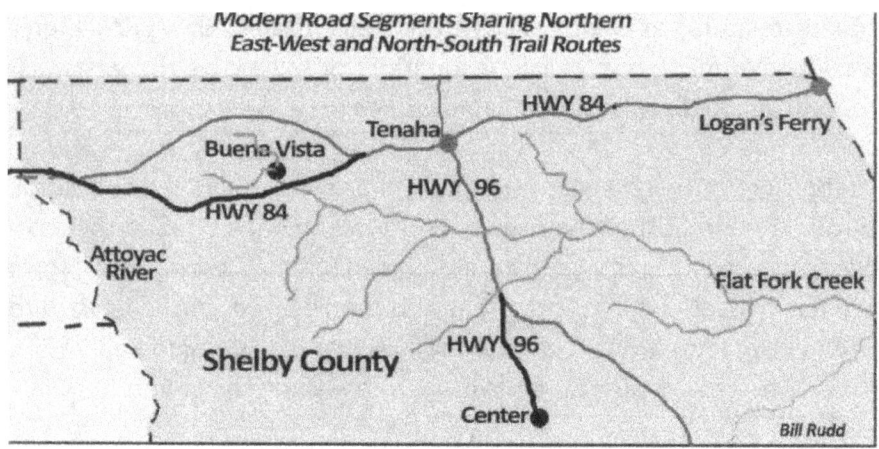

Map by Bill Rudd

Southern East-West Trail Routes

Texas State Highway 7 closely follows the southern east-west wagon trail from Nacogdoches, crossing the Attoyac River, continuing to the Mt. Herman Community. There the trail turns eastward, leaving Texas 7 to continue to Center. Segments of the east traveling trail are county roads. It proceeds eastward on CR 1168 to Word. Word, one of the earliest Post Offices in Shelby County, was closed in 1912. The trail from Word, passing south of Pearl Lake to the western end of CR 1273 has fallen into disuse, but the old roadbed is still clearly visible. The trail continues along CR 1273 past Mt. Pleasant, crossing FM 711 at the future site of Jericho. It passed just outside our kitchen window when my family owned the Jericho crossroad grocery store and station in the 1940s. Starting at FM 711, the trail becomes CR 1005 to the Short Community. From Short to Shelbyville and beyond much of the trail's identity is lost, except for a potential segment of FM 417.

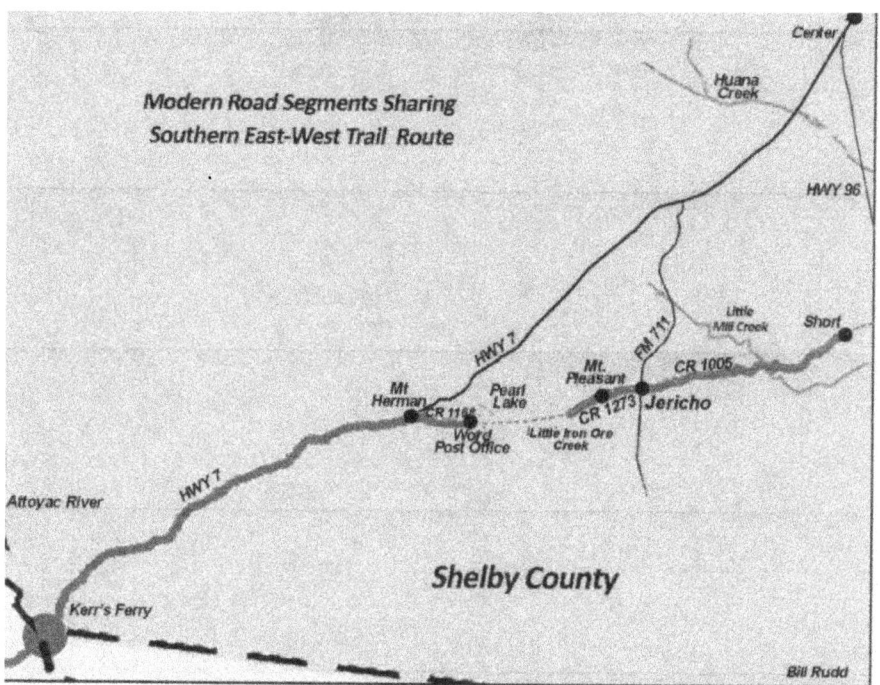

Map by Bill Rudd

Southern North-South Trail Route

State Highway 87 going south from Center intersects the north-south wagon trail route at Shelbyville and goes with it for a few miles to the intersection of Texas 87 and 147, where T 87 turns eastward and 147 continues south with the trail to the intersection of El Camino Real at San Augustine.

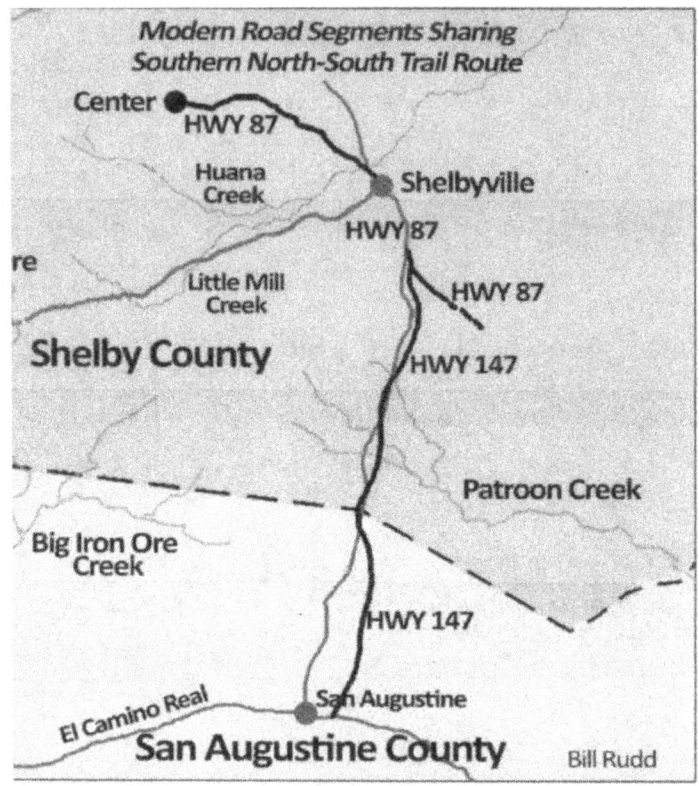

Map by Bill Rudd

So, when you travel some Shelby County roads, you will be joining uncountable hosts of those who have gone on before you; Native Americans who created and traveled footpaths, Pioneers who converted the footpaths to wagon trails and modern travelers who converted the wagon trails into highways and byways. (Swanzy, n.d.)

Royce Lynn Johnson: The old road bed is clearly visible south of Pearl Lake, going to the January place. The road we call "the lane", connecting 1273 and 1168, was more recent. Edward Johnson, my grandpa, told me all this, he being raised just south of it, next to the Youngblood place, where your mother was raised.

William Rudd: Royce Lynn, when I was young, 5 to 8 years old, your Grandpa Edward Johnson gave me a nickel on my birthday every year, because he said that I was named Edward after him, William Edward. When I was 6 he also bought me a billy goat and a 2 wheel riding cart for the goat to pull. That worked well for a short while, but Billy got so mean we couldn't get anywhere near him without having a major butting attack. Good memories.

Royce Lynn Johnson: The old road crossed Ironore Creek and Clear Branch and the narrowest points, probably following old Indian trails.

William Rudd: In retrospect, it's kinda interesting to know that an old Indian trail and/or an early settlers' road was right outside our kitchen window when my family lived in the house portion of the Jericho crossroads store in the 1940s.

Thanksgiving

Jan Akridge: Our Thanksgiving in Mt. Herman and Aiken will be different this year because of covid 19. Back when I was young we never had a turkey, we had a big fat hen. We always did the wringing of the necks up at my aunt's house. She would hang them on her clothes line to let them bleed out. She would have a big fire under the wash pot with hot water in it to dip the chickens in it where the feathers could be plucked out. The smell was awful but it sure didn't keep any of us from eating them. I don't remember big Thanksgiving dinners until at Maw Akridge's. Billy's mother would have the table full of all kinds of good cooking. I swear she had bowls as big as dish pans. The best banana pudding ever! Share some of your Thanksgiving stories. Everyone have a safe and happy Thanksgiving.

Brenda H: I sure miss her and she was the best cook!

Rhonda Chandler: I miss those family get togethers! Especially at the roadside park. Great memories.

Lea Osborne: I don't remember Thanksgiving being anyone but just us. I think 1 time my grandparents on the Osborne side came, and we all got so sick with a stomach bug.

Christmas

Jan Akridge: Going Christmas tree hunting was exciting when I was a little girl. I can remember my brother climbing a cedar tree to cut the top out for our tree that year. Being little the tree might not have been that tall, but it sure looked it. Our first Christmas I think we went somewhere around Big Ditch, and Billy cut our first Christmas tree. Later on we would just look around here. Mt. Herman and Aiken had a lot along the dirt roads. I still see some, and think that would be a cute Christmas tree. Wonder if many still go to the woods to get one? When I see a fence row that has cedar trees lined along it and see the top is gone. I have a feeling of what happened to that tree years ago.

Mila Justice Smith: For a number of years after we married, we'd cut a cedar for our Christmas tree. Gene Edward would locate a nice one early in the year and trim it a little so it would be a little bushier and a nice shape. They did make the prettiest Christmas trees.

Jill Fountain Parker: Only kind of Christmas tree Mamaw (Rachel) ever had.

Pam Adkison: We always went Christmas tree hunting. The first Christmas tree that I remember was the one my aunt, Henry Faye Hooper, put up. She had decorated it with those bubble lights. It was mesmerizing.

Kelley Hancock: Daddy used to take us tree hunting every year. He would tell us that we had to listen for the tree to call to us.

Brandon Jones: Feeling nostalgic. What I would give for another Christmas at Granny & Pawpaw Hooper's and Mawmaw and Pawpaw Jones'.

Pamela Warr Weaver: I've been lost in those old memories of the good ole days. I have a notebook Granny wrote in about Christmas when she was little. I feel like I'm there every time I read it. Love it.

Helen Windham: I have been thinking of Granny and Grandpa Hooper today! I remember being there for Christmas, and Cynda and I played with our sparklers on the bricks in front of the fireplace. I believe they let us do that because it was so cold outside.

Brandon Jones: Helen, I baked some sweet potatoes. I may have to roast some peanuts now!

Helen Windham: I saw that, and they looked tasty! I have not had roasted peanuts in many years! Mama used to make some in the oven, but Grandpa's were so good!

Nelda J C: Those precious Christmas memories make me cry too. Merry Christmas.

Kimberly M: Love it Brandon! Thank you! Nothing beats the love of being at Granny's and Grandpa's house with everyone there. We have to make sure our kids feel that same love during the holidays. Especially now.

16

Church

Days Gone By

Joy Tarver: Becky, Pam, sometimes Brenda, and I would sing specials. I played, very poorly, but I tried. Then we would sit in the back pews and get tickled. Everything is funny when you have to be quiet.

Pam Adkison: Joy, we had lots of fun. You are talented.

Providence Church

Jan Cruse: My parents, Travis and Bennie Wilson, attended Providence Baptist where the revival was the first week in August. It seems we attended a church revival every evening all summer long.

Providence Church, Courtesy of Barbara Scates, Original from Mila Smith

Mila Justice Smith: Back row: Randi Michelle Rudd held by Anthony Tomlin, Paul Dane Hughes, Ken Muckelroy, Ronnie Livingston, Wesley Livingston, and Bro. Lewis Johnson.

Front row: Randy Folsom, Deanne Lovell, Dewayne Lovell, Reese Smith, Craig Livingston, Bryan Livingston, Katha Muckelroy holding Scotti Smith.

Aiken Pentecostal Church

Sharon Fenley Prince: I remember seeing the building before the woods took it over. I was told Dolly Hooper is the one behind the beginning of the Pentecostal Church there.

Cynda Jones: Momma [Dolly Hooper] and Mrs. Leta Lucas took up money to have a building moved there for church. At one time I remember seeing a paper with names of people that donated money. Aunt Jewell donated the land for the building. I'm not sure when the last services were held there.

Royce Lynn Johnson: Jesse Hudspeth and I went once when we were in high school...60 yrs. ago! How long since services were held there? Building is still intact!

Tammy D: My grandpa played the fiddle in that church.

Jan Akridge: I went there after I married Billy. Bro. Lee Lout preached there then. Sister Nettie Johnson played the piano. Wanda Ree Peace and her daughter came with her. Sis. Vivian Lucas and her children. Bro. Green and his wife, and more. I think Gene and Zandra got married there. The first building burned after a car ran into it and it caught fire. They rebuilt it not sure of the year. I posted a picture last year of the members in front of the old building. I will try and find it.

__Joy Tarver__: James [Chandler] is moving it to his place to make him a little house.

__Eldora Gilchrist__: Rev. M.D. Lamon preached there at some point, as it was mentioned in his obituary.

Aiken Pentecostal Church 1950s, Courtesy of Mildred McSwain

Courtesy of Mildred McSwain

Days Gone By

Aiken Pentecostal Church 1965 Courtesy of Cynda Kay Hooper Jones,

<u>Joyce Bright</u>: Nettie Johnson was my great aunt and Wanda was my second cousin. R J Johnson was my grandmother's brother. He was a brother to Edward Johnson, who was Royce Johnson's dad and Royce Lynn Johnson's grandad. They were some fine people. We lived on my Uncle Edward's place down in the Sandhills when I was a little girl. I went to that church a few times with my grandma, Leta Lucas. Kenneth Hooper's Mom and Dad went to church there also.

<u>Karen Bittick</u>: I do not know when the original old church building at Mt Herman was torn down. I remember laying on a pew to sleep with my head in my grandmother's lap. I could not have been over 3 years old. It is this building I remember.

Eldora Gilchrist: I have read that the reason the old churches had two doors on the front was because the ladies went in one door and the gentleman the other, and they sat on separate sides of the church.

Delores Harris Brown: Rodger, each one had their own views about denominations, Ma was Church of Christ and Pa was a Baptist. I don't ever remember them attending church together. Pa didn't go regularly, but he did on occasion and usually by himself. I went with him a few times.

Rodger McLane: Delores, That's interesting that married people didn't go to church together. Mother's people in Panola Co were Methodist until the Great Depression when they became Pentecostal. I always thought it was interesting Mammaw Ruby was interested in the Pentecostal Church.

Delores Harris Brown: Rodger, I guess the Church & the people were what she needed. My mother was disappointed in me when I became a Baptist. I need to add though that she was proud that I did join a church and was baptized.

Helen Windham: I was always told that the family did go to church together before EC and LC were killed. They lived in West Texas at that time.

Rodger McLane: Helen, what church did they go to? Dad doesn't know.

Delores Harris Brown: Helen, do you know if that was the same time my grandparents & Mama were in West Texas too? It was before I was born, but Helen was with them.

Helen Windham: Rodger, I think quite a few family members went to West Texas at the same time, but I am not sure who all went.

Delores Harris Brown: Helen, I think you are right because I remember them talking once and my grandma's sister & her husband went also. So it must have been a large group. I know that Gr Grandpa George Luman's 2nd wife (Julie) died out there. Pa said she died from poison.

Helen Windham: Rodger, I am not sure. All I know about West Texas is that EC was fighting in Korea at that time. His picture was in the local paper, because he helped put up telephone poles so the army could communicate or something like that. LC was in high school, and he was a good baseball player. There is an article in the paper about the car wreck he was in.

Rodger McLane: Helen, I have the original clippings and the pictures from the graveside of their funerals. I'd be glad to share copies with you. I have a little wooden box that Aunt Shirley gave Daddy before she died.

Summer Revival

By Pam Hooper Adkison

"Why are all those people standing out there?" I asked Mother, as we drove by Mr. Lowell's one day.

"It must be a baptism," she said.

Church

Summer time is the season for revivals around Aiken. We got a lot of the hell fire and brimstone and the love of Jesus in those services. We sang and prayed and enjoyed each other's company. The revival services ran about a week. They were held at night after the farmers had completed their chores. The next week another church would have a revival with a different preacher. More than just the church people came. Not all of the families from the community would go to church every Sunday, but they would try to make it two or three nights of the revival.

White Rock Church was designed around the cross in a simple country style. It was a one-room rectangle building. The layout had a wide aisle from the double doors to the pulpit, with long benches on each side of the aisle. The transcript separated the pulpit from the congregation completing the cross. About four rolls of deacon benches were on each side of the pulpit, facing it. A piano was in front of the pulpit arranged so the pianist's back was toward the congregation.

There was no sound system. Sound amplified along the plank walls out to the congregation. The reverse was also true. If someone spoke in a slightly raised voice from the front doors, it amplified back to the pulpit. The preachers, that I knew, didn't need a microphone anyway. Anyone passing by on Highway 7 could clearly hear them.

Another thing that the church didn't have was a baptistery. The deacons would ask a nearby landowner for permission to have a baptism on his property. Lowell Russell allowed the church to use his place. He would pen his cattle in another pasture away from the stock pond. His pond could be seen from the highway. It is still there, but it's much larger now.

Early evening was usually hot and still. With both sides of the church full, the room became stifling even with the windows raised and the doors opened. Mangum (funeral home} provided paper fans with wooden handles stapled to them. On one side, these usually had a reproduction of a biblical scene by some famous artist. On the other side, there were Mangum's telephone number and address.

It is said that a hummingbird can flap its wings faster than any other bird. That may be true, but I would like to see a competition between a hummingbird and one of the women with a Mangum's fan during a summer service.

Even the men, who were acclimated to the heat, found it suffocating inside. They would take out their starched, white handkerchief to wipe the sweat from their brow and the back of their neck. It helped some, but anything starched is slightly moisture proof at first.

The families of that time usually had more than three children. There were one in diapers, one around two-four years old, one on his way to first grade in the fall, and one or two older siblings. The heat affected the children first. The mother would pop a bottle into the mouth of her crying baby. She would help the next youngest with water from a canning jar, pint-sized with the screw-top on it. The father would keep an eye on the soon-to-be first grader. Even that child would have a meltdown in some services. When people nearby started glancing in their direction to see what the ruckus was about, the mother would take the distressed child outside. We couldn't have a frantic child competing with the preacher for everyone's attention.

After the intensity of the service, and the mellowing out from the altar call, everyone moved outside. The evening would have cooled off by then. Even though there were no street lights, there was plenty of light from the porch fixture and from the open windows. Small groups formed, split up, and then reformed into different groups. The children ran out into the darkness, then back through the light pooling on the ground from the windows. The soft mummer of voices, and occasional laughter, drifted about and settled the night. People didn't leave right away. They stayed around for thirty or forty-five minutes and planned to be back the next night.

There was an authentic revival the summer of '65. I was between the fifth and sixth grades. Brother Travis Fenley was the pastor of White Rock. The invited speaker was Brother Lee Collum. The house was full every night. At the end of the week, everyone wanted to continue for another week. Even though his voice was failing, Bro. Collum agreed to return. During the second week, I answered the altar call. There were many who answered the call those two weeks. The church made arrangements with Bro. Lowell for the use of his pond. Later that summer, we all were baptized.

I like to think that some little girl or boy passing by Bro. Lowell's that day asked, "Why are those people standing over there?"

Tommie O T: Will never forget being baptized in Mr. Lowell's pond.

Pam Adkison: Tommie, Baptisteries are nice today, but the service itself is no longer public. I kinda miss that.

Tresa Danley Konderla: This brought back so many memories. I remember going to the baptism pond and hearing Bro. Lee preach...and even him losing his voice.

Paul Hughes: I was baptized in Pearl Lake by Bro. Lewis Johnson.

Sue E.: Our church used Uncle Jimmy Eddins' pond. Mother and Daddy were both baptized there. They used car headlights for light.

White Rock Baptist Church, VBS, 1970, Courtesy of Pamila Hooper Adkison

Map of White Rock Church VBS 1970

Days Gone By

1 David Danley	21	40 Beverly Hooper
2 Robert Luman	22 Ronny Davis	41 Brenda Hooper
3 Tonya McSwain	23 Jason Ward	42 Ira Lee Holt
4 Ginia Hooper	24 Mark Adams	43 Janie Raines
5 Kathy Fancher	25 _____ Mora	44 Bernice Adams
6 Randy B	26 Debra Hooper	45 Shawn Danley
7 John Ward	27 Shelia Stephens	46 Wesley Rains
8 Jackie Berg	28 Tresa Danley	47 Shelia Fountain
9 Randy Fountain	29 Dana Adams	48 Wanda Fountain
10 Cole Hooper	30 Ricky Davis	49 Miriam Oliver
11	31 Wanda Adams	50 Joyce Tindale
12	32 Kip Adams	51 Marie Mora
13 Tonya Cruse	33 Curtis Holt	52 Audrey Oliver
14 Melissa Cruse	34 Carolyn Williams	53 Vivian Jernigan
15 Larry Berg	35 Judy Jernigan	54 Lillie Smith
16 Kimberly Smith	36 Pam Hooper	55 Caroline Warr
17 Jana Adams	37	56 Kathy Oliver
18 Dana Adams	38 Karen Brown	57
19 Brenda Stephens	39 Debra Brown	58

Corresponding names to White Rock VBS There must have been another picture taken that day at White Rock Church, because many of the organizers/teachers are not in this group.

Bibliography

Burns, A. (n.d.). *"Shay" Steam Locomotive*. Retrieved March 2021, from American Rails: http://www.american-rails.com

Burns, A. (n.d.). *Logging Railroads: History and Operations*. Retrieved March 2021, from American Rails: https://www.american-rails.com

Dillinger, M. (n.d.). Box 744. *The Champion*.

Gabel, C. R. (1992). *The U.S. Army GHQ Maneuvers of 1941 {U253 G33 1991]*. Washington, D. C.: CENTER OF MILITARY HISTORY: Superintendent of Documents, U.S. Government Printing Office. Retrieved from Center of Military History, U.S. Army,: http://www.history.army.mil/html/books/070/70-41-1/CMH_Pub_70-41-1.pdf

Harris, L. (2019). *Dedication of Historical Marker & First Ever School Reunion; Excelsior Common School No. 47*. Center.

Minton, J. (1991, May-Dec). The Waterman Train Wreck, Tracking a Folksong in Deep East Texas. *Journal of Folklore Research, 28*(No. 2/3, Special Double Issue :), 179-219. Retrieved August Monday, 2020, from http://www.jstor.com/stable/3814503

Old Farmer's Almanac. (2020). Retrieved 2020

Swanzy, D. (n.d.). *Before the 150-Year Life of The Village of Center,"* …. Retrieved from http://www.uniqware.com/magazine19/index.htm.

Tindall, N. (1996, Sept. 12). Clarence Fountain. *San Augustine Tribune.*

Wikipedia Creative Commons Attribution-Share alike License 3.0. . (2022, February).

Works Progress Administration. (2023, August 2). In *Wikipedia.* https://en.wikipedia.org/wiki/Works_Progress_Administration

Acknowledgments

Barbara Scates recognized the importance of recording our memories for our families. Everyone believed in her vision of a community book, so we added our stories. Thank you also for the charming stories that you contributed, the work on the esign forms, and the inspiration for our book.

Thank you, Jan Akridge, for introducing new topics which led to heartwarming discussions.

Thank you, Laura Wheeler Harris, for your entertaining pamphlet on Excelsior School with the timeline to other national events.

Thank you, William Rudd, for the well-researched topics. Your explanations added to our understanding of the area and informed us of events that we were unaware of. Your personal stories tied historical events to our area.

Thank you, Linda Johnson Winder, for the interviews of the Tabernacle School.

Thank you, Jana Adams Ivy for the George Adams Family Story.

Thank you, Ginia Hooper and Anittra Phillips Adkison for editing our book.

Thank you Gwen Taylor Stewart for work on the esign form and mailings.

Thank you Paul and Henry Faye Hooper for letting me interview you.

Days Gone By

Thank you Ann Crain Hooper for your interview.

Thank you, Nina Jo Hudspeth Walker, Jimmie Nell Adkison Lee, Joyce Bright, Mila Justice Smith, Linda Johnson Winder, Delores Harris Brown, Laura Wheeler Harris, Jana Adams Ivy, Joye Taylor Hodges, Jeff Davis, Jason Adkison, Eldora Gilchrist, Jill Fountain, Venorah Williams McSwain, Edwena Williams Higginbotham, Merle Howard, Pamela Johnson Sanford, Tonya McSwain Andrews, Tresa Danley Konderla, Erma Bush Parrish, Theresa Bush Bradshaw, Tammy Fenley, Sharon Fenley Prince, Shane Fenley, Joy Tarver, Ellen Luman Hearne, Terri Lacher, Cherry Martin Murphree, Ginger Russel, Katha Watts, Bobbie Sue Scates, Michael Scates, Sandra Wilson, Phyllis Adams, Jerry H, Phillip Holt, Paul and Henry Faye Hooper, Ann Crain Hooper, Ginia Hooper, Clinton Adkison, Shirley Adkison Di Verdi, Jill Fountain Parker, Elaine Belanger, Rhonda McSwain, Cecilia McSwain Boles, Cynda Kay Hooper Jones, Mildred Hooper McSwain, Pamela Warr Weaver, Helen Windham, Brandy McLane Kelly, Rodger McLane, Royce Lynn Johnson, Angela Johnson Lawson, Karen Bittick, Brenda H, Rhonda Chandler, Alec C, Mitchell Anthony, Matt Sims, Brandon Jones, Lori Goodwin, Nadine Windham, Bruce Britt, Fred Borders, Mack Borders, and Shelby Johnson.

The Ones Behind Our Book

Barbara Williams Scates

Barbara Williams Scates was born and raised in Shelby County, just a stone's throw from Aiken, Texas, in the Mount Herman Community. Only an imaginary line separates the two communities. Scates attended school in Center, Texas, but was closely associated with all the events that took place at Excelsior School in Aiken. Barbara's three children attended Excelsior ISD and she later became employed there. At long last, she achieved her dream of being a part of Excelsior School and is dedicated to making every student a part of the Excelsior family. Her love for the school and all the students will last a lifetime. [Barbara Scates is kind and gentle hearted. I am blessed that she is my friend…..Pam]

Jan Mavis Adams Akridge

Jan Akridge lived with her husband and raised her three children in the Mt Herman Community. In her own words she claimed to be a "transplant" to the area. She worked at a flower shop and at a gift shop in Center. Later, she became an antique dealer. She was generous with her time and gave new dealers pointers on how to make their business grow. She had a classic style. In this photograph of her, you can see the pin where she hung her readers when she didn't need them. She was my friend......Pam

Pamila Hooper Adkison

www.ingramcontent.com/pod-product-compliance
Lightning Source LLC
Chambersburg PA
CBHW050833230426
43667CB00012B/1981